Avril

With my personal thanks
for a great 'Pinafore'
1983

Dennis Sayer.

THE SAVOY OPERAS

The Savoy Operas

A New Guide to Gilbert and Sullivan

by
Geoffrey Smith

ROBERT HALE LIMITED · LONDON

To the Smiths
of 1110 Tenth

First published in Great Britain 1983

ISBN 0 7090 1011 7

Robert Hale Limited
Clerkenwell House
Clerkenwell Green
London, EC1

Phototypeset by
Rowland Phototypesetting Ltd
and printed by St Edmundsbury Press
Bury St Edmunds, Suffolk
Bound by Hunter & Foulis Ltd

CONTENTS

ILLUSTRATIONS

PREFACE

For almost a century, Gilbert and Sullivan meant D'Oyly Carte. That traditional bond was weakened in 1961, when the Savoy Operas came out of copyright, bringing non-D'Oyly Carte productions with them. In 1982, it seemed to break altogether, as financial difficulties forced the old company out of business. At the same time energetic new productions overturned all the conventions of 'proper Savoy style'. D'Oyly Carte may return, but Gilbert and Sullivan will never be the same. Henceforth the Savoy Operas are on their own, free to be seen as fresh works of art with new potential.

It's high time, really. A la D'Oyly Carte, the G & S operas have been a national institution for so long—'as British as bangers and mash', one writer put it—that they have received little of the critical attention they deserve. And they *do* deserve it. Whether one has been a G & S fan or not, the Savoy series is an entertainment phenomenon, an extraordinary achievement that is much more than a quaint slice of British Victoriana. This book sets out to show why, to give the operas a dusting, to illuminate some features of the unique Savoy range.

It is a personal guide, the result of an exploration that has been tantalizing, diverting and delightful. It is not a gazetteer. There are G & S dictionaries and handbooks a-plenty that trace every one of Gilbert's allusions. I have found the 'in-joke' aspect of Gilbert's art less important—and less persuasive—than his quirky point of view and skill as a dramatist. If a reference is particularly significant or mysterious, I have explained it, but I have been more concerned to consider what makes the operas go, what accounts for their special character and survival—or neglect.

Throughout, the play's the thing, which in this case very much includes the music. Critics have argued that the Savoy Operas are not properly operas, but they are not operettas either, or *opéra bouffe.* They are simply Gilbert and Sullivan, and while they all share a family resemblance, there are intriguing differences between them, as their creators try to determine exactly what 'Gilbert and Sullivan' is. Of course each piece blends acerbity and amiability, sentiment and sarcasm, topsy-turvy and tenderness. But the balance shifts considerably as the series goes along. How much satire is permissible? How 'serious' can the partners be? Above all, what is the proper relation of words to music—a perplexing point when Gilbert's words and Sullivan's music tended in the often contrary directions of crispness and romanticism.

The personal and artistic differences between librettist and composer are part of the G & S canon. Though my concern is more with the individual operas than with their creators, the works do reflect these differences. Artistically, the two men complement each other, fill in each other's gaps. The human conflicts, however, were finally and unhappily irreconcilable and left their mark on the collaborators' output too. The story of the operas is to an extent the story of the partnership, and I have related the joint G & S biography as it pertains to the production of specific works. I have tried to resist anecdotes for their own sake, but they are always a temptation when dealing with two such remarkable men—the sharp-tongued writer with a will so strong he would lengthen his tennis court rather than shorten his ground strokes, and the charming, greatly gifted musician constantly veering between high art and high society.

But the two men live most for us in their operas, and their operas have first claim on our attention. For each work I provide a fairly detailed plot summary, both to ensure that everyone is *au fait* with the action and to show Gilbert's talent for turning out a tight, fast-moving if eccentric story. I look at the circumstances of the piece's creation and first production, as well as later 'unauthorized' versions. But chiefly I try to get at its individual character, its strengths and weaknesses, its effect as entertainment. Gilbert's virtues are not only amusing lyrics and dialogue, but surprisingly distinctive characters and the ability to deploy them with pace and variety. Sullivan's most obvious contributions are elegant, seductive melodies and bracing rhythms, but his scores abound in wonderful subtleties of orchestral wit and colour.

These qualities make up the real Savoy tradition, which will keep the operas alive and flourishing in the post-D'Oyly Carte era. West End productions of *The Pirates of Penzance*, *H.M.S. Pinafore* and *The Mikado* have already proved this beyond a doubt, as will new versions of the other operas that are sure to follow. Paradoxically, after years in the public eye, Gilbert and Sullivan have been rediscovered. This book contains one person's happy discoveries and the hope that it will entice others to make their own.

ACKNOWLEDGMENTS

This book has had a rather complicated history, and it is a pleasure to thank those who helped it on its way. Clive Unger-Hamilton introduced me to George and Pat Sharp, whose idea it was in the first place. They supplied considerable aid, comfort and hard work, and only unfortunate circumstances kept them from seeing the project through to its conclusion. Sheila Watson brandished stick and carrot and represented me in the marketplace. My wife wiped away tears and sweat in very trying conditions. My friends Hugo Cole and Ivan Zmertych read various parts of the manuscript, commented and encouraged. Other friends provided friendship, chief among them the Demon Decorator of East Kennington who, assisted by the usual cast of thousands, at least kept away boredom.

My research was facilitated by the humane efficiency of the staffs at the Westminster Music Library, the Victoria and Albert Theatrical Museum, the Mansell Collection and the Pierpont Morgan Library in New York. Decca Records kindly contributed a set of the D'Oyly Carte recordings of the operas. At Robert Hale, Antony Wood has proved a tactful and sympathetic editor.

My ultimate debt is acknowledged in my dedication—to my family in America who, years ago, gave me a love of Gilbert and Sullivan along with everything else.

THE GILBERT AND SULLIVAN OPERAS

	First Production
Thespis; or, The Gods Grown Old	Gaiety Theatre, 26 December 1871
Trial By Jury	Royalty Theatre, 25 March 1875
The Sorcerer	Opera Comique, 17 November 1877
H.M.S. Pinafore; or, The Lass that Loved a Sailor	Opera Comique, 25 May 1878
The Pirates of Penzance; or, The Slave of Duty	Royal Bijou Theatre, Paignton, Devon. 30 December 1879. Fifth Avenue Theatre, New York, 31 December 1879. Opera Comique, 3 April 1880
Patience; or, Bunthorne's Bride	Opera Comique, 23 April 1881
Transferred to	Savoy Theatre, 10 October 1881
Iolanthe; or, The Peer and the Peri	Savoy Theatre, 25 November 1881
Princess Ida; or, Castle Adamant	Savoy Theatre, 5 January 1884
The Mikado; or, The Town of Titipu	Savoy Theatre, 14 March 1885
Ruddigore; or, The Witch's Curse	Savoy Theatre, 22 January 1887
The Yeomen of the Guard; or, The Merryman and his Maid	Savoy Theatre, 3 October 1888
The Gondoliers; or, The King of Barataria	Savoy Theatre, 7 December 1889
Utopia, Limited; or, The Flowers of Progress	Savoy Theatre, 7 October 1893
The Grand Duke; or, The Statutory Duel	Savoy Theatre, 7 March 1896

1

G & S: The Makers

Any look at the Gilbert and Sullivan operas has to begin with Gilbert and Sullivan. This may seem obvious, but the partnership that produced the Savoy classics is as unique as the operas themselves. Never, perhaps, has such a string of collaborative successes—such an institution—been created by men who were personally so different.

Towards the end of their mutual and regularly stormy career, the librettist himself said that the composer was 'like me in one respect (only in one) . . . no interruptions when working'. They had talent, energy and professionalism in common, but similarities ended there. Sullivan was ingratiating, social, charming; Gilbert quick-tempered, strong-willed, master of a slashing wit that was always ready to leap out of its scabbard. Thus armed, the librettist was famous for feuds and lawsuits, continuing campaigns, public and private, against critics, actors and fellow writers—anyone in fact who provoked his displeasure. He called it honesty, telling the critic Clement Scott, 'I always speak openly, without fear or favour—and I am quite incapable of an act of social treachery.' Maybe; but Scott was one of Gilbert's oldest comrades until an ill-advised quip at the expense of one of Gilbert's plays put an end to their friendship. Twenty-six years later he attempted a reconciliation, but Gilbert spurned him in a curt note that ended 'I have a long memory.' That elephantine memory and deadly tongue rather limited Gilbert's social relationships. In his combative prime, he once entered the dining-room of his club and stopped in amazement. 'A dozen men,' he exclaimed, looking around, 'and I'm on terms with them all!'

Sullivan, on the other hand, was on effortless good terms with everyone, and his friendships tended to be life-long. He was known in part for the company he kept: the aristocracy of several countries, particularly his own, as well as the leading figures of art and society. But he was no sycophant. His claim to the attention of the great was first of all his remarkable and precocious talent. He had been hailed as a prodigy and the new hope of British music almost from his first appearance on the scene. But along with his ability went a genuine enjoyment of people that was as deep-seated as Gilbert's contentiousness. Sullivan exuded a graceful bonhomie that appealed to whomever he was with, whatever their social rank. Gilbert gave the impression of being constantly on guard. One critic, in fact, has said he had 'a grudge against life'. This is rather strong, but it is undoubtedly true that the writer did not project the pleasure at giving and receiving good will that was one of the musician's main characteristics.

As a contemporary noted, the differences between the partners were summed up simply in the way they took their bows after a triumphal opening night at the Savoy. Sullivan was dark, short and rather roly-poly, beaming the delightful smile that seemed reflected in his twinkling monocle, smoothly and sincerely acknowledging the cheers. Gilbert looked like a military man taken by surprise—tall and ramrod-straight, he seemed to have been coerced on stage, and his bow was a kind of gruff jerk. They might have been a comedy team in their ill-assortedness. But there was no humour for them in their differences. The wonder was that these conflicting personalities should complement each other so ideally in their art and produce so many of those glittering first nights.

As might be expected, they came from totally dissimilar backgrounds. Born in 1836, William Schwenck Gilbert was an Englishman of the truest blue. His forebears were hardy Hampshire yeomen who had left the soil and achieved a certain prominence in London. Gilbert's grandfather was a tea merchant, an acquaintance of Dr Johnson and Sir Joshua Reynolds, and, Gilbert avowed, 'the last man in London to wear Hessian boots and a pigtail'. The playwright's father was a proper block for the young chip. He had sailed as a midshipman with the East India Company until a Gilbertian insistence on his rights deposited him ashore. He later became a naval surgeon but retired from the sea once and for all when he received his family inheritance. After his son's success, Dr Gilbert turned to literature himself, showing a special interest in the absurd and fanciful, the supernatural and the psychologically macabre. He was a crusty character, easily piqued by critics and publishers. Passages from his books indicate that kinship with his son was more than just familial. A character in one of his novels observes that 'the longer I live . . . the more fully I am convinced that the world is one monstrous sham.'

Despite his obvious affinity with his prickly father, Gilbert's home-life was not idyllic. In fact he once referred to childhood as 'the most miserable period of one's existence'. The family was well-off and travelled a good deal, but relations between Dr Gilbert and his wife were strained. She compounded the difficulties of his personality by her aloofness and severity. In the '70s the couple finally separated, and their son attempted mediation. He failed. In his early letters to his mother he calls her 'Dear Mama'; in reply she addresses him as 'Schwenck', the name he had received from his grand-aunt and loathed. At length he complains of her 'cold and formal' attitude to the affair, and his last letter commences with a frigid 'Madam'.

One episode in Gilbert's early life deserves special mention because it seems so charmingly prophetic. At two, little William was snatched from a gullible nursemaid by a pair of fast-talking Neapolitans during a family visit to Italy. He was returned without delay for a ransom of £25, but who knows what secret marks the experience may have left on a writer who specialized in strange infant adventures?

Nothing so exotic disturbed Sullivan's infancy. His family found mere survival adventure enough. Born in a working-class neighbourhood in South London in 1842, Arthur Seymour was the second Sullivan child and son. His father earned a meagre income playing the clarinet in a theatre orchestra, copying music and giving lessons. The family ancestry was Irish and Italian (and, it has been alleged, Jewish as well). Sullivan's paternal grandfather was a poor but rakish country squire from County Cork, who, after a late night revel, suddenly found he had enlisted to fight Napoleon. He served with distinction through several campaigns, including Waterloo, and wound up as part of the guard attending the defeated Emperor on St Helena. Sullivan's mother was part of the Righi family, one of whose ancient members was said to have been Michelangelo's assistant.

Economic strains had no effect on the family's internal strength, except perhaps to increase it. The Sullivan ménage remained loving and good-humoured in the face of any difficulty and could rely on each other unfailingly for encouragement and support. His family continued to be the emotional centre of Arthur Sullivan's life. When death diminished that circle of comfort, his anguish was profound. His father died suddenly in 1866, and within a month Sullivan had poured his grief into an impassioned concert overture, *In Memoriam*. Ten years later, as his brother Fred lay mortally ill, he wrote his most famous song, 'The Lost Chord', during a long, painful bedside vigil. Soon after his mother's death in 1882, Sullivan drew up instructions for his own funeral, specifying that it be conducted in the same manner as hers 'and if possible, by the same undertaker'. During his own final illness, he gently remonstrated with his weeping valet: 'You must not cry for me. How do you think I could be otherwise than happy when I am going to see my dear mother?'

Along with this deep legacy of affection, Sullivan received at home the art that would be his life's work. When he was three, the family's fortunes brightened with his father's appointment as bandmaster at the Royal Military College in Sandhurst. Young Arthur thrived in the musical atmosphere, constantly in attendance at rehearsals and gradually mastering all the wind instruments. His love of the winds, as he later said, was 'not merely a passing acquaintance, but a real, life-long, intimate friendship'. The result of that intimacy can be clearly heard in the operas, which sparkle with deft writing for the brass and woodwinds.

Thomas Sullivan was clearly raising a musician. His little son was not only an accomplished multi-instrumentalist but a composer, turning out his first anthem at the age of eight. However, all too aware of the precarious nature of a musician's life, the bandmaster sent the likely lad to a proper academy, hoping to inspire wider interests and a more sensible career. But it was not to be. His letters home did mention the fascination of a chemical set, but also his regular visits to Miss Matthews, a lodger at his teacher's house, who let him play her piano. He briefly considered buying his own piano, before deciding that the down payment of 15s.6d was 'rather dear', at least for a ten-year-old.

The real passion of his life had become singing, and his great ambition to sing as a chorister of the Chapel Royal at St James's Palace. His father was reluctant to see his son's education jeopardized by concentrated musical study, but Arthur was not to be denied. 'It means everything to me,' his letters insisted. Ultimately he had his way, despite the additional fact that he exceeded the formal age limit for a new boy at the Chapel. At the audition the examiner was impressed with his voice, his musical knowledge and his personal charm. For his part, young Arthur was utterly self-possessed, reporting to his parents that 'he seemed very pleased with me'. Almost as soon as he had donned his splendid red and gold uniform, the new chorister was singing solos.

The Chapel Royal was Sullivan's entrée not only to a new world of musical riches but also to the opulence of life at court. The choristers performed every Sunday at the palace and for special royal occasions as well. Arthur's clear, sweet voice and curly-headed good looks soon brought him into direct contact with the great. The Duke of Wellington gave him a pat on the head, a pleasant word and a gift of ten shillings. Ten more shillings came from Prince Albert, along with his personal congratulations and the express pleasure of Queen Victoria herself, when Sullivan sang at Prince Leopold's christening. Newspaper reporters noticed him; a military audience voted 'three cheers for the young gentlemen, especially the one with the black hair'.

His talent was blooming. At a performance of an oratorio, he heard a march that he thought would be just the thing for his father's band. The piece was unpublished, so Arthur wrote out the instrumental parts from memory. In 1855 the choristers performed one of his own anthems. The same year saw his first publication, the song 'O, Israel'.

Another golden opportunity presented itself and, typically, fell into the remarkable chorister's lap. The dominant influence on mid-Victorian music was Felix Mendelssohn, and in his memory a scholarship had been established for a year's study at London's Royal Academy of Music. Sullivan, after being officially over-age for the Chapel Royal, found himself the youngest of eighteen competitors for the award. He won, of course, after a special run-off against a boy three years older than he who had already studied at the Academy for two years.

Arthur's reaction was pure rapture. But none of the honours and recognition he was gaining so quickly impressed him in themselves. They simply represented his progress in what he loved most. 'I have chosen music,' he wrote home, 'and I shall go on, because nothing in the world would ever interest me so much. I may not make a lot of money, but I shall have music, and that will make up if I don't.' His genuine delight in music-making, and in the people around him, saved him from the jealousy and resentment that his special status might have aroused. 'He was so free and unconstrained,' a fellow student remembered. He became conductor of a little tissue-paper-and-comb band and dazzled his mates by improvising fugues at the piano from motifs they suggested, and turning popular songs into chorales.

He worked hard and happily. The flow of courtly tips and compliments continued, since he was still singing at the Chapel Royal. He gained further rewards and professional experience by selling songs to young gentlemen. His ears were open to the music London had to offer and his opinions—even at fifteen—were decisive. When the Russian pianist Anton Rubenstein played an original concerto, Arthur declared that the soloist 'had a lot of clap-trap about him' and that the piece 'was a disgrace to the Philharmonic'.

At the end of his first year of study, the Mendelssohn scholar re-entered the competition and won a second year. His progress and talent were so obvious that he was granted a third year of tuition, to be spent at the Leipzig Conservatory on Mendelssohn's own hallowed ground. His time there repeated his successes at the Academy. He studied piano, composed and conducted, earning the respect and devotion of his classmates as well as his professors. He became friendly with such giants as Franz Liszt, through the standard Sullivan combination of musical and social talent. A girl friend of his Leipzig days recalled his charm: 'It was part of [his] nature to ingratiate himself with everyone that crossed his path. He always wanted to make an impression, and what is more, he always succeeded in doing it. . . . In this way he got into personal touch with most of the celebrities. . . . He was a natural courtier, which did not prevent him, however, from being a very lovable person.'

His first Leipzig year was supposed to be his only one. But the usual circumstances presented themselves. His teachers exhorted him to stay on, and his father somehow found the necessary money, which

Arthur scrupulously stretched and accounted for. The Conservatory made its own gesture by remitting his tuition expenses, because, as the Director himself said, 'We all like you so much that we can't let you go!' He crowned his Leipzig stay with the first performance of his music to Shakespeare's *The Tempest*, a full-length concert work that was enthusiastically received. It represented a kind of homage to Mendelssohn, suggesting the bright, melodic music that the German composer had written for the bard's *A Midsummer Night's Dream* when *he* was a rising young prodigy. And yet *The Tempest* was as winning and assured as Sullivan himself. In April 1861 he returned to London, his student days at an end, with the credentials, promise and personality that seemed to ensure a great career.

Gilbert's early years convey no such sense of fate pouring out blessings on a favourite son. He showed some early inclination to the stage, but nothing like Sullivan's foreordained commitment to music. His first schooling came in France, in Boulogne. (Gilbert remained adept in French all his life, translating *Les Brigands* by one of the fathers of comic opera, Offenbach, in 1871 and even, during his last years, writing his laconic diary in the language. Perhaps the biting metrical precision of his verse owes something to this influence.)

When his peripatetic family finally established themselves in England, Gilbert was sent to the Great Ealing School in London. He was thirteen and at first did not distinguish himself. Bright enough, but lazy, he liked writing and drawing and was somewhat disdainful of his classmates. Their academic success, however, fired his strong competitive streak, and by the time he was sixteen Gilbert was head boy.

His achievements included prizes for verse translation from Latin and Greek. He was a handsome youth, too—as a small boy the portraitist Sir David Wilkie had asked to paint him. He organized plays among his classmates, which he wrote, designed and directed. He acted as well, starring as Guy Fawkes in his own melodrama. But already the Gilbertian will to power was revealing itself. The fledgling man of the theatre insisted on having his productions exactly as he wanted them and brooked no other opinions—particularly from his actors. Gilbert was perfectly willing—and, being a strapping lad, perfectly able—to enforce his dramatic theories with his fists. Reminiscing about his school years, Gilbert told a biographer, 'I was not a popular boy, I believe.' This was probably an understatement. Possessing none of Sullivan's natural gift for being at home anywhere, Gilbert was restless and impatient. Ability and ambition he had, but so far no direction.

He made a brief, impetuous attempt to join a professional theatre company, but it was foiled when the manager turned out to be an old friend of his father. Thereafter, he followed the normal course for a middle-class boy, entering university (King's College, London) in 1853 and duly earning a general arts degree. His only public distinction there was becoming secretary of the Scientific Society and helping to engineer the small coup that transformed it into a Dramatic Society. Privately, he developed his talent for satiric verse and caricature.

Gilbert's hunger for action of some kind received an outlet with the eruption of war in the Crimea. The new Bachelor of Arts applied himself vigorously to studying artillery, hoping to win a commission. But the war ended in 1856 while he was still fighting his own battle with ballistics. He satisfied his martial longings by joining the West Yorkshire Militia as an ensign, ultimately becoming a captain with the Royal Aberdeenshire Highlanders. He cut an impressive figure in his kilt and proved a somewhat unlikely master of the Highland Reel. Military life suited Gilbert's temperament ideally, at least as long as he was giving the orders, and he remained in reserve army service for almost twenty years, until a naval commitment—*H.M.S. Pinafore*—took too much of his time.

But meanwhile civilian life demanded he do something with himself. At a loose end, Gilbert sat a competitive examination for an assistant clerkship with the government. He was successful but soon found he had let himself in for 'four uncomfortable years' of 'detestable thraldom'. By now he had left home, no doubt partly to escape family friction. Lodging in a boarding-house, working in a job he despised, Gilbert devoted his spare time to writing and drawing. He had begun to try his hand at plays once more, but his first break came from a family friend, the soprano Mlle Parepa. She requested he translate the 'Laughing Song' from Auber's *Manon Lescaut* for a series of promenade concerts—programmes of popular classics presented at a number of theatres, ancestors of the Henry Wood Proms. Gilbert did, and later said he attended the proms again and again 'to enjoy the intense gratification of standing at the elbow of any promenader who might be reading my translation, and wondering to myself what the promenader would say if he knew that the gifted creature who had written the very words he was reading was at that moment standing within a yard of him.'

The little feather in his cap presented a chance for a typical bit of Gilbertian humour. Vague word that he had theatrical connections got around his office, and one of his fellow-clerks asked if Gilbert could write him an order for free tickets to a play. Gilbert said indeed he could, inquired what kind of seats were preferable and handed his colleague the completed order. Of course at the theatre it produced only a blank look and considerable embarrassment. Confronted the next day, Gilbert defended himself: 'You asked me whether I could write you an order for the play. I replied that I could, and I did, but I never said that it would be of the least use to you.'

It was probably just as well for all concerned that an inheritance permitted Gilbert to leave the office behind him. Certainly for him his resignation in 1861 marked 'the happiest day of my life'. But he hadn't altogether wasted his time. Professional boredom had sharpened his determination to make a success of popular literature. By his own account he had composed fifteen farces and burlesques, though not one had come close to gracing a stage. His version of the 'Laughing Song' had succeeded modestly; he had even had a letter published in *The Times*, complaining of the rowdy conduct of soldiers, one of whom had jostled him in the street. (Gilbert's mixed feelings about uniforms, and the people in them, thus appeared early.) Various magazines had rejected his humorous drawings and articles. But the year that freed him from clerking was about to produce his first literary foothold.

Officially Gilbert had become an aspiring barrister, picking up studies he had begun at university and using his inheritance to pay for chambers and his call to the bar. But more importantly one of his comic pieces had so impressed the editor of *Fun*, a newly founded humour magazine, that he put the unknown author on his regular staff. Gilbert contributed to *Fun* well into the '70s, building a reputation for unique, and even perverse, wit. It also gave him, at last, the means to some status in his true profession and to the friendship of kindred spirits. In 1861 Gilbert had finally started on his way, but it had taken him much longer than his future partner, the graceful Sullivan, just as it would take him longer to arrive.

Meanwhile, that future partner had returned home from Leipzig full of prospects and honours, but faced with the mundane problem of earning a living. He put an advertisement in a music journal soliciting private pupils. An introduction to George Grove, later the editor of the monumental *Grove's Dictionary of Music and Musicians*, yielded a position as Professor of Pianoforte and Ballad Singing at the Crystal Palace School of Art, where Grove was secretary. But Sullivan's main desire was composing music, not teaching it. The Crystal Palace was a renowned venue for concerts, and when he had completed extensive revisions in his *Tempest* music, he sent it off to Grove for possible performance. It was a bold stroke, but it paid off handsomely. On 5 April 1862 this ambitious work by a young, unknown and British composer took its place in a programme of standard European classics. It was an instant success with both critics and public. On what he looked back on as 'the great day of my life', Sullivan's name was made. The piece had to be repeated a week later in an atmosphere of great

Gilbert in 1874 as a doughty captain with the Royal Aberdeenshire Highlanders. Two years later he almost resigned his commission in a dispute over his mess bill

The very handsome, very talented Sullivan in 1858, on the eve of his departure to study in Leipzig

Even in the traditional pose and costume, Gilbert makes a stern-looking Harlequin in 1878

Sullivan (at left) with the fun-loving Moray Minstrels in 1867. On his left is the famous actress Ellen Terry. The other lady is her sister Kate, grandmother-to-be of Sir John Gielgud. Between them sits George du Maurier, cartoonist and novelist. Behind Kate Terry stands John Tenniel, the classic illustrator of *Alice in Wonderland*

excitement. Its nineteen-year-old composer was hailed by various eminent Victorians. One of the most eminent of all, Charles Dickens, rushed backstage, clutched Sullivan's hand and exclaimed, 'I don't pretend to know much about music, but I do know I have been listening to a very great work.'

Doors opened everywhere. Musical London, hitherto largely dependent on the products of Europe, suddenly found a champion in its own breast. Sullivan thankfully gave up his teaching and accepted a post as organist at St Michael's Church, Chester Square. His fashionable congregation supplied him with sufficient female voices for his choir, but for tenors and basses he had to seek the help of the local police station. The force never failed to carry out this unexpected constabulary duty, and Sullivan found them 'capital fellows', whom he thought of years later when composing *The Pirates of Penzance.*

Established as a new musical star overnight, he turned out original works of every kind to extend his reputation. His songs were particularly in demand and made him a good deal of money, especially when he discovered the advantages of the royalty system. But orchestral works, hymns, chamber music, even a cello concerto poured from his pen in the next few years. He had become a celebrity—'shown about like a stuffed gorilla', he told a friend, describing the Birmingham triumph of *The Tempest*. He consorted with celebrities as well. The great soprano Jenny Lind gave him motherly advice against overwork. He spent a holiday whirling about Paris with Dickens, amazed at the novelist's energy. He met one of the old lions of opera, Rossini, who took a great fancy to both the young musician and his *Tempest*, which the two composers played as a piano duet.

Sullivan made royal conquests too, just as in the days of the Chapel Royal. For the wedding of the Prince of Wales and Princess Alexandra in 1863, he produced a song, 'Bride from the North', and a wedding march. Both pieces were performed at a gala concert at the Crystal Palace. Afterwards Sullivan was introduced to the Prince and to his brother the future Duke of Edinburgh, both of whom—the latter in particular—were to become personal friends.

The young composer was, as he himself said, 'getting on' in a number of ways. But both he and his public felt he had a responsibility to revive British music, which meant creating serious, large-scale works. *The Tempest* was a noble start, and Sullivan followed it with a masque, *Kenilworth* (1864), his *Irish Symphony* (1866), *In Memoriam* (1866) and an oratorio, *The Prodigal Son* (1869). Each piece lifted the hearts of the *cognoscenti* and made Sullivan seem a musical messiah, or at least a missionary. What was expected of him was spelled out clearly in a letter from one of his old teachers after the success of the symphony, urging his pupil to go 'on—on—on—on until . . . you may prove a worthy peer of the greatest symphonists'. After the oratorio, he wrote again, exhorting Sullivan to 'show yourself *the best man in Europe!'* Sullivan himself held very earnest views on the proper use of his gifts, writing to his mother, 'There are so many things I want to do for music, if God will give me two days for every one in which to do them.'

But there was so much to do—composing, travelling about the country to conduct. And there were the claims of his friends. One specific claim produced a fateful new direction for Sullivan. He was an habitué of a glittering, good-natured circle that met at Moray Lodge, Kensington, the home of Arthur Lewis, a well-to-do businessman. It included artists, aristocrats and other amusing characters, who put on musical evenings. One of the number was F. C. Burnand, editor of *Punch*. He suggested to his fellow-reveller Sullivan that they collaborate on a rather madcap skit he had adapted from a farce, *Box and Cox*. (One of his more straightforward adaptations was reversing the original title to *Cox and Box*.) Ever amiable, Sullivan agreed and knocked the piece off hurriedly. Burnand presented it at his house in late 1866, and it was given a benefit performance in Manchester in December of the same year. But the little operetta really came into its own at Moray Lodge on 27 April 1867. There was no proper musical score; Sullivan improvised an accompaniment on the piano. But his tunes were so delightful and the whole work so jolly, if silly, that it would not be kept private. The Moray Minstrels, as the Lewis group called itself, put it on as a benefit for a member of the *Punch* staff at the Adelphi Theatre two weeks later. It attracted critical cheers and was picked up for one more performance by the impresario Thomas German Reed. Reed, dedicated to presenting entertainment of a more respectable nature than the loose, risqué fare generally available, saw a winning combination in Sullivan and Burnand. Here was theatre that was clean, melodious, rib-tickling and thoroughly British. He commissioned a full-length piece, *The Contrabandista*, which opened on 18 December 1867. It had a run of three months. But when *Cox and Box* was brought back in March 1869, the one-acter kept the boards for three hundred performances.

Sullivan had proved his mastery in a totally new musical context. Reviews hailed his light touch and his gaiety and talked of the development of native comic opera. Rarely before had a musician of such accepted stature participated in a popular medium. But not everyone was heartened by Sullivan's versatility. More sober observers complained that the champion of British music was debasing his God-given gifts when he wrote a lullaby to a slice of bacon, as he had for *Cox and Box*. Sullivan himself was guiltily sensitive to such arguments. But these comic pieces took so little time and paid so well. Surely he might do both. *Cox and Box* was playing to capacity houses while its composer worked at his oratorio *The Prodigal Son*—whom he described in the prologue as 'a buoyant and restless youth . . . led gradually away into . . . follies and sins.'

On 1 June 1867 a slightly double-edged review of the first German Reed production of *Cox and Box* appeared in the pages of *Fun* magazine. 'Sullivan's music,' it said, 'is, in many places, of too high a class for the grotesquely absurd plot to which it is wedded. It is funny here and there, and grand or graceful where it is not funny; but the grand and graceful have, we think, too large a share of the honours to themselves.' The score was *too* good, attracted too much attention to itself. This was precisely the kind of grievance that Gilbert (who wrote the *Fun* review) would hold against Sullivan in years to come. By now the ex-clerk was a thoroughly professional journalist. He turned out verse, drawings, criticism, articles and stories for several magazines and was acquiring something of a reputation. A bit of money was coming in too, which was fortunate because his legal practice—probably more from his own lack of interest than incompetence—had brought him few cases.

For *Fun* his regular features included a series called the 'Comic Physiognomist' and another called 'Snarler'. Under each of these pen-names Gilbert delivered mordant, even cynical views of human activity, such as 'Man was sent into the world to contend with man, and to get the advantage of him in every possible way. . . . The great object in life is to be first at the winning-post. . . .' His verse and drawings gained special notice because their similarly dark perspective was brightened by a streak of pure nonsense. Sometimes it was satiric, sometimes merely violent. Throughout his merry stanzas, people were skewered and chopped, babies were eaten, love was not triumphant and pomposity was ventilated. They shocked and dismayed some people. A critic of Gilbert's first collection shuddered, saying his rhymes contained neither 'a thread of interest, nor a spark of feeling' and that his cartoons were 'inhuman'. Indeed, the editor of *Punch* had turned down his maiden ode, 'The Yarn of the Nancy Bell', which concerned a shipwrecked crew blithely devouring each other, as 'too cannibalistic for his readers' tastes'. But many readers found Gilbert's gleefully wicked energy hilarious. The *Bab Ballads*, as he called them, giving them his childhood nickname, earned him a distinctive reputation in the '60s and '70s. They remain true Gilbertian utterances, and he often returned to them for material for the operas.

But the rising humorist still hungered for theatrical success. He got his chance when one of his friends, the playwright Tom Robertson, recommended him to a manager who needed, on two weeks' notice, a burlesque for the Christmas holidays of 1866. Burlesque was one of the reigning genres of the time, featuring very broad comedy, outrageous puns, pretty girls dressed alluringly as boys, other pretty girls in what the Victorians considered shocking undress, and a general air of high-spirited confusion. (The singing, the dancing and the girls led to the more full-frontal mode of American burlesque.) The shows were often take-offs of the plots of grand opera, and the music was cheerily borrowed from operatic and popular sources of all kinds, to which the playwright added his own elbow-in-the-ribs lyrics. Gilbert's baptismal effort was roughly based on Donizetti's *L'Elisir d'Amore*. He called it *Dulcamara; or, The Little Duck and the Great Quack*. It gave him a hit and taught him a lesson when the stage manager, after writing Gilbert a cheque for the £30 he had asked for his play, advised him never to sell so good a piece so cheaply again.

Other burlesques followed, similarly outlandish in title and inane in humour. Typical is *Robert the Devil; or, The Nun, the Dun, and the Son of a Gun*, which contains lines like 'Men shun him and do not mention him.' But these extravaganzas were successful. Gilbert was making a name and learning his trade. And he also shaped his material to his own purposes, using the burlesque form as a medium for the same kind of satire he had practised in his other work. Critics recognized him as a writer who 'hates humbug of all sorts with a ferocity that is not of this planet.' But the free-wheeling nature of burlesque was most uncongenial to him. Gilbert had an almost military vision of the well-made play, with every effect calculated, every word and movement weighed. He was a moralist too, and it was this combination of qualities that took him to German Reed's Gallery of Illustration, where more orderly entertainment was promoted and where *Cox and Box* had had its triumph.

Gilbert began to produce more refined pieces, which still retained his patented saritiric wit, as well as exhibiting an unexpected sentimentality. In his quest to have his works performed the way he wanted them, he had already begun to earn a reputation for being difficult, hot-tempered and uncompromising. He reduced actresses to tears. He stormed, or sent actors storming, out of rehearsals. (Once *both* he and his adversary stormed out, only to find themselves reunited on the same railway platform. They fumed for a while, then patched it up and returned to the theatre, to discover everyone else had gone home.) There was even an occasional reprise of his schooldays: in mid-performance one cast was amazed to see emerging through a trapdoor, not the character they expected but Gilbert, who had disagreed with the intended actor, knocked him down and taken his place.

Not much of this happened at the Reed theatre, where the goings-on were relatively decorous. But that was the scene, in 1869 or 1870, of the first meeting between this vigorous, acerbic and ambitious playwright and the pleasant, sociable and ambitious Arthur Sullivan. Nothing came of the initial encounter, but, as recalled by Gilbert in later years, it does capture some flavour of the relationship to come. The two men were introduced by Fred Clay, a composer friend of Sullivan who was writing music for one of Gilbert's plays. We can imagine names exchanged and Sullivan smiling beautifully, murmuring his pleasure. But Gilbert responds, 'I am very pleased to meet you, Mr. Sullivan, because you will be able to settle a question which has just arisen between Mr. Clay and myself. My contention is that when a musician, who is master of many instruments, has a musical theme to express, he can express it as perfectly upon the simple tetrachord of Mercury (in which there are, as we all know, no diatonic intervals whatever) as upon the more elaborate disdiapason (with the familiar four tetrachords and the redundant note) which, I need not remind you, embraces in its simple consonance all the single, double, and inverted chords.' Sullivan blinks, asks to hear the salvo again, then says he will have to give careful consideration to such a nice point before making a reply. He can't know that his new acquaintance is simply trying out a passage from one of his plays, cribbed verbatim from the *Encyclopaedia Britannica*. Sullivan is slightly taken aback, but his suavity is unshaken; Gilbert chuckles inwardly, maintaining a straight face. For the moment the two men return to their different courses, the playwright to assault the follies of the age and stage, the composer to try to reconcile his friends, his talent and his responsibilities to High Art.

2

Thespis, Trial By Jury, The Sorcerer

It would have been fitting if the first Gilbert and Sullivan collaboration had seen the light at German Reed's Gallery of Illustration, where the two men had met, but it only almost happened. In 1870 the impresario sent a note to Sullivan: 'Gilbert is doing a one-act entertainment for me—soprano, contralto, tenor, baritone and basso. Would you like to compose the music? If so on what terms? Reply at once as I want to set the piece going without loss of time.' But the high-flying musician was too occupied with his customary round of social and artistic activities. The honour of launching the partnership went to John Hollingshead, who represented a quite different face of Victorian theatre from Reed. Reed called his establishment the 'Gallery of Illustration' to remove it as much as possible from the unsavoury associations of the stage. We have seen that it was to the Gallery that Gilbert turned when he sought more refinement than was attainable in the heady, leggy world of burlesque. But it was precisely that world in which Hollingshead reigned supreme. He gloried in burlesque, dubbing himself the keeper of its 'sacred lamp'. *His* theatre was proudly named the Gaiety, and it had opened in 1868 with Gilbert's scatty, pun-laden *Robert the Devil* (etc).

However shamelessly giddy Hollingshead's view of entertainment might have been, he also believed in style. The Gaiety was very handsome, a great improvement on the dingy, smelly houses of his competitors. Its patrons were liberated from the old, extortionate system of tipping, provided with perfumed programmes and invited to enjoy a large, well-appointed restaurant. Thus, with his reputation for quality, it was not a great surprise when Hollingshead announced that the Gaiety's Christmas bill would include '*Thespis*, a new operatic extravaganza', by the top-ranking talents of Messrs Gilbert and Sullivan. What was a surprise was that Sullivan, the golden boy of establishment music, should have accepted Hollingshead's proposal. But accepted he had, perhaps for money or amusement or the change that an 'operatic extravaganza' would offer his restless ability. Certainly it would differ from what he had been writing: his productions for 1871 included music for *The Merchant of Venice* and the evergreen hymn 'Onward Christian Soldiers'.

The prospect of the Gaiety, Gilbert and Sullivan provoked a flutter of anticipatory excitement. At the very least, said one newspaper, 'we may, indeed, expect a treat.' But more than that, the writer foresaw a 'great step in favour of English *Opéra Bouffe*'. Perhaps the new team could challenge the dominance of Jacques Offenbach, the witty Frenchman who had created the modern style of comic opera. A prophetic editorial advised anyone with 'a lively interest in the history of the stage' to take himself to the Gaiety.

Clearly something was in the wind. But in the event what transpired on 26 December 1871 was a distinct anti-climax. Instead of being remembered as a milestone in the annals of the theatre, the first fruit of the greatest of stage partnerships, *Thespis* has been counted a failure and largely forgotten. Gilbert sniffed at it in later years as 'crude and ineffective', merely thrown together. First-night reviews were mixed, many attributing the piece's difficulties to inadequate rehearsal. Writing to his mother, Sullivan mentioned a personal ovation when he appeared to conduct, but agreed the performance had been unfortunate, with one of the singers a semi-tone sharp throughout. Most unfortunate of all, modern audiences have no way of evaluating the first G & S opera for themselves, since the music to *Thespis* seems to have disappeared for good.

A moment spent considering what the maiden effort had to contend with will show why its first night was ill-fated and what a revolution its creators would have to bring about before their work got the hearing it deserved. We have seen that the Hollingshead company dealt in broad entertainment. People came to the Gaiety to ogle the lovely legs of Nelly Farren, who made a speciality of playing boys, and roar at the antics of J. F. Toole, the star comedian. Every performance was rife with 'gagging'—funny bits of business or asides the players would throw in on the spot. None of this suited the kind of production Gilbert had in mind. He had written *Thespis* for the Gaiety company, but its effectiveness depended on more precision than they were used to.

Another problem was musical. The new opera was original throughout, instead of borrowing its melodies burlesque-fashion from a hodgepodge of sources. So it required a higher level of vocal skill than usual. Even Hollingshead, with his devotion to Farren and Toole, did not vouch for them as singers, though they were expert at 'talking' a song artfully. But knowing this put a burden on Sullivan, who found himself 'rather restricted as a composer in having to write vocal music for people without voices!'

Then too, *Thespis* was a Christmas piece, which meant the audience expected the elements of pantomime traditional in Yuletide entertainment. These included the magical scene change known as the Transformation and above all the manic comedy of Harlequin and Clown.

Harlequin's specialities were agile leaps and athletic escapes, and the power to change one object into another with a blow of his slapstick (hence 'slapstick comedy'). Clown played practical jokes, hurled custard pies and jabbed people's bottoms with his supposedly red-hot poker. Since the Gaiety company featured the Payne brothers, famous for playing the pantomime characters, Gilbert had at least to leave room for their high jinks.

The Christmas season also meant that rehearsal time was in short supply. Hollingshead's company were running daily double and triple bills of other productions right up to *Thespis*'s première as well as playing a simultaneous matinée season miles away from the Gaiety at the Crystal Palace. In addition, sharing the bill with the opera was a new three-act play which also had to be learned. Gilbert, who had just opened a new play of his own two weeks before *Thespis*'s first night, read the hapless piece to the Gaiety troupe on 14 December—giving them twelve days to prepare it. And of course he was determined to see his work done as he wanted it. His great innovation was making the chorus part of the action, creating a genuine, unified dramatic effect. Standard Victorian staging put the stars in the centre while the chorus stood randomly about. But Gilbert told *everyone* where he wanted them, which caused the usual strained feelings. 'Really, Mr Gilbert,' objected one of the principals, 'why should I stand here? I am not a chorus girl!' 'No, madam,' Gilbert replied briskly, 'your voice is not strong enough, or no doubt you would be.'

The play's final misfortune was opening on Boxing Day night. The day after their Christmas festivities, audiences tended to be huge but undiscriminating, eager for simple diversion. As several critics pointed out, the playwright's clevernesses were 'over the heads' of the Gaiety throng. Things were made worse by the muddle resulting from inadequate rehearsal, which not only diminished the play's effect but caused it to run an hour over time, leaving the ill-tempered audience, after midnight, 'in a fidgety state to get away'. No wonder the first-night curtain fell 'not without sounds of disapprobation'. But many of the critics recognized that the piece had been ill-done-by and that further rehearsal and more favourable conditions would bring a work 'so rich in humour and so delicate in music' the success it deserved. And in fact this is what happened, despite the contrary testimony of many later G & S chroniclers. *Thespis* ran sixty-four performances, a perfectly acceptable record for what was intended as a Christmas novelty. Judging by the quality of the libretto, it might be regularly performed today if Sullivan's music were extant. But even in its truncated condition it has been revived by amateur companies, who have cobbled together a score from other Sullivan compositions or attempted a Sullivan pastiche.

The story itself is a mixture of standard Victorian elements and Gilbertian ingenuities. The curtain rises on the fog-bound summit of Mount Olympus, where we first meet a chorus of stars coming off duty after a hard night's shining, and then a varied assortment of Greek gods, all of whom complain of old age and fatigue. The fog lifts to reveal a picturesque ruined temple, to which the gods withdraw when a group of mortals appear—the theatrical troupe managed by Thespis, out for a picnic. After they are settled, the Olympians re-emerge. Jupiter scares the actors off with a display of his powers, except for Thespis, from whom he seeks professional advice. The gods feel they are out of touch with their earthly subjects; they are not the gods they were. Thespis suggests they go to earth as a band of touring players. There they can gauge public opinion and decide how best to recover their influence. In the meantime he volunteers his troupe as stand-ins for the Immortals—they are used to long parts on short notice. Everyone seems delighted with the arrangement, roles are assigned among the actors, and the gods set off to tour the earthly provinces, with only Mercury left behind to act as Jupiter's steward.

In Act II the Thespians have been in charge for a year and are utterly content with their Olympian status. They have had some difficulties in adapting the proper mythological relationships to the real-life alliances of the actors—Deputy Venus, for instance, objects to being married to Vulcan, who is played by her grandfather—but everything else is going swimmingly, without any need for discipline. Only Mercury sees the chaos that has been caused on earth by the whims and experiments of the fill-in gods. The real state of things becomes clear when Jupiter and the deities return in wrath and begin to examine the year's backlog of petitions from earth. Athens' complaint that it has been subjected to a wet Friday in November for the last six months is only one example of the Thespians' absurd ineptness. The troupe is banished back to earth, condemned to 'be eminent tragedians/Whom no one ever goes to see!'

Victorian theatre-goers would have recognized Offenbach's influence in the general setting of Gilbert's play. The Frenchman's two most popular operas, *Orpheus in the Underworld* and *La Belle Hélène*, were also mythological, deriving much of their humour from the spectacle of the gods conducting themselves like bored Second Empire Parisians. But Gilbert did not imitate Offenbach's use of sexual intrigue as the main business of the action. He was content with the possibilities afforded by the topsy-turvy, wholly Gilbertian notion of substituting mortals for immortals and putting them in charge of the basic forces of nature. Like Offenbach, he also jested with anachronisms—the gods complain that they used to be worshipped by human sacrifice, whereas now they are offered preserved Australian beef.

Some of Gilbert's wit clearly shows his Victorian roots and, no doubt, his awareness of the expectations of a Gaiety audience. Puns, if not as unrelenting and outrageous as in his earlier burlesques, still crop up. Thespis laments his 'unhappy lot' in having charge of his actors, 'and it is rightly termed a lot, because they are many'. The same tendency occurs in the mock-Greek names of his actors and actresses, like Sparkeion, Nicemis and Pretteia. Gilbert moderated this habit, at least, but he would always have a weakness for the alliterative thump of 'I'm Thespis of the Thessalian Theatres.'

The Boxing Day crowd must have been delighted with the presto-changeo transformation of a foggy stage to the ivied columns of Olympus, just as they would have appreciated Jupiter's imperious demonstration of his powers—flash-paper in his fingers igniting an explosive 'calling-card', a thunderbolt sending the Thespians screaming off stage. And the scholar Terence Rees, whose research has resuscitated *Thespis*, has suggested that the picnic scene must have given the Payne brothers, as Stupidas and Preposteros, ample opportunity to do their stuff as Harlequin and Clown. As Thespis and Mercury, J. F. Toole and Nelly Farren had plenty of scope for their specialities.

But *Thespis* already shows traits that were unmistakably Gilbert's own, particularly the topsy-turvy premise of the plot and his wicked logic in applying it. If the actors deputizing for the gods Apollo and Diana are married, then of course the sun and the moon (which they control) will go around together—a man wouldn't let his wife out alone at night. Nothing is more Gilbertian than these paradoxical conflicts between people's roles, and in *Thespis* we already hear one of the abiding questions of the Savoy operas: 'Who are we all and what is our relation to each other?'

Many of the G & S operas satirize a particular institution. In *Thespis* it is the stage. Toole must have been wonderful as the strutting title character, snubbing people with 'Don't know yah! Don't know yah!'. And writing the part must have been positively therapeutic for Gilbert, especially since it is the stage manager's lack of control of his company that brings about their downfall. He also uses the character of Preposteros as a hilarious jab at the heavy villain of melodrama, a figure as unreasonably moody and unpredictably explosive as Heathcliffe in *Wuthering Heights*. Among the Immortals, a choice target is poor Venus, the goddess who is distinctly 'past it', the first in a long line of middle-aged women who suffer at Gilbert's hands.

Any Savoyard can recognize archetypes among *Thespis*'s songs. Mercury's two solos, 'Oh, I'm the celestial drudge' and 'Olympus is now in a terrible muddle', along with Thespis's tale of 'a chap who discharged a function/On the North South East West Diddlesex junction', look forward to the classic patter songs in which a comic figure introduces himself in galloping polysyllables. 'Little maid of Arcady' is a wry pastoral ballad which was published separately and thus survived whatever fate overtook the rest of Sullivan's score. 'Climbing over rocky mountains' also escaped to posterity, because Sullivan used it again in *The Pirates of Penzance*. As it stands in *Thespis*, it is the first of the blithe choral entrances that brighten every Savoy opera. The Act II quartet, 'You're Diana, I'm Apollo', is the prototype of the so-called 'ensemble of perplexity', in which a group of characters discuss the intricacies of the dramatic situation in stirring counterpoint. In G & S, these moments are purportedly parodies of the clichés of Italian opera—such notable ensembles, for instance, as the sextet from Donizetti's *Lucia di Lammermoor*. But Sullivan manages to make them exciting as well as amusing, although sadly we will never know what his original, Thespian effort sounded like.

In addition to the main objects of its satire—the paradoxes of roles and the excesses of the stage—*Thespis* also reveals some other characteristic Gilbertian fixations. Mercury's 'celestial drudge' ditty contains in its refrain the librettist's sceptical view of titles versus ability:

> 'Well, well, it's the way of the world,
>   And will be through all its futurity;
> Though noodles are baroned and earled,
>   There's nothing for clever obscurity!'

Thespis's song relates the significant story of a chairman of a railway who treated his employees with too much consideration:

> 'He was hand in glove with the ticket inspectors,
> He tipped the guards with bran-new fivers,
> And sang little songs to the engine drivers.'

The problems inherent in such 'easy breeding' originally appeared in the *Bab Ballad* tale of 'Captain Reece', who treated his crew in just this way. He is also an ancestor of Captain Corcoran on the good ship *Pinafore*.

There can have been little doubt in anyone's mind after the *Thespis* rehearsals that Gilbert was utterly in command of *his* ship. Similarly, he must have realized that his future productions would require conditions quite different from those at the Gaiety. But *Thespis* had not been a failure. Sullivan himself had written to his mother that he had 'rarely seen anything so beautifully put upon the stage'. The music and lyrics had been praised. Only another opportunity was needed. That, however, was three years in coming.

In those intervening years the erstwhile collaborators met socially from time to time. They still frequented different circles, but they did have success in common. Sullivan had written a *Te Deum* in thanks for the Prince of Wales's recovery from typhoid fever; it was given at the Crystal Palace in May 1872 by two thousand performers before a huge audience liberally adorned by royalty. The next year his oratorio *The Light of the World* was hailed as 'a triumph' by the Duke of Edinburgh in person and the critics in the papers. Queen Victoria herself (who had already requested a complete set of Sullivan's works) declared it would 'uplift British music'. The composer advanced on all fronts, turning out more incidental music, ballads and hymns and travelling tirelessly through the provinces to conduct.

Gilbert had made his mark with several plays, his biggest hit being *Pygmalion and Galatea*, which ultimately earned him £40,000. He continued to write for magazines and published a second collection of *Bab Ballads*. There were the usual vigorous defences of his professional and private rights.

But a sequel to *Thespis* was not forthcoming, at least directly. One would-be backer had briefly appeared, proposing to back another G & S effort with £1,000, but had failed to produce any money. Gilbert was approached, however, by the operatic impresario and composer Carl Rosa, who wanted a libretto for a short piece to feature his wife, the same soprano for whom a frustrated young clerk had translated the 'Laughing Song' years before. As he would almost invariably in the future, Gilbert found inspiration for the new work from his earlier output. For the *Fun* issue of 11 April 1868, he had written and illustrated a one-page 'operetta' called *Trial by Jury*, about a breach-of-promise suit. It presented sprightly satiric verse and a small but complete cast of characters and chorus. Gilbert expanded it into a one-acter and sent it to Rosa, who intended to provide the music. But very suddenly, in 1874, the unfortunate Mme Parepa-Rosa died, and her widowed husband returned the manuscript to its author.

Then early the next year Gilbert happened to stop by the Royalty Theatre, where Offenbach's *La Périchole* was about to open. The manager of the Royalty, a rising power in the theatrical world named Richard D'Oyly Carte, mentioned that he was looking for an afterpiece to strengthen the bill. (He already had an opener, a piece of pure Victorian nonsense called *Cryptoconchoidsyphonostomata*.) Gilbert described *Trial by Jury*; Carte thought it sounded just the thing and suggested that Sullivan set it. The librettist duly called on the composer to go over the work with him. It was another characteristic meeting, with Gilbert in Gilbertian mood. Sullivan later recalled the scene in which his partner-to-be introduced him to *Trial by Jury*: 'He read it through, and it seemed to me, in a perturbed sort of way, with a gradual crescendo of indignation, in the manner of a man considerably disappointed with what he had written. As soon as he had come to the last word he closed up the manuscript violently, apparently unconscious of the fact that he had achieved his purpose so far as I was concerned, inasmuch as I was screaming with laughter the whole time.' The composer accepted the project with pleasure and had the music ready in two weeks.

The first announcement of 'A New Comic Opera' to be given at the Royalty appeared on 23 January 1875. It mentioned only Sullivan's name, reflecting perhaps both Carte's opinion that the Queen's favourite composer would attract more attention than the merely commercially successful playwright, and standard operatic practice: the man who wrote the words received much less credit than the spinner of the melodies. Gilbert would become the first librettist to receive equal billing, indeed to have his name come before the composer's. But in these early days he still had to assert his claims. A later notice did include him, but with his middle initial changed to C. It was only in the advertisements just prior to the opera's opening on 25 March that matters were wholly rectified, though he still had to accept second place both there and in the theatre programmes.

With two months between the first notice and opening night, we can imagine Gilbert at last getting the kind of rehearsal time he desired. He was free alike from the Christmas rush and the Gaiety's requirements. (It is not surprising that John Hollingshead had made no attempt to follow up *Thespis* with another G & S collaboration. He had admired it but thought it contained 'defects'—probably those parts that were 'over the heads' of his audience. And he knew Gilbert's conception of gaiety was not Hollingshead's. When the playwright himself once appeared as Harlequin in a benefit pantomime, the manager quipped that his performance gave you an idea of how Oliver Cromwell might have played the role.)

These favourable conditions produced a little masterpiece. Not only were the words and music delightful, but in *Trial by Jury* Gilbert was able to carry through every aspect of his intention. He designed the set, basing his realistic courtroom on the Clerkenwell Sessions he had known well in his barrister days. The women's costumes were tasteful, flowing creations in the best style of the period. The staging extended the revolution Gilbert had begun in *Thespis*, with the movements of soloists and chorus planned to the smallest detail, so that the action was continuously effective. The result was a new kind of theatrical experience. It combined charming music and satirical nonsense with refined taste, presenting it all with absolute precision.

None of this was lost on critics and audiences. Everyone was captivated by the little 'Dramatic Cantata', which one reviewer summed up as 'a burlesque of the wildest sort'. It was, said another, 'the happiest idea caught to perfection by Mr. Arthur Sullivan's music and faultlessly executed by the company'. The smoothness of the production was only impeded by its own success: 'Laughter more frequent or more hearty was never heard in any theatre than that which more than once brought the action . . . to a temporary standstill.' Honours were fairly divided between author and composer, though a serious musical journal raised an eyebrow at 'the versatile composer of *The Light of the World*' being involved in such goings-on. But most of the audience would have endorsed the praise lavished on the duo's remarkable joint effect: ' . . . so completely is each imbued with the same spirit that it would be as difficult to conceive the existence of Mr. Gilbert's verses without Mr. Sullivan's music, as of Mr. Sullivan's music without Mr. Gilbert's verses. Each gives each a double charm.' And *The Times* recognized that the evening represented an historic confrontation. Here was an English challenge to Offenbach, appearing on the same bill as the Continental master. The paper's verdict was unequivocal: '. . . *Trial by Jury* suffered nothing whatever from so dangerous a juxtaposition. On the contrary, it may fairly be said to have borne away the palm.'

Even now it is possible to recreate something of the excitement of that opening night and the emergence of this new musical and dramatic force. Though *Thespis* is rather unluckily forgotten, *Trial by Jury* deserves its customary place as the first Gilbert and Sullivan opera. Everything that makes the partnership great is already here in miniature, and some Savoyards still regard it as the essential G & S production. Part of its special appeal is due to its being the only one of the operas in which every word is sung. There is no spoken dialogue, so its creators' remarkable compatibility is displayed throughout.

The story is simple and outrageous, full of Gilbertian absurdity. The curtain rises on a courtroom, where jurymen and spectators announce that a breach-of-promise suit between Edwin and Angelina is about to be heard. The usher calls them to order and reminds the jury of its duty to be impartial—while displaying his own bias for the plaintiff. Edwin, the anxious defendant, appears to justify his change of heart toward his 'old, old love', but the jury is clearly disposed against him. Amid great solemnity the judge enters and gives a candid account of his rise to eminence, which was due purely to having proposed to 'a rich attorney's elderly, ugly daughter', whom he subsequently jilted. The jury is sworn, and in trips a chorus of bridesmaids. They introduce the distressed plaintiff, also in bridal dress. The judge and jury are obviously impressed, which gives the plaintiff's counsel an even greater advantage. To add to the emotion of the scene, the lady opportunely faints. The jurymen rush to her aid and shake their fists at the hapless Edwin, who pleads that he has only obeyed nature's laws. He offers to marry *both* the plaintiff and his new sweetheart, which the judge finds 'a reasonable proposition', until the learned counsel points out that it would constitute 'burglary'. Everyone agrees they face 'a nice dilemma', which is intensified by both parties' attempts to influence the jury. Finally the judge, furious at the impasse, throws his papers about and declares that *he* will marry the plaintiff. The dilemma is resolved, and everyone rejoices.

A typical Gilbert production, extravagant, amusing, with a goodly number of satiric bristles. But, also typically, it comes into its own only with Sullivan's music. His skill gives life to the opera's opening. The chorus excitedly declaims, 'Hark, the hour of ten is sounding', and Sullivan sets the first three lines (and most of the fourth) to a single repeated note. This is not a failure of inspiration but a recognition that these scene-setting words must come across with absolute clarity. In addition, the resulting chant creates a feeling of breathless anticipation. In the next four lines Sullivan bursts into a lively, rhythmic melody that derives its character from the natural accents of Gilbert's words: '*For* today in this arena,/*Sum*moned by a stern subpoena,/ *Ed*win, sued by *An*gelina. . . .' The proceedings are scarcely thirty seconds old and we are already captivated.

The mood changes to mock-gravity as the usher advises the jury, and Sullivan provides just the air of pomposity and slyness his backhanded counsel requires. But when the defendant appears, supposedly presenting his case to his own guitar accompaniment, the composer produces a lilting, ballad-like refrain. It is this variety of pace, these utterly controlled alterations in rhythm and colour, that Gilbert sought; Sullivan never fails to capture them and to add dimensions of his own. As a critic observed, in Sullivan 'Gilbert found his piano, and something more.'

One of *Trial by Jury*'s best moments is the judge's song 'When I, good friends, was called to the bar', which is the first of the biographical patter numbers that become such a feature of the operas. As a former barrister, Gilbert had had considerable experience with judges, and it gave him more than a slight suspicion of the breed. (This antipathy was increased in later life as he went through a long series of lawsuits, which often left him feeling badly treated. He described the judge in one notable action as 'a drunken monkey' and 'a monument of senile incapacity'.) His operatic judge is an amiable fraud, quite pleased with his lordly position. He enters to wonderfully august music, a Sullivan wink in Handel's direction. Indeed, the chorus are so carried away by their sonorous counterpoint that the judge must repeatedly demand 'Let me speak!' His song is a merry affair, full of the telling details that Gilbert delights in. The great irony, of course, is that he is just the man to hear a breach-of-promise suit since he himself threw over the girl whose father's influence got him where he is. *Trial by Jury* as a whole, in fact, offers a classic view of its author's reservations about love. The judge faked the emotion with success; the defendant pleads that in going from one girl to another, perfectly sincerely, he is just obeying nature, which is 'constantly changing'. The operas show again and again that for Gilbert love is inexplicable, unstable and untrustworthy. It is yet another area—perhaps the central one—where he believes in order and good sense.

The plaintiff's and defendant's songs attractively demonstrate the collaborators' skill at characterization. Angelina is winsomely pathetic, Edwin anxious. (Accompanying his 'Oh, gentlemen, listen I pray', the bridesmaids rush prettily to the jury box, a nice touch by Gilbert the director.) But the musical climax of the opera is the 'ensemble of perplexity' in which the whole company consider their 'nice dilemma'. Sullivan's importance can be appreciated by a glance at the libretto on its own. It simply reads 'ALL: A nice dilemma, etc.' Sullivan makes this 'etc' into a glorious ten-part concoction of interlocking lines, soaring melody and a certain harmonic grandeur. It may have been intended as a take-off of Italian opera, like the florid recitatives that precede it, but it gives a genuinely operatic effect all the same. In a way it is the forerunner of the great G & S Act I finales to come. The ensemble brings these proceedings to a final peak, resolved by the judge's well-considered decision to marry the plaintiff. The charming cantata dances to a close with 'Oh, joy unbounded', which quite resembles a British version of an Offenbach can-can.

As the critics had sensed at *Trial by Jury*'s first night, the British version of comic opera, in spite of Offenbach's reputation, was something distinctive and triumphant. Its effect was dramatic. Not long after the opening, the Frenchman's *La Périchole,* supposedly the main item on the Royalty's bill, was withdrawn. But the British one-acter picked up new supporting pieces and carried on and on. At a stroke it had proclaimed a re-birth of native comic opera and the brilliant team that would foster it. And it had created a new kind of audience for a new kind of theatre.

Trial by Jury might well have exceeded its original one-year run but for the illness of one of its stars. This was Fred Sullivan, the composer's older brother, who had made a great personal success as the judge. A witty and companionable man, he had worked as an architect before taking to the stage. (As he once explained, 'I still draw big houses.') He was expected to be an integral part of future G & S productions, but, though only thirty-six, he never recovered his health. His death in January 1877 shattered his brother. 'The Lost Chord' was Sullivan's tribute and an attempt to ease his own suffering. It was also the last piece he could bring himself to write for several months.

Gilbert, meanwhile, had turned out further successful plays, but his most celebrated production may have been his virulent, long-running feud with the actress-manager Henrietta Hodson. Quintessentially Gilbertian, it began at a rehearsal of one of his works in 1874. Miss Hodson, starring, misjudged the position of a chair and sat heavily on the floor. 'Very good,' snapped Gilbert. 'I always thought you would make an impression on the stage one day.' Miss Hodson was not amused, having objected for some time both to the playwright's high-handed manner and to his questionable wit. The ensuing acrimony deepened over the next few years, fed by letters, pamphlets and threats of legal action. Observers tended to favour the plaintiff against her too-blunt adversary. As *The Theatre* said, 'Mr. Gilbert has yet to learn that he is a servant of the public and amenable to public opinion, and Miss Hodson must be congratulated on the courage she has shown in appealing to her profession against him.'

With Sullivan bereaved and Gilbert embattled, the great cause of native opera was being pursued by Richard D'Oyly Carte alone. His uniting of librettist and composer in *Trial by Jury* had been no accident. *Thespis* had convinced him they would be an ideal team. Since 1869 he had been bent on 'the starting of English comic opera in a theatre devoted to that alone'. He called it 'the scheme of my life', frustrated so far by lack of money. But the proven success of the Gilbert and Sullivan partnership convinced him the moment was at hand.

Carte was as much a master in his sphere as his two associates were in theirs. In interesting ways he combined certain of their personal characteristics. His background recalled Sullivan's. His father too had been an impecunious musician; his grandfather had fought at Waterloo. On his mother's side he was descended from Welsh and ancient Norman stock. Paternal objections to her marrying a penniless flautist had forced the young couple to elope, but at length the family was reconciled. Richard Carte made a success of a musical instrument business, and the Carte home became a place of refinement, with French spoken two days a week and lively discussions of painting and the theatre.

Young D'Oyly Carte (named for his Norman forebears) inherited his father's talent. After university, he composed operettas, three of which were performed. But he became more and more drawn to the management side of the music business, for which his affable manner and keenly analytical brain ideally suited him. He opened an agency in the late 1860s and was soon representing opera singers, touring companies and lecturers alike. As we have seen, he expanded into theatre management, with light opera a speciality. Everywhere he was such a success that he became known, darkly, as 'Oily' Carte—a dubious compliment to his instinct for manipulation. Outwardly he resembled Sullivan—easy-going, charming, almost self-effacing. But inwardly what has been called his Napoleonic strain related him to Gilbert. He had an *idée fixe*, a driving ambition to be the impresario who would revive English opera, and comic opera in particular. It was the conjunction of these three diverse but complementary and necessary personalities that spawned the Savoy Operas.

To follow up on *Trial by Jury*, D'Oyly Carte wanted Gilbert and Sullivan to compose a full-length, two-act comic opera. Before committing himself, Gilbert in particular wanted to see the colour of Carte's money. Carte's proposal for a Christmas run of *Thespis* had fallen through in 1875 for lack of funds, and the author had written to the composer sceptically: 'It's astonishing how quickly these capitalists dry up under the magic influence of the words "cash down".' So Carte began the hunt for backers, touting the project on artistic, patriotic and commercial grounds. By late 1876 he had assembled a syndicate whose members contributed £500 each and whose directors included three music publishers and the man in charge of watering London's streets. The Comedy Opera Company Ltd would finance the theatre, the cast, the costs of production—and an advance for Gilbert and Sullivan.

Carte's quest for a theatre turned up the Opera Comique, an auspiciously named but ill-favoured house off the Strand. It was cramped and dingy; one of its entrances was a tunnel from the street. It was also said to be jinxed, having ushered a number of productions to oblivion. But it was available, and Carte took it.

Choosing performers for the Comedy Opera Company was a ticklish task. Gilbert and Sullivan opera would be lively and tasteful, fast-paced and disciplined. In order for the works to have their proper effect, the author, for once, would have absolute control of staging—contrary to the standard Victorian view that he was the least important person in the house. Thus the new company was suspicious of established stars, who would be temperamental and tainted with the old extravagant habits of pantomime, melodrama and burlesque. Another problem was that, generally, singers couldn't act and actors couldn't sing. As his careful setting of the texts shows, Sullivan was sensitive to Gilbert's desire that the clarity of the words be paramount.

But where to find players who could be both accurate and at least musical to some degree?

Ultimately the partners did their recruiting from amateurs, non-London professionals and students. The Royal Academy of Music supplied a substantial portion of the chorus. From a provincial touring company came the featured contralto and, at her insistence, a young actor who would be a Savoy star for years to come. His name was Rutland Barrington, large of frame and seemingly inexpressive of countenance. But Gilbert could see that this 'staid, stolid swain' would take direction and that was what mattered.

Another future star, the great George Grossmith, was primarily a solo entertainer, presenting songs and recitations for private gatherings, including the 'Penny Readings' that were a respectable alternative to the sordid stage. Gilbert and Sullivan both knew something of his work (he had played in two different productions of *Trial by Jury*), but it was the composer who suggested he audition for the title role in the next G & S piece, *The Sorcerer*. Grossmith's subsequent dealings with the three executive heads of the Company are instructive. Nervous about his ability to carry off an important singing part, he appeared first before Sullivan. After hearing him deliver one note, the composer beamed—Grossmith recalled that 'even his eye-glass seemed to smile'—and said, 'Beautiful!' Gilbert in his turn was 'very kind', outlining the role of the sorcerer. Grossmith was intrigued but still apprehensive. 'For the part of a magician,' he said tentatively, 'I should have thought you required a fine man with a fine voice.' Gilbert thought of singers and their egos. 'That,' he replied, 'is exactly what we don't want.'

With the creative team satisfied, Grossmith met with D'Oyly Carte to talk salary. Supported by his father, the little comedian was worried that his appearance on the stage would blast forever his sterling reputation with groups like the YMCA. He thought the risk was worth eighteen guineas a week; Carte's estimate was fifteen. The manager was amiable and understanding and suggested that a lunch of oysters and champagne would do them both good. It certainly did Carte good. Mellowed by the repast and his host's bonhomie, Grossmith waived the extra three guineas.

The difficulties of casting had caused a delay in the new opera's opening. So had Sullivan's tardiness with the score. After shaking off the numbing effects of his brother's death, he had another commission to fulfil before embarking on *The Sorcerer*. He finished the music just prior to the first night, which became his usual practice.

But Gilbert had his libretto well in hand. He had based it, according to his usual practice, on a previous work, in this case a story called 'The Elixir of Love', which he had published at Christmas 1876. In it a clergyman doles out a love potion to villagers to promote peace and harmony. The topsy-turvy effects of such an idea appealed to Gilbert; he had, after all, based his first operatic burlesque on Donizetti's *Elisir*.

The Sorcerer is set in the village of Ploverleigh, which is already love-obsessed. The opening chorus hymns the coming marriage of Alexis Pointdextre and Aline Sangazure, scions of two ancient and honourable families. Straightaway we meet Mrs Partlet, a pew-opener, and her daughter Constance, who confesses that she too is suffering Cupid's pangs. To her mother's amazement, the secret object of her passion is the white-haired village vicar, Dr Daly. With weddings in the air, he too has been thinking of the contrast between his present solitude and his happy past, when he received admiring feminine attention. But he considers himself too old to marry now, much to Constance's distress.

Alexis comes in with his father, Sir Marmaduke, who congratulates his son but chides him for being too overt in his expressions of love to Aline. Years ago he loved Aline's mother, but they were properly restrained in their addresses. Father and son withdraw and the lovely Aline enters, accompanied by a girls' chorus and followed by her mother, Lady Sangazure, whose gladness for her daughter is tinged with regret for the past. Alexis and Sir Marmaduke return, and the lovers embrace and wander off, leaving their parents to exchange decorous compliments. But the secret love they still feel for each other bursts out in passionate asides.

Having signed the marriage contract, Aline and Alexis agree that 'true love' is 'the source of every earthly joy' and 'that in marriage alone is to be found the panacea of every ill'. Alexis's ambition, in fact, is to convince the world that 'men and women should be coupled in matrimony without distinction of rank.' His proposals to use love to break down social barriers have been welcomed by the working classes; the aristocracy is less enthusiastic. Now, determined to realize his vision, he has contacted an old family firm of London sorcerers about providing a love potion for the village. The firm's representative, the natty John Wellington Wells, arrives to describe his wares. After assurances that the elixir will inspire love at first sight in everyone but married people, Alexis has Wells mix the liquid in the teapot set up for the nuptial celebrations. Aline is apprehensive, and a harrowing incantation only increases her misgivings. When the innocent villagers partake of the brew, they all fall insensible.

Misrule reigns in Act II. Everyone is in love, but with the wrong people. Alexis still believes in his project, though he is shaken to see his father arm-in-arm with Mrs Partlet. He is also offended that Aline refuses to drink the potion with him: she maintains their love should be based on trust alone. Finally she does drink, but by herself, and fatefully encounters Dr Daly, despondent because everyone is engaged but he. He and Aline are immediately, helplessly smitten. Alexis is furious, and all turn to Wells, who himself has been fighting off Lady Sangazure, to undo the confusion. The magician relates that the spell can be lifted only by his death or that of Alexis. The honour quickly passes to Wells, and all are restored to their proper partners as he descends to the netherworld, in red fire.

The Sorcerer's opening night, on 17 November 1877, augured very well for the syndicate, the triumvirate and the cause of English opera. A packed house sent wave after wave of applause rolling over the stage, with separate ovations for Gilbert, Sullivan and Carte. The Press praised all aspects of the production, from the careful and efficient ensemble acting to the starring roles of Grossmith and Barrington. *Punch* called the former 'the Sorcerestest Sorcerer that ever I did see or hear' and noted the clarity of his enunciation, which must have pleased Gilbert. Barrington was singled out for the restrained humour with which he played Dr Daly. No one had been sure how the public would take to a comic clergyman, but, as a reviewer said, Barrington's 'good taste and freedom from exaggeration . . . preserved the character of the Vicar from any suspicion of impropriety'. The only criticism of the treatment of Dr Daly would come later from no less a figure than Lewis Carroll, author of *Alice in Wonderland*. A true Victorian, he found the curate's song 'simply painful', because it called into contempt earnest and hard-working young churchmen.

Sullivan's music was acclaimed, though one critic expressed 'a sense of disappointment at the downward art course Mr. Sullivan appears to be now drifting into. . .'—not the last time that admonition would be heard. But another writer noted that 'above all, the music is spontaneous, appearing invariably to spring out of dramatic situations' and that those situations were 'full of genial humour and . . . droll fancies'. The general reaction was summed up by one critic who observed that in this operatic partnership 'the importance of the playwright is at least as great as that of the musician.'

The promise of *Trial by Jury* had been fulfilled by its full-length successor, and *The Sorcerer* has retained its place in the G & S canon. It is true, however, that it suffers from comparison with the best of the series. The plot is weak, really nothing more than a sequence of results from a single premise. The village setting is charming but makes for a certain lack of contrast. Only the wedding festivities give Sullivan a chance to turn on the pageantry, and a rural occasion is less splendid than a military or noble one. There is a similar lack of contrast in the songs, because love is so exclusively the business of the tale, and this sort of love is so abstract and artificial. For Gilbert the emotion tends to be rather mechanical at the best of times, a kind of biological distemper, however pleasant, in an otherwise healthy brain. The potion lets him show helpless people in its grip. The libretto is Gilbert at his most topsy-turvily theoretical, seeing what would happen if. . . . Though the results are amusing, they lack real human interest, which is what Sullivan thrives on. The music, therefore, is inclined to be a little pallid, though as always with Sullivan it is graceful enough.

But there are undoubted moments of distinction. The curate's song, 'Time was when love and I were well acquainted', is very good Sullivan, warm and ruefully elegiac. Barrington made a great hit with his rendering, though everyone recognized that vocal technique was not his strong point. (It never would be, and the partners accepted this good-naturedly. After another première, someone remarked to Gilbert that Barrington had sung surprisingly well in tune. 'Oh, I know those first night nerves,' said W. S. 'They soon wear off.')

Lady Sangazure ('blue-blood' is Gilbert's Gallic pun) claims pride of place as the first lovesick matron in the Savoy operas, but she receives much milder treatment than that meted out to Ruth and Katisha. 'Welcome joy, adieu to sadness', her duet with Sir Marmaduke, shows Sullivan's skill at interweaving melodies of different character; the singers express politeness and passion alternately at first, then simultaneously. The Act II quintet of ill-assorted lovers is an early example of Sullivan finding feeling where his colleague may imply amusement. 'She will tend him, nurse him, mend him/Air his linen, dry his tears' is rather unpromising emotional territory, but the music does call up an image of marital sweetness. And the villagers' celebration of the tea-time banquet (replete with 'the gay Sally Lunn') is fresh, bucolic and charming.

Though Gilbert is more interested in the topsy-turvy than the satiric here (at his best, the two go together), the character of Alexis, the upper-class do-gooder, did cause some comment. He manages to be both patronizing (the working man 'is a noble creature when he is quite sober') and hypocritical: he renounces his plan for universal harmony as soon as it may cost him Aline. Perhaps with Alexis in mind a critic sounded what would become a familiar complaint: he doubted that 'conveying moral lessons' was 'suitable for the purposes of comic opera'.

A fine Sullivan set-piece is the Incantation scene, which he makes effectively spooky. Grand-opera buffs would have recognized a general resemblance to the forest scene in Weber's *Der Freischütz*, where the occult is similarly invoked. Another connoisseur's delight is the little minuet in Act I, which accompanies Dr Daly's florid congratulations to Alexis. As one of Sullivan's best critics, T. F. Dunhill, says, 'it might almost have been signed by Henry Purcell.'

But undoubtedly *The Sorcerer*'s central strength is the sorcerer himself. John Wellington Wells is a classic G & S creation, a go-ahead Cockney tradesman with infernal connections. His entrance transforms the proceedings. His patter song is as intoxicating to hear as it is demanding to execute, and author and composer contribute equally to its giddy precision. Gilbert's fiendish string of syllables recalls the motto he appended to the *Bab Ballads*—'much sound and little sense'. But the sounds scamper brilliantly, right down to that most euphonious of addresses, 'number seventy, Simmery Axe'. (Wells's pronunciation of 'St Mary Axe' proves him a true Londoner.) In each of the song's sections Sullivan catches perfectly its manic, diabolical tone.

The number made George Grossmith, though the part of the sorcerer had originally been conceived for 'poor Fred Sullivan', as Gilbert eulogized him, who had been responsible 'in no slight degree' for the success of *Trial by Jury*. It has subsequently made every revival of *The Sorcerer*, for despite the infirmities of the piece at other points, the jaunty magician will not be kept down. It was at one of those revivals, in fact—a gala celebration of the twenty-first anniversary of the original production in 1898—that the two begetters of *The Sorcerer* saw each other for the last time. By then, years of misunderstanding had taken their toll, and, as Sullivan recorded sadly in his diary, the two men did not speak. But in 1877 all was amity, and the horizon was bright.

3

H.M.S. Pinafore;

or, The Lass that Loved a Sailor

It might be said that the Gilbert & Sullivan phenomenon had a four-stage beginning. *Thespis* was a sort of test run, carried out under adverse conditions, promising but forgotten. *Trial by Jury* was a curtain-raiser, a brilliant inkling of what was to come. *The Sorcerer* showed that the elements of a unique form of comic opera had been fully assembled. And on 25 May 1878 those elements produced a work which served notice that a theatrical institution had arrived. Fifty years after the event, a member of *H.M.S. Pinafore*'s première audience could recall proudly that he had 'heard that night for the first time words and airs that . . . straightaway became a part of the national inheritance'. The good ship's maiden voyage lasted for seven hundred London performances. At the same time, across the Atlantic, American pirates sailed her for thousands more. A hundred years on, she is as trim and delectable as ever, still bearing the G & S colours in triumph.

The Sorcerer's friendly reception in 1877–8 encouraged its begetters to strike again. By the usual standards of comic opera the piece was very successful, finally running 175 nights. The Comedy Opera Company had momentum behind it, and Gilbert and Sullivan were ready to provide another work. But there were administrative problems. Carte's four director-capitalists had shown themselves rather short on nerve during *The Sorcerer*. (Before it, they had also shown themselves rather short on judgement, wiring Carte, 'Whatever you do, don't engage Grossmith.') Attendance had been good, but whenever it seemed to be slipping, the anxious businessmen wanted to take the work off. Several times they gave the cast two weeks' notice, only to retract it when the box office improved. Their fretting worried the actors and irritated Carte. When the new production came to be discussed, the directors tried to reduce the size of the advance Gilbert and Sullivan had received for *The Sorcerer*. The duo stoutly resisted, and the new project went ahead on the old terms.

Ever the thorough professional, Gilbert had begun mulling over a sequel not long after its predecessor had opened. Just after Christmas

1877 he sent his partner a sketch of the proposed work. He had high hopes for the piece and 'very little doubt' that Sullivan would be pleased. For one thing there was 'plenty of story in it', which Gilbert knew *The Sorcerer* lacked, and 'good musical situations'. The demon stage manager was already imagining how well the crew's uniforms would look on stage and planning to have them made by a naval tailor at Portsmouth. A nautical yarn would generally provide the kind of pageantry *The Sorcerer* also lacked, but it might have appealed to its author on a personal level too. His father had been at sea, after all, and he liked to fancy that Queen Elizabeth's great sailor Sir Humphrey Gilbert had been a distant ancestor. The playwright himself owned a series of yachts with which he sailed along the English coast.

Whatever the ultimate source of Gilbert's pleasure, Sullivan shared it immediately. They began to carry out their standard collaborative pattern, with Gilbert polishing his scenario, then working on the songs, which he sent off to the composer. If Sullivan encountered difficulties, Gilbert would revise his lyrics until they were manageable. Only with the songs well under way would he begin the dialogue.

The musician's share of *Pinafore* was painfully hampered by sickness. Since 1872 Sullivan had suffered sporadic attacks of a kidney disease which left him in agony, unable to work or rest. The affliction would beset him all his life and was at its worst during the new opera's composition. Sullivan himself noted the ironic difference between the fetching melodies and sparkling orchestrations he was creating and what he was enduring: 'It is, perhaps, rather a strange fact that the music to *Pinafore*, which was thought to be so merry and spontaneous, was written while I was suffering agonies from a cruel illness. I would compose a few bars, and then be almost insensible from pain. When the paroxysm was passed, I would write a little more, until the pain overwhelmed me again. Never was music written under such disturbing conditions.'

In the summer of 1879 he underwent an operation for kidney stone which, at least initially, seemed to be successful and prompted congratulations from the Duke of Edinburgh and the Prince of Wales. As of Febuary 1878, however, with Gilbert hard at work on their new creation, he was still seeking relief in the sun and gambling-casinos of southern France, advising Carte that he was 'not in very good cue yet for writing anything fresh and bright'.

But by April both partners were in harness, and work was proceeding apace. During the genesis of an opera, they kept in close touch with each other. Gilbert always asked the composer's opinion on the structure and character of the story, as well as the suitability of the lyrics. He did not insist that Sullivan mind his own musical business and leave the words to him. It was the musician, in fact, who came up with a title for the new opera. Gilbert wanted something that would rhyme with 'and three cheers more', as the line then ran. His first notion was 'semaphore', but Sullivan felicitously topped it with 'pinafore'.

Both men travelled to Portsmouth in the middle of April to absorb some on-the-spot atmosphere. Sullivan's friend Lord Charles Beresford, of Her Majesty's Navy, gave them lunch and access to several ships of the line. Gilbert made careful sketches on board one of the most historic of all vessels, Lord Nelson's *Victory*, aiming at an exact re-creation of the deck of a British man-of-war. He might also have felt the imposing presence of the legendary admiral as he planned his own campaign. Later the operatic commanders went to check on the progress of the uniforms Gilbert had ordered.

Armed with his sketches, the playwright-manager retired to his study and the miniature stage he had constructed there. As he would with every opera, he blocked out the set and planned all the stage business, using striped pieces of wood to represent his characters. Men were three inches high, women two and a half. Different colours indicated the pitch of their singing voices. With these models Gilbert could work out exactly the movements and effects he wanted long before live rehearsals began. When he came to the theatre, it was simply a question of drilling the cast in what he had already prepared with his little bits of wood.

Gilbert's critics have wondered if he occasionally forgot he was working in a living rather than a ligneous medium. What he certainly never forgot was the bad example of the mid-Victorian stage, which was alive to the point of chaos. It was this moral and artistic licentiousness that Gilbert worked with all his might to reform, which required discipline and the 'absolute control' of staging he demanded at the Opera Comique. Part of his vision was his own very definite idea of what was funny. It depended on detail, realism and a highly ordered, even stylized kind of acting. He once said that his intention in *Pinafore* had been 'to treat a thoroughly farcical subject in a thoroughly serious manner'. In a note to his comedy *Engaged*, Gilbert set out what his approach required of his actors: 'It is absolutely essential to the success of this piece that it should be played with the most perfect earnestness and gravity throughout. There should be no exaggeration in costume, make-up or demeanour; and the characters, one and all, should appear to believe, throughout, in the perfect sincerity of their words and actions. Directly the actors show that they are conscious of the absurdity of their utterances the piece begins to drag.' He knew what he wanted; knew too that it could not be achieved by the free-wheeling gags and leers so typical of contemporary productions. Thus the meticulous care with sets, costumes, stage action, even vocal inflections, and thus the tight but patient rein at rehearsals. For Gilbert the stage *was* a living medium, but it owed its life to the particular play being performed. Every aspect of the stage had to be marshalled and directed to put that life across. Topsy-turvy humour demanded military precision, with nothing left to chance.

As we have seen, his crusade was made easier because the theatrical side of the Comedy Opera Company had been set up exactly to his and Sullivan's specifications. D'Oyly Carte played no artistic part but provided all the conditions the collaborators required to realize their ideas. From the outset, the acting company had no doubt who was in charge. However different they were, Gilbert and Sullivan were both famous and formidable men, and, as Rutland Barrington said, their performers 'were in awe of them'. In addition the whole group shared the patriotic aura of the enterprise. Barrington related his pride at being part of this 'home of English talent'. Everyone involved felt 'a kind of patriotic glow combined with a determination to show other nations (and *inter alia* our own) what we could do. . . '.

Thus a powerful combination of fear, fervour and *The Sorcerer*'s recent success enabled Gilbert to have things largely his way in the *Pinafore* rehearsals. The resistance he had sometimes encountered in his straight plays (as when an actor had sniffed, 'Doubtless you think yourself a very clever person, Mr. Gilbert, but I, for one, fail to see it') appeared only infrequently. Once a leading soprano he had positioned to one side of the stage objected that she had always occupied the centre in Italian opera. 'Unfortunately this is not Italian opera,' Gilbert replied gravely, 'but only a low burlesque of the worst possible kind.'

All he asked of his players were the limitless patience and effort he was willing to give himself. As an actress recalled, there was no sign of his quick temper or sarcasm when he was trying to correct 'honest stupidity; but what he could not stand were the people who could do and wouldn't'. One older actor summarily announced he would not repeat a passage Gilbert and he had been going over and over. 'I've been on the stage quite long enough,' he objected. 'Quite,' Gilbert agreed, and the actor left *his* stage for good.

The company began to feel a real affection and trust for their blunt-spoken chief. For one thing it became clear that his crustiness hid kindness. On rainy nights, when rehearsals finished late and the buses had stopped running, he would pay the cab-fare for the ladies of the cast—'whether they were pretty or not', one of them recalled. Everyone marvelled at his quick wit. He told Barrington once to sit on a skylight on the deck of the *Pinafore* 'pensively'. Unfortunately the prop, only sewn together, collapsed under the bulky actor. 'That's *ex*pensively,' said Gilbert, quick as a flash. Going over a scene in which sailors and ladies were to be paired off, he was vexed to see one seaman regularly winding up with a girl on each arm. He was informed that one member of the crew was absent, and the next time the threesome popped up, Gilbert said brightly, 'Ah, now I see: you've just come off a very long voyage.' Rehearsing with the librettist may have been demanding, but it was not usually oppressive. And his alertness became legendary. On a bet, Barrington displaced one of the *Pinafore*'s ropes. He won his wager when Gilbert noticed the fault before starting rehearsal.

Sullivan had rather less contact with the company because music rehearsals began closer to opening night than acting rehearsals. Though more benign in temperament, he had strict standards too. The chorus were drilled in their vocal responsibilities as thoroughly as they were in their dramatic paces. The composer had as little time for individual vanity as his partner. When a tenor was tempted to linger over a high note, Sullivan's twinkle became slightly steely. 'Yes, that's a fine note, a very fine note,' he said, 'but please do not mistake your voice for my composition.' He was as much a reformer in his sphere of comic opera as Gilbert was, insisting that more voices be added to the chorus to bring out the richness and vitality of his music. When *Pinafore*'s run was under way, he visited the theatre to find that the present orchestra was not up to the calibre of the band he had rehearsed. In a stiff note to his friend Carte, the composer threatened to withdraw his music unless matters were rectified.

So, with precision, patience and good humour, *H.M.S. Pinafore* was fitted out for launching. Its two commanders were altering, polishing, refining almost until the opening. Final rehearsals went on all day and well into the night of 24 May. Gilbert continued keen and tireless, though he himself was not perfectly well, feeling the first signs of the gout which would be his unwelcome life's companion. In his diary he reported that the dress rehearsal had gone smoothly; he had been in the theatre until 3.35 in the morning, and *then* gone to his club for supper.

The première saw Gilbert and Sullivan acting out their personal rituals, the composer arriving to conduct, smiling, confident, joking, the playwright putting on finishing touches, becoming increasingly nervous, giving last minute instructions to the principals and finally rushing from the theatre as the overture began. Poor Gilbert couldn't bear opening nights. He had asked a party of friends to dine on the first night of *Dulcamara*, years ago, but long since had decided he 'would as soon invite friends to supper after a forthcoming amputation at the hip-joint'. As *Pinafore* sailed blithely along, he stalked along the Thames, returning to the theatre three or four times to allay his worst fears. He need not have worried. The production yielded everything the collaborators had put into it. The performance went like clockwork,

The pleasantly outlandish first production of *Thespis,* with Nelly Farren (right) displaying her charms as Mercury

Richard D'Oyly Carte, without whom there would almost certainly have been no Gilbert & Sullivan

The programme for the maiden production of *Trial by Jury*. The image of Jacques Offenbach beams from the top of the cover, but the newly fledged Gilbert & Sullivan will carry the day. Inside, Sullivan receives first billing. Above the title his brother Fred is depicted, starring as The Learned Judge

To conclude with a novel & entirely original Dramatic Cantata, entitled

TRIAL BY JURY.

Music by ARTHUR SULLIVAN.
The Book by W. S. GILBERT.

CHARACTERS.

The Learned Judge ... Mr. FREDERIC SULLIVAN
Counsel for the Plaintiff, Mr. HOLLINGSWORTH
The Defendant ... Mr. WALTER H. FISHER
Foreman of Jury ... ... Mr. C. CAMPBELL
Usher ... Mr. C. KELLEHER
Associate ... ... Mr. B. B. PEPPER
The Plaintiff ... MISS NELLY BROMLEY
(Her first appearance this Season)
Bridesmaids Mesdames VERNER, AMY CLIFFORD, VILLIERS LASSALLE, DURRANT, PALMER, JULIA BEVERLEY, LEE, ETC.
Gentlemen of the Jury.
Messrs. BRADSHAW, HUSK, ETC.

Scene . . . The Court of Exchequer.

Chef-d'Orchestre ... Mr. SIMMONDS.

Prices of Admission. Private Boxes, £2 2s. and £3 3s.
Stalls, 7s. 6d. Dress Circle, 5s.
Upper Boxes, 3s. Pit, 2s. Gallery, 1s.

Seats may be secured at all the Libraries and at the Box Office, open daily from 11 till 5, under the direction of Mr. COLLIVER.

REFRESHMENT SALOONS,
Under the management of Mr. H. DODSWORTH.

The Sorcerer indeed, John Wellington Wells fulfills his eerie contract

Inimitable Gilbert drawings from three Bab Ballads that influenced *H.M.S. Pinafore: Above*—'Captain Reece', 'adored by all his men'; *left*—'Joe Golightly' who 'adored the First Lord's daughter' and *right*—'The Sailor Boy to his Lass', in which an honest tar objects to his captain's refusal to return him to his sweetheart

A poster advertising the original production of *H.M.S. Pinafore*, showing off its handsome set and still giving Sullivan first billing and the curtain fell to extravagant approval, with, as Gilbert's diary recorded, 'enthusiastic calls for self and Sullivan'.

What pleased *Pinafore*'s first-night audience and critics most was that the opera was effective as well as ingenious, beautifully done as well as amusing. Indeed, they realized that, in Gilbert and Sullivan, those qualities were inseparable. The enthusiasm began the moment the curtain rose. 'So perfect a quarter-deck as that of *H.M.S. Pinafore* has assuredly never been put upon the stage,' declared one reviewer. He was equally delighted to find 'that marvel of marvels, a chorus that acts, and adds to the reality of the illusion'. Carte received his share of the tribute too, since he 'had evidently spared no pains to make the representation as complete as possible'. The note of inspired efficiency carried over into the journals' praise of author and composer. Gilbert's libretto, said one, showed 'perfect proportion. The humour is sustained throughout, and . . . there is no superfluous dialogue. . . .' For his part, everyone agreed, Sullivan had 'entered thoroughly into the spirit of the jest'.

Thus these early days were already revealing what should still be clear now: the G & S operas succeed because they *work* superbly. At their best, at least, every facet shows scrupulous planning and serious purpose. This care in preparation lets the ample nonsense, satire and sentiment come pouring out.

The collaborators exercised the same care in constructing their stories. As Gilbert recalled years later, 'we resolved that our plots, however ridiculous, should be coherent.' *H.M.S. Pinafore* displays both the cheerful ridiculousness and the coherence. It begins on that impeccably rendered quarterdeck where all the action will take place. The audience sees what seems to be an actual ship's crew going about their duties, manning the ropes or at work on deck. But an actual ship's crew probably would not burst into Sullivan's rousing chorus 'We sail the ocean blue.' The motherly Little Buttercup appears; she is the 'bumboat' woman, who vends various homely goods to the ships in port. Despite her 'round and rosy' appearance, she implies that her gaiety is only a façade, hiding some dark secret. Dick Deadeye comes forward at this, a one-eyed, hunchbacked sailor who delights in dark secrets. His shipmates hate him for his ugliness, his deformity and his 'beast of a name'. In shining contrast is Ralph ('Rafe') Rackstraw, 'the smartest lad in all the fleet', who has his secret too, a hopeless love for his captain's daughter. All agree that differences in rank are unnatural but unavoidable.

In comes the well-bred Captain Corcoran, popular with his crew despite his rank. But, as he confides to Little Buttercup, he has his sorrow as well: the First Lord of the Admiralty, Sir Joseph Porter, wants to marry his daughter Josephine, but she will have none of him. When he tries to dispose Josephine more kindly to His Lordship, she horrifies him by revealing that her heart is already given—and to a common sailor! But she knows such a match can never be and promises to keep her feelings to herself.

Directly 'Sir Joseph's barge is seen', and the First Lord boards the *Pinafore*, accompanied by the small crowd of female relatives that follow him everywhere. He smugly relates his rise from office boy to 'monarch of the sea'. The experience has left him a radical democrat, and he reminds Captain Corcoran that only an accident of birth has placed him above his crew. He insists that every order should include 'if you please,' because 'a British sailor is any man's equal, excepting mine.' When Sir Joseph and Corcoran withdraw to discuss Josephine, Ralph Rackstraw takes the First Lord's fine sentiments as a call to action. Boldly he opens his heart to his captain's daughter, who is inwardly thrilled but manifests only cold indifference because of her duty to her position. Before his shipmates and Sir Joseph's ladies, Ralph, in despair, prepares to dispatch himself with a pistol (while they block their ears). But at the last instant Josephine rushes in and confesses her love for him. In great excitement everyone plans a midnight elopement, while Dick Deadeye meditates betrayal.

Act II begins with Captain Corcoran reflecting on the unforeseen complexity of his relations with his daughter, Sir Joseph and, now, his crew. Little Buttercup sympathizes. But for their difference in class, they would be attracted to each other, and Little Buttercup hints mysteriously that there may be something about this that the captain does not know. Sir Joseph comes in, complaining of Josephine's recalcitrance. Her father suggests she may be in awe of his exalted station and advises Sir Joseph 'to assure her officially that it is a standing rule at the Admiralty that love levels all ranks'. The First Lord does, and Josephine, still somewhat in a quandary about Ralph, announces she will 'hesitate no longer'. The delighted, misguided Sir Joseph thinks this means she will accept *him*.

After the trio celebrate, Dick Deadeye creeps in to reveal to Captain Corcoran whom his daughter really plans to marry. The outraged officer waylays and denounces the absconding couple. Ralph defies him, provoking the captain to swear, which appals the company and the late-arriving Sir Joseph in particular. He sends the captain off in disgrace but is even more appalled when he learns what caused the outburst. Irate at the lovers' radical misconduct, the First Lord has Ralph cast into the 'dungeon'.

But Little Buttercup provides a lightning dénouement. She reveals that in her youth she practised 'baby farming' and switched two infants who were in her charge. One was high-born, one lowly, and she returned them to the wrong families. To everyone's astonishment, she declares the two babies were Ralph and Captain Corcoran, whose present stations in life and on board should be exactly reversed. And in an instant, they are. Corcoran enters as a common sailor, Ralph in a captain's uniform. Since Josephine's true origins have been revealed, Sir Joseph obviously cannot condescend to marry her. She embraces Ralph, Corcoran pairs off with Buttercup, and the First Lord winds up, reluctantly, with his first cousin.

Like all Gilbert's plots, this one mingles satire and nonsense. Like almost all of them, it is derived from themes and characters used in his previous work. Few authors have been as thrify as W. S. G.; he was extraordinarily adept at recycling his old bottles for new wine. Sometimes the wine tasted slightly familiar too. His great repository of inspration was the *Bab Ballads*, the wonderful verses-with-caricatures he turned out for *Fun* magazine and later collected in book form. *H.M.S. Pinafore* contains smatterings from at least eight of them. We have already mentioned Captain Reece, whose concern for his crew is even more benevolent than Captain Corcoran's. Lieutenant-Colonel Flare is another kindly officer, while Private James persuades the aristocratic General John that they were switched at birth and should change places. The same ploy is practised in 'The Baby's Vengeance'. Like Ralph Rackstraw, Joe Golightly and Little Oliver sue for a high-born hand, but without Ralph's success. 'The Sailor Boy to his Lass' pleads the rights of man against naval authority with chaotic results; 'The Bumboat Woman's Story' speaks for itself.

But despite its complex pedigree, *H.M.S. Pinafore* is, as the first programme said, 'An Entirely Original Nautical Comic Opera'. Gilbert has woven his motifs into whole cloth, not simply stitched up a patchwork. The themes of rank and privilege are examined cunningly in each of the characters, chief among them the hilarious Sir Joseph Porter KCB. As a pompous, hypocritical reformer, he reminds us of Alexis in *The Sorcerer*. As a grandee whose rise to eminence has nothing whatever to do with merit, he recalls the learned judge in *Trial by Jury*. His patter song, 'When I was a lad I served a term', was an immediate hit. Its catch-line, 'He polished up the handle on the big front door', was heard everywhere, partly because it so deftly expresses how Sir Joseph got where he is and partly because it is such a memorably crisp line of musical verse, a small example of the joint artistry of G & S. (Sullivan was amazed and tickled when, on a visit to Germany with the Duke of Edinburgh, he was solemnly greeted by the future Kaiser Wilhelm with this very phrase.)

Sir Joseph was part of Gilbert's plans right from the beginning, but he was afraid the character might cause some grimly furrowed brows by its (purely coincidental) resemblance to the actual First Lord of the Admiralty, W. H. Smith. Smith had been appointed by the Prime Minister, Disraeli, because he was an efficient administrator. But it was true that his public position was due to his founding a chain of newsagents; he had no naval experience at all. Gilbert had tried to placate Sullivan in advance by insisting there was 'no *personality* in this'. The real First Lord was a Tory, while Sir Joseph would be 'a *Radical* of the most pronounced type'. But no one was fooled by the political shift. Even Disraeli, whose brow *was* furrowed by the opera's gleeful satire, referred to his Admiralty chief as 'Pinafore Smith'.

Still, it was the type that Gilbert was after, not a personal attack. Captain Corcoran represents another type, to which the librettist is more sympathetic. If it is true, as Sir Joseph reminds him, that the captain owes his naval rank to his upper-class standing, it is also true that, unlike Sir Joseph, he seems to know his job. As he declares in his song, 'though related to a peer,/I can hand, reef, and steer.' He is rather puffed-up, but no more than any military man, and does admit, endearingly, that he is 'very far from clever'. His relations with his crew are affectionate, as seen in the famous exchange when his claims that he is 'never sick at sea' or swears 'a big, big D' are challenged *en masse* with 'What, never?', to which the captain must confess, 'Well, hardly ever.' Despite his liberality, he does believe in the necessity of class distinctions. By contrast, Sir Joseph, being of the very highest class, can preach that everyone is equal, because no one will ever be equal to him. Gilbert might well go along with the realism of the captain's observation to his daughter that 'I attach but little value to rank or wealth, but the line must be drawn somewhere.'

Josephine herself, while a rather standard girl-in-love, does realize 'what I am giving up and whither going' in choosing Ralph. And the choice, Gilbert clearly shows, is not between rank and noble virtue but between rank and physical attraction. Sex appeal has its claim to status too, and Ralph is a handsome lad. He is also something of a prig. Nothing is more characteristic of Gilbert than to expose weaknesses in *everybody* in his plays, which is why it is so difficult to decide 'what he is really saying'. Ralph is quite prepared to agree that 'there's not a smarter topman in the Navy . . . though I say it who shouldn't.' No doubt he loves Josephine. He certainly loves the sound of his own voice (and his singing voice too—naturally he is a tenor) and his passionate ideals. Gilbert uses him to satirize the literary figure of the lowly swain whose humble expressions of passion sound as if he has spent every spare moment studying rhetoric: 'In me there meet a combination of antithetical elements which are at eternal war with one another. Driven hither by objective influences—thither by subjective emotions—wafted one moment into blazing day, by mocking hope—

plunged the next into the Cimmerian darkness of tangible despair, I am but a living ganglion of irreconcilable antagonisms.' To which Josephine can only sigh, 'His simple eloquence goes to my heart.' Gilbert summed up his view of Ralph in a book version of *Pinafore* written for children years later. 'Unhappily,' he said, 'he had got it into his silly head that a British man-of-war's man was a much finer fellow than he really is.'

The one character excluded from the democratic ardour is Dick Deadeye, reviled by everyone despite their humanitarianism. He is a remarkable creation, showing in part that we all make distinctions simply by how we respond to other people physically, merely substituting one 'class system' for another. Poor Dick Deadeye (with whom Gilbert himself does not seem to sympathize) cannot even agree with general sentiments without being shouted down. When Ralph holds up the 'strange anomaly' by which one man is not free to love another's daughter although all men are equal, Dick mildly observes, 'Ah, it's a queer world,' only to have Ralph accuse him of 'a revolutionary sentiment'.

But it is Dick whom Gilbert chooses to deliver a moment of straight talk. After Sir Joseph has incited the crew, and Ralph in particular, to an exalted sense of their status, the hunchback puts in: 'You're on a wrong tack, and so is he. He means well, but he don't know. When people have to obey other people's orders, equality's out of the question.' Though here he is the dramatist's spokesman, Gilbert also employs Dick to be simply what he looks like—the stock villain of melodrama, a character we have already seen parodied by Preposteros in *Thespis*. In this guise he skulks about, foils the lovers' plans and sets up the dénouement.

Providing the dénouement is Little Buttercup's major function, along with adding a contralto voice to the lead singers and giving the ex-captain a marital mate. Her baby-switching seems rather crudely grafted on the satiric plot, bringing the piece to an artificially speedy resolution, though she has been hinting that something is up almost every time she appears. The topsy-turvy climax promotes a happy ending; does it undermine Gilbert's criticism of rank and privilege? Ralph, who looks and sounds like a noble fellow, turns out in fact to *be* a noble fellow, which paradoxically supports the theory of birth and class. Positions may be reversed, but the validity of the system remains. But Gilbert has no programme of political or social reforms in mind. No one ever went from a Gilbert and Sullivan opera to the barricades. What he despises anywhere and in anyone is sham and self-importance, which are the real targets of his satire.

A more valid objection can be lodged against the switching of these particular babies. If they were crib-mates, Ralph and Captain Crocoran must be the same age, and yet the seaman is a strapping youth while the captain is middle-aged, old enough to be the father of Ralph's beloved and the intended spouse for Buttercup—supposedly his old nurse. Clearly this won't do for plausibility. It is a weakness, further ammunition for sober souls who maintain that Gilbert's satire is cancelled out by his nonsense, that the operas are merely amusing, high-spirited and delightful. But satire, nonsense and delight in Gilbertian proportions are exactly what he intended.

Of course an essential ingredient in the mixture is Sullivan, whose contribution to *Pinafore* is perfectly vivacious despite the distress in which it was composed. As always, he responds aptly and resourcefully to the varied opportunities of the text. Supposedly he once maintained that there was no such thing as humour in music. But he is very much the subtle humorist in the simple, blandly strutting accompaniment to Sir Joseph's entrance, which nicely sets off the chattering ensemble of 'his sisters and his cousins and his aunts'. (The female retinue is Gilbert's clever means of getting a woman's chorus on board a naval vessel, but it is also what you might expect of the First Lord.) Humour of a different kind appears in the second-act duets between Captain Corcoran and Little Buttercup, 'Things are seldom what they seem', and the captain and Dick Deadeye, 'Kind Captain, I've important information'. In each the mood is mysterious, and, perhaps since the officer's partners are respectively a baby-switching woman with gipsy blood and a hunchback, Sullivan creates textures that recall the darker moments of Verdi's *Il Trovatore* and *Rigoletto*.

Throughout, the composer shows his usual acuteness at catching and heightening moods. His blithe treatment of the 'Never mind the why and wherefore' trio makes it one of the opera's highpoints, giving Sir Joseph a chance to execute some devilishly clever dance steps and the actor playing him a sure-fire chance for encores. The same festive atmosphere graces the first-act hornpipe, which rises out of the efforts of a sailors' trio to render the rather tortuous 'glee', 'A British tar is a soaring soul', composed by the First Lord himself.

The glee's laboured counterpoint demonstrates Sullivan's skill at parody, a vital strength for anyone working with a hungry satirist like Gilbert. Critics were always keen to call attention to such moments, particularly the way in which the partners deflated the overblown genres of grand opera. And yet many times the critics seem to have been rather too keen, expecting consistent parody from Sullivan in the same way they wanted consistent satire from Gilbert. The writer's orientation was toward absurdity, the composer's toward sentiment, and Sullivan often responded genuinely to emotion when Gilbert had intended a spoof. These contrasting but complementary impulses account for the peculiar charm of the operas. Sullivan can take the sting out of Gilbert's acidities and turn parody into musical pleasure.

A good example of this process—and the confusion it can cause—occurs in Ralph's song, 'A maiden fair to see', which expresses his dolorous passion for Josephine. After the first night, the *Times* critic admonished listeners against taking seriously what was to him a delicious take-off of operatic ballads. A take-off is what you might expect, given the kind of chap Ralph is. And yet the song itself is quite lovely, distinguished by a simple, touching melody and the standard stirring Sullivan climax with the singer rising to a top note with the chorus resonant beneath him. Again and again Gilbert pokes fun at tenors while Sullivan gives them good tunes.

Pinafore's most striking example of cross-purpose collaboration emerges in the famous 'He is an Englishman'. Clearly Gilbert intends it satirically, a testament that patriotism can be the last refuge of a lover. Caught making off with Josephine, Ralph invokes nationalism as his defence, and all join in a hymn of praise at the very idea of Englishness. It is just the kind of thing to make a Tory quiver, except that Sullivan turns the tables by creating an anthem that is authentically noble. As T. F. Dunhill observes, 'the librettist is making us laugh, but the composer is in earnest. . . . This is not merely a good tune: it is a glorious tune.' Even in its miniature compass and perverse context, it conveys the kind of grand emotion natural to Sullivan but alien to Gilbert.

The key phrase of the anthem also illustrates the most fundamental of the composer's skills, his instinct for effective word setting. The octave leap of 'he *is*' gives stirring expression to the splendour of simply *being* English. Conversely, Sullivan creates a pleasant, rather self-effacing melody for Little Buttercup so that her precisely detailed list of wares is heard clearly. Another of his customary virtues is his masterly handling of ensembles, particularly in the finales to both acts, where he interweaves soloists and chorus, alternates effects and reprises the best melodies that have gone before. Altogether, Sullivan's *Pinafore* concoction—a blend of gusto, invention and good taste—is as irresistible as Gilbert's, and their mutual efforts still send audiences away as happy as they were on *Pinafore*'s first night.

One of the curiosities of *Pinafore*'s history is that she almost foundered despite her auspicious launching. Attendance was very erratic for most of the summer of 1878. Some nights the house was quite respectable; on others the takings plummeted. One account insists that the second night's receipts were an infinitesimal £14. Various reasons are proposed for the show's rough early run. Perhaps good Victorians felt that Sullivan's charming melodies did not quite disarm Gilbert's aggressive satire. Prime Minister Disraeli, for one, though he might privately wink at 'Pinafore' Smith, thought the opera as a whole was a scandal—

he had 'never seen anything so bad' since Wycombe Fair in his youth. In addition the tender craft was decidedly unfortunate in its weather. The summer was a scorcher; people were not readily inclined to spend a wilting June or July night in the stuffy Opera Comique.

Whatever the cause, *H.M.S. Pinafore* was in trouble. D'Oyly Carte's fellow directors reacted just as they had during *The Sorcerer*. Notices of closure were put up six times, to be revoked only at the last minute, if the show seemed less becalmed or Carte had persuaded his jittery colleagues to wait out the doldrums. Not knowing whether they were employed from one night to the next, the cast were understandably on edge. Nevertheless, they did their part in the crisis, volunteering to take a one-third cut in salary until business improved. At length it did, and emphatically. Sullivan conducted a series of Prom concerts in mid-summer and included an arrangement of tunes from *Pinafore*. The piece was an instant hit, encored three times at its first performance. The sparkling samples sent audiences clamouring to the source. By the end of August the Opera Comique was full every night, and *Pinafore* was triumphantly on course.

But an even more mammoth success came unexpectedly from across the water. *Trial by Jury* and *The Sorcerer* had both been performed in the United States without much effect. *Pinafore*, however, opened in Boston on 25 November 1878, and within four months a correspondent reported to *The Times* that, '*H.M.S. Pinafore* has fairly taken our leading cities by storm. In Philadelphia it has been successfully running at half-a-dozen theatres at one time. In New York and Boston it has been similarly successful, and it is running in the South and West. Its melodies are sung by everyone and its jokes have got firmly fixed in our newspaper literature. Such a furore as this opera has created I have never known before in the history of the American stage.'

The phenomenon was dubbed '*Pinafore* mania'. There were church choir productions, black productions, children's productions, puppet productions. Barrel-organs cranked out nothing else. New York alone floated eight *Pinafores* simultaneously. A news story reported, deadpan, 'At present there are forty-two companies playing *Pinafore* about the country. Companies formed after 6 PM yesterday are not included.' But the actual count was closer to one hundred. Utterances public and private were peppered with the opera's catch-phrases. The 'What, never/Well, hardly ever' exchange became notorious. A newspaper editor summoned his staff to complain that every article was polluted by the deadly quote; they must never use it again. 'What, never?' the reporters whooped joyfully. 'Well,' returned their hopeless boss, 'hardly ever.'

This delirium would have been very welcome to *Pinafore*'s creators, except for two reasons. First, the lack of a copyright agreement with the

States deprived them of any financial return from American productions. Over the bright blue sea, their doughty ship was being manned exclusively by pirates. Secondly, the native versions took the most painful liberties. It was bad enough that their musical arrangements had to be faked, since Sullivan's score had not been published. But all of them freely interpolated popular songs, sea shanties, new lyrics, local gags and topical references. They fiddled with the casting. In Boston, Ralph was played by a girl. One Baltimore Buttercup was a man seven feet tall. It was worse than Hollingshead and the Gaiety.

The ship's rightful owners felt both the artistic and monetary injuries. Sullivan wrote to an American friend that he was 'gratified beyond measure' by the piece's success but greatly regretted that 'my music is not performed as I wrote it.' The lack of proper orchestral colouring distressed him more than the financial injustice, though he did prefer to be paid for his work. Gilbert merely grumbled, 'I will not have another libretto of mine produced if the Americans are going to steal it. Not that I need the money so much, but it upsets my digestion.' Carte proposed that they should go to America to claim their rights and in June 1879 made a preparatory voyage himself. He wrote back that local performances were 'atrocious' and that conditions were ripe for the real thing.

While he was away, an even more bizarre piratical attempt signalled the end of the Comedy Opera Company. Carte had had enough of his fellow-directors' bad faith and interference. He announced that when the lease on the Opera Comique, which was in his name, expired on 31 July, the partnership would be dissolved and he would assume complete business control himself. All the directors' earlier misgivings had vanished with *Pinafore*'s great success, and they were very reluctant to give up their share in it. On the night of 31 July, with Carte still in America, two of them appeared at the Opera Comique's stage door with wagons and a gang of hooligans, determined to carry off the sets and scenery of *Pinafore*, which they insisted were their property. The opera was actually going on at the time, and very soon the audience became aware of a considerable commotion backstage. For some while there was more action behind the scenes than in front, with the loyal *Pinafore* hands refusing to give up the ship to the intruders. Grossmith (as Sir Joseph) made a short speech to calm the audience, the show continued, and at length the would-be boarders were repelled. Subsequently the disgruntled directors mounted their own *Pinafore*, which resembled the American versions more than the original, but bankruptcy and Carte's successful court action scuttled them.

That autumn the G & S triumvirate began its campaign against the transatlantic buccaneers. They would show the colonials the authorized version of *Pinafore*. It would be the polished London production, but with a cast more suited to the wide-open American character. As Carte had already observed, 'They like "emotional" singing and acting. The placid English style won't do. . . .' The British contingent received a large dose of emotion when they arrived off New York on 5 November 1879. A flotilla of ships representing native *Pinafores* brazenly greeted their steamer, ecstatically pouring out music from the opera. The only discordant note came from a tug hired by a minstrel version with a flag demanding 'NO PINAFORE' and a whistle that tried to shriek down all sounds of welcome.

Interviewers flocked around the librettist and composer, noting that they both conveyed 'animation, high spirits and the jolliest kind of bonhomie'. But the obvious differences were noted too, with Sullivan's appearance expressing 'gentle feeling and tender emotion' as strongly as Gilbert's did 'cold, glittering, keen-edged intellect'. The two men agreed, however, in mildly disparaging *H.M.S. Pinafore*, 'a frothing trifle' compared to the more serious work they had done individually.

They were fêted everywhere, so that they scarcely had a moment to themselves. Sullivan was bowled over by the hospitality, writing to his mother that, 'The moment a man sees you, he wants to know what he can do for you, and means it too.' All the same, he felt rather 'bewildered and dazed', wondering 'where these Americans end?' Gilbert was approached by an enthusiastic New Yorker with a great idea—a real *native* version of *Pinafore*, with USS replacing HMS, Jersey Beach substituted for Portsmouth, and the chief of the US Navy standing in for the First Lord. Gilbert opined that the local idiom would defeat him, but he did extemporize an ironic version of his 'English' anthem:

'He is Ameri-can!
Though he himself has said it,
'Tis not much to his credit,
That he is Ameri-can!

For he might have been a Dutchman,
An Irish, Scotch, or such man,
Or perhaps an Englishman!
But in spite of hanky-panky,
He remains a true-born Yankee,
A cute Ameri-can!'

The first business of the trip, however, was establishing the authentic version of the piece. Gilbert and Sullivan prepared their forces, and their *Pinafore* opened at New York's Fifth Avenue Theatre on 1 December. The staging was a revelation (with Gilbert himself an unobtrusive member of the crew at the opening, making sure things went as planned), and so was Sullivan's scoring. The production clearly seemed a hit, and Gilbert made a graceful speech after the final curtain, hoping he and his partner had created an entertainment 'innocent but not imbecile'. Sullivan wrote to his mother that at last he thought he would 'get a little money out of America'. But the glut of rival *Pinafores* did cramp the style of the original, and attendance began to waver. The collaborators had another project afoot, however—what Carte, months before, had called 'our trump card, the New Opera'. Reasoning that what had not yet been performed could not be stolen, they set out to fight pirates with *Pirates*.

While author, composer and impresario laboured at this second stage of their American campaign, their first hit opera sailed contentedly along in London without them. For Christmas 1879 Carte's stage manager introduced a mild innovation—a *Pinafore* manned by children that would run as a matinée concurrent with the adult production. This juvenile version became a hit in its own right, charming audiences until *Pinafore* made way for *The Pirates*. Only Lewis Carroll objected, as he had to *The Sorcerer*. He found the passage in which 'a bevy of sweet innocent-looking girls sing, with bright and happy looks, "He said Damn me! He said Damn me!" . . . sad beyond words'. Part of Carroll's displeasure might be due to Sullivan's earlier refusal to set *Alice in Wonderland* to music. At any rate, when Gilbert, Sullivan and Carte saw the production, they were enchanted. Ever a soft touch for children, the curmudgeonly librettist declared his adult actors should see it to learn how the piece should be played, and bought the whole cast boxes of candy.

4

The Pirates Of Penzance;

or, The Slave of Duty

At 45 East 20th Street in New York, a plaque records that 'On this site Sir Arthur Sullivan composed "The Pirates of Penzance" in 1879.' The boast is in fact only partly true, but all the same the fifth Gilbert and Sullivan opera does have authentic American roots. After *H.M.S. Pinafore* had been shamelessly misappropriated by Yankee companies, its authors had made up their minds to retain the local rights to their next production as absolutely as they could. This meant mounting their own American production and keeping their words and music out of the hands of greedy theatrical entrepreneurs. So, hard on the heels of the D'Oyly Carte *Pinafore, The Pirates of Penzance* opened its world première run at the 5th Avenue Theatre in New York on 31 December 1879. The day before, across the Atlantic, the actual first performance had been given in a makeshift version on the English coast. But, for the first few months of its life, all the interest in the latest G & S piece centred on the United States. How appropriate that one hundred years later an American company should have reasserted the native claim on *The Pirates* with a production so gleefully outrageous that it could have made both Gilbert and Sullivan apoplectic.

As might be expected, the original audiences were keen to compare the new work with its famous predecessor. Many of them, British and American, declared that in essentials only the names had been changed. *The Pirates*, it was said, was *Pinafore* on dry land, or Act III of *Pinafore*.

At first glance the resemblance is obvious enough. The later opera begins with a hearty pirates' chorus, while its naval sister began with hearty seamen. On the rocky coast of Cornwall they are celebrating the twenty-first birthday of Frederic, their apprentice, who can now become a full-fledged buccaneer. But Frederic tells his shocked comrades that he intends to leave them and that his indenture was a mistake in the first place, which he honoured only because he is by nature 'the slave of duty'. His nurse, Ruth, who brought him to the gang and has remained with them, confesses that she misunderstood

Frederic's parents, who wanted him apprenticed to a *pilot*. Now free of his bond, Frederic must devote himself to his old companions' extermination, despite his affection for them.

The pirates accept his decision sympathetically. Besides, buccaneering pays them so poorly they see little incentive for him to stay. As a last dutiful act, Frederic reveals that they are too tender-hearted. They never attack a weaker force and are always thrashed by stronger ones. Worst of all, they never molest orphans, since they are all orphans themselves. Word of this dispensation has spread, and the ships they have captured lately have, curiously, been 'manned entirely by orphans' and had to be released.

Ruth, faithful but middle-aged, is in love with Frederic and wants to go away with him. But he is afraid that, since she is the only woman he has ever seen, she may suffer by comparison with others. The pirates vouch for her but hastily decline his offer to leave her with them. They also decline to return to civilization since, as the Pirate King says, their way of life is relatively honest, compared to respectability.

Left alone with Frederic, Ruth assures him her charms are perfectly acceptable, when girls are heard singing in the distance. As soon as he sees them, Frederic is entranced, and enraged at Ruth's deceit. He drives her away and hides as the maidens enter but dutifully emerges to tell them they are being watched. All sisters, they are horrified to learn he is a pirate. They pity him when he explains he intends to leave his evil trade, but, despite his good looks, none of them is willing to marry him—except their sister Mabel, who scolds them for their lack of charity and accepts Frederic's proposal.

After a blissful duet, Frederic cautions the girls that his former companions are about and that they should move to a safer place. But at that instant the pirates appear, seize the maidens and threaten them with marriage. The vigilant Mabel warns the brigands to take care: the girls' father is a Major-General. Straightaway that officer enters, declaring he is indeed 'the very model of a modern Major-General' and is quite taken aback by the prospect of having pirates for sons-in-law. But the crafty old man has heard of the Pirates of Penzance and appeals to them not to take away the only comfort of his old age because he is—an orphan. The pirates disgustedly accept their fate but warn that if he is 'telling a terrible story' the consequences will be dire. As it is, the Pirate King makes them all honorary members of his band and sets them free. Poor Ruth comes in to plead with Frederic, but he thrusts her aside, and the act ends in flag-waving high spirits.

Act II opens some time later, at night, in the ruins of a Gothic chapel, part of an estate that the Major-General has purchased. He sits brooding over the lie he has told, his guilt increased by the silent presence of the ancestors around him, even though they are not actually his. Meanwhile, Frederic's expedition against his old comrades is prepared, and his 'lion-hearted' corps of police come marching in. Unfortunately they seem none too eager for combat, and the girls' war-like encouragement only increases their misgivings. When they move off at last, Frederic exults at this chance to expiate his criminal past. But all at once Ruth and the Pirate King appear. They have come to relate an amusing paradox. Since Frederic was born on 29 February in a leap year, his twenty-first birthday will not officially occur until 1940, and he is still bound to the pirates. Aghast, Frederic bows to his duty. He also dutifully exposes the General's lie, and the King and Ruth resolve on the spot to return in strength and claim revenge.

Mabel is shocked by Frederick's revelations but swears she will wait for him till 1940. He runs off, leaving her to explain things to the constables, who are ready to be led against the foe. They stoically prepare to march alone, reflecting that 'a policeman's lot is not a happy one' at the best of times. But when they hear the buccaneers advancing, they hide at once.

'With cat-like tread' the gang thunder in but also conceal themselves when the Major-General approaches. Still conscience-stricken, he sings a ballad in praise of nature's peace, accompanied by the hidden men-at-arms. When his daughters enter, the pirates strike. Mabel appeals fruitlessly to Frederic, but the police come to the rescue. They are no match for the buccaneers, however, until the bobbies demand they 'yield in Queen Victoria's name'. Loyal to a man, the pirates do. Then Ruth reveals that they are in fact all noblemen, led astray by youthful folly. The Major-General embraces them at once as sons-in-law and encourages them to return to society and the House of Lords. All the 'poor wandering ones' regain their rightful places, and the opera ends in celebration.

The connections between *Pinafore* and *The Pirates*' scenario are apparent enough. There are the two crews, land-based and sea-going, and their leaders—though, because of his bass voice and villainous character, the Pirate King's *alter ego* on the *Pinafore* is Dick Deadeye, not Captain Corcoran. Stoic mildness and a baritone range relate the captain and the police sergeant, both of whom were played by the blandly comic Rutland Barrington. The First Lord of the Admiralty, a puffed-up commoner ignorant of ships and shadowed by a crowd of female relatives, obviously resembles the Major-General, whose military knowlege is extremely limited, whose family ancestry is purchased and who is attended by a chorus of daughters. Finally the conventional Ralph and Josephine have their counterparts in the conventional Frederic and Mabel.

But these resemblances are superficial. The operas are quite different pieces, and *The Pirates* sprang from other sources than a bald attempt to repeat *H.M.S. Pinafore*. On the most basic level, Gilbert was working in a stage tradition that employed a standard cast: the young lovers, a villain, a comedy figure. The roots of the convention went back to pantomime and provided staple ingredients for a variety of dramatic situations. They were certainly used in Victorian melodrama, and in the extravagant operatic plots which melodrama influenced. These are the real sources of Gilbert's inspiration. For, though many of its specific barbs have long been lost on audiences, *The Pirates* is intended as a theatrical satire very like the burlesques Gilbert once wrote for John Hollingshead. Its first programme described it as a 'melo-dramatic opera', and the Pirate King is a tender-hearted version of the heavy brute people loved to hate. The sergeant is the comic policeman of pantomime, right down (or up) to his traditional red hair. (Years after the Savoy Operas, this lovable figure would receive perhaps his ultimate incarnation in Mack Sennet's Keystone Kops.) As for the Major-General, Gilbert certainly did not need the success of a naval caricature to encourage him to have a shot at the army: the *Bab Ballads* are full of broad jokes at any uniform's expense. Nor do the Stanley daughters have to thank Sir Joseph's ladies for their existence. The two groups represent independent solutions to the same problem, that of providing a female chorus in a masculine setting.

Besides the overall model of the melodrama, Gilbert had specific influences at hand. In 1871 he had translated Offenbach's *Les Brigands*, whose subject is roughly similar. Swashbuckling settings were very popular in plays and books, like the classic *Treasure Island*, which came out not long after *Pirates*. Indeed, Gilbert had already used the theme in his own writing. In 1870 he produced *Our Island Home*, which contains not only a Pirate King, Captain Bang, but the device of the mistaken 'pilot/pirate' apprenticeship. Captain Bang also has an overdeveloped devotion to duty, and his would-be victims escape a nasty fate in the Pacific by proving that in terms of Greenwich Meridian Time the date of his indentures has already passed.

Though this seems a classic case of Gilbert's self-borrowing, as of August 1879 his melodramatic opera dealt with bandits, not pirates. Its provisional title was *The Robbers;* the most famous sea raiders in theatrical history were an afterthought. It is hard to say why the change was made. Perhaps Gilbert did think staying close to the ocean would boost the new work's chances of repeating *Pinafore*'s success. Or perhaps, with his digestion upset by American liberties with the earlier piece, he had pirates on his mind.

Whatever the cause, Gilbert must have found it very satisfying that the new opera had New York in a great state of anticipation throughout December. One rumour maintained that the plot had to do with six burglars and the six maidens they stumbled on while robbing a house. Gilbert fed the speculation with teasing interviews, but in fact his libretto was largely complete, and rehearsals were proceeding even while *Pinafore* was ploughing its rather unsteady course. As Sullivan wrote to his mother, the earlier work's inability to attract a city surfeited with *Pinafores* made it imperative that they bring *The Pirates* forward at once. With their profits reduced, the partners were having to find ways to reduce their expenses. 'We shall begin,' he told his mother gaily, 'by not paying the postage of our letters home!'

In the same nonchalant tone Sullivan confided that, though Act II was in hand, he had somehow left all his sketches for Act I in England. It was a great nuisance, he said, because it meant rewriting everything he had done, in addition to scoring the complete opera. Despite the composer's sang-froid, this new burden coupled with his other labours was almost too much for him. He was writing new music, orchestrating, rehearsing, occasionally conducting *Pinafore* personally and meeting his usual busy round of social obligations. To Gilbert's amazement and admiration, he did manage to reconstruct all his intentions for Act I, except for the sisters' entrance, for which Gilbert suggested they substitute a chorus from a similar point in *Thespis*.

As if the pressure of work were not enough, Sullivan was being afflicted by his old kidney complaint, adding pain to exhaustion. His diary records that for three weeks he seldom got to bed before five or six in the morning. With opening night scheduled for 31 December, the last week was almost unbearably gruelling. He finished the full score at 7 a.m. on the 28th. The next day's rehearsal lasted till 1 a.m. with the composer 'in despair because it went so badly'. Prospects were brighter on the 30th; in fact Sullivan declared 'everyone enthusiastic'. But at one in the morning he, Gilbert and their friends the musicians Fred Clay and Alfred Cellier all set to work on the overture that would, in sixteen hours, begin the new opera. Sullivan produced the main outline, Cellier filled it in, Gilbert and Clay copied parts. At 5 a.m. it was finished. At eleven it was rehearsed. That afternoon Sullivan could neither eat nor sleep, and at 5.30 he 'got up feeling miserably ill'. He made his way to the theatre, stopping at a club for twelve oysters and a glass of champagne, and entered the orchestra pit 'more dead than alive'. But his concentration on the music and the enthusiasm of the audience brought him through. That night, 'utterly worn out' after a month of the most punishing labour, he could record a 'grand success'.

The newspapers agreed completely, reporting endless encores, laughter and applause. Opinions varied as to whether the new entry surpassed the almost notorious *Pinafore*, but no one denied it was a worthy rival. Several critics noted that the two works had somewhat different qualities. While *The Pirates*, one writer observed, was 'brighter, prettier and more artistic', its music was 'hardly of that character which may be termed strikingly popular, and there are few bright, brisk airs or flowing melodies such as abound in *Pinafore*. . .'. Sullivan himself thought his new creation was 'infinitely superior in every way . . . "tunier" and more developed, of a higher class altogether'. He and the critics alike concurred in praising Gilbert's libretto, sets and direction.

The production was slightly less lucky in its performers. While most received good notices, the reviewers had reservations about the interpreters of Mabel and Frederick. Assessing Blanche Roosevelt—born in Sandusky, Ohio, but engaged by G & S in London where she sang opera as 'Madame Rosavella'—the papers toasted her spectacular beauty but found her voice thin and wavery. One gallant critic suggested she evidently had a cold. To the tenor Hugh Talbot quarter was neither given nor, from the sound of it, deserved. The reporters roasted him, in witty variations on the verdict Sullivan later gave his mother: 'the Tenor . . . is an idiot—vain and empty-headed. He very nearly upset the piece on the first night as he didn't know his words, and forgot his music.'

One potential disaster was averted by a display of gambler's nerve from Sullivan, the more remarkable considering the terrific pressure he was under. Only a few days before opening night the orchestra announced that the music of *The Pirates* seemed to them much closer to grand opera than comic opera—and under union rules that meant they should get more money for playing it. Sullivan met their last-minute threat of a strike by thanking them for the compliment to his composition and regretting their proposed course of action. But nothing would be easier, he said, than to cable England and arrange for the orchestra of Covent Garden to come to New York to take their place. In the meantime he and his friend the accomplished Alfred Cellier would fill in on the piano and harmonium. After delivering with a straight face an ultimatum worthy of one of Gilbert's plots, Sullivan requested an interview with a New York newspaper in which he exposed the mean-spirited and inhospitable scheme. Between the publicity and Sullivan's bluff, the band gave in.

Amid the intense interest surrounding the American production, the real world première of *The Pirates of Penzance* received scant attention. A bizarre event in the little town of Paignton, in Devon, it was a purely formal means of securing *The Pirates*' British copyright. The site was chosen because a *Pinafore* company was already touring the area. The performance itself was decidedly informal, supervised by D'Oyly Carte's invaluable secretary Helen Lenoir, who later became his wife. Scheduled for 29 December, the production had to be postponed till the 30th because the parts had not yet arrived from America. As it was, the company had only one rehearsal, after the evening show of *Pinafore*, to get the new work into roughly presentable shape. When the piece did go on, at 2 p.m. on the 30th, it offered no more than an approximation of what New York would enjoy in a few hours. The Paignton pirates were indistinguishable from the crew of the *Pinafore*, except for coloured kerchiefs on their heads. All the members of the cast carried their parts and no doubt referred to them often. At times the melodies must have sounded improvised. A piano supplied the only accompaniment, and of course there was no overture. Even with a perfect performance, however, this version of *The Pirates* would have been quite different from what either New York or London would see, since Gilbert and Sullivan were constantly tinkering with their material. At Paignton there was no 'Poor Wandering One' or 'Come, Lads Who Plough the Sea'—that robust anthem that Americans would soon transform into 'Hail, Hail, the Gang's All Here'. The opera ended with a harshly Gilbertian blast at the House of Peers. Nonetheless, its audience of fifty applauded vigorously, and several reviewers could clearly discern another G & S triumph.

Back in New York, Gilbert, Sullivan and D'Oyly Carte wanted to capitalize on the enthusiasm of the gala opening. Foiling would-be native pirates had to be their first concern. Contrary to his usual custom, Gilbert had not printed his libretto for distribution to the first-night audience. If the Americans wanted to steal his material, he would make them work for it. Sullivan's music, still in manuscript, was locked in a safe every night. The orchestra members were offered bribes to hand over their parts, but their loyalty on this account seems to have made up for the abortive strike. The leader of the band was under particular pressure because his part contained cues to the full orchestration, a great bonus to any musical thief. Even with these precautions, unscrupulous types scribbled down melodies during performances, hoping to make off with the score piecemeal.

While *The Pirates* remained in its owners' hands, the one sure way to American profits was to send out authorized D'Oyly Carte touring companies. Determined to 'strike whilst the iron is hot', as Sullivan wrote to his mother, the partners plunged into preparing the junior companies with all the energy they had shown in readying the original show. They would send three to different parts of the country and have them all in rehearsal at once. Sullivan conducted the first performance of each tour, in Philadelphia on 9 February, Newark, New Jersey, on 16 February and Buffalo on the 21st, and everywhere the opera repeated its New York success.

The Buffalo tour—which began with the partners making an impassive ritual visit to Niagara Falls—brought their theatrical business in America to a close. They were scheduled to leave for London on 3 March, to arrive in time to rehearse for the 3 April opening there. Gilbert returned to New York to see to administrative matters. Sullivan, as he had throughout their American stay, minded his social obligations, visiting Ottawa as the guest of the Governor-General of Canada and Queen Victoria's daughter Princess Louise. Then he came back to New York for the voyage home.

Biographers have suggested that the fatal discord between the two men had its beginnings in the States. It is said that Gilbert was jealous of Sullivan, not as much because of his social celebrity as from the public's tendency to rate his music at the expense of Gilbert's words. Sullivan was fêted everywhere, introduced as an honoured guest at conservatories and invited to conduct programmes of his 'serious' pieces. He represented culture; perhaps it seemed to Gilbert that he was regarded merely as a clever wordsmith, an exalted hack. For his part, Sullivan complained to Fred Clay that he felt Gilbert mocked him subtly when they were in company together.

Neither of these responses would be uncharacteristic. They were both sensitive men in their different ways, and Sullivan could no more help his enjoyment of public acceptance than Gilbert could his instinct for finding chinks in people's armour. But on the surface, at any rate, their relations appeared very amicable. When, while they were still in America, the Leeds Festival engaged Sullivan as its conductor and commissioned a large-scale choral piece, the composer asked his operatic partner to provide the libretto. This involved rewriting sections from a religious drama, *The Martyr of Antioch*, and Gilbert performed his task efficiently and without charge. After the work was produced in October, Sullivan presented him with a silver loving-cup inscribed 'Martyr of Antioch; W. S. Gilbert from his friend Arthur Sullivan'. Gilbert responded that the honour of assisting in Sullivan's composition was sufficient in itself and would always be 'the most highly prized . . . of the many substantial advantages that have resulted to me from our association. . .'. Meanwhile, following an enthusiastic reception in April, *The Pirates of Penzance* was filling the Opera Comique, and there seemed no reason why the association should not go on and on.

By the time *The Pirates* appeared, audiences were becoming more attuned to Gilbert and Sullivan's appeal. As one reviewer summarized the new opera, 'the humour of the piece consists in the gravity of the music applied to the most ridiculous situations imaginable.' But a writer in the *Times* of London approached the question more thoughtfully. 'Mr. Gilbert's characters are not comic in themselves,' he said. 'but only in reference to other characters chiefly of the operatic type, whose exaggerated attitude and parlance they mimic. He writes in fact not comedies but parodies, and the music has accordingly to follow him to the sphere of all others most uncongenial to it—the mock-heroic.'

The writer seems to be one of those who wished Sullivan would attempt a serious dramatic theme, but his views still help to define why *The Pirates of Penzance* is such a different work from *Pinafore*, despite their supposed resemblances. *The Pirates is* a parody, and all its comic business is based on that principle. It abounds in Gilbertian topsy-turviness, which either adds to the parody or advances the plot. But *Pinafore* is a combination of satire and sentimental comedy, and its only real topsy-turvy episode is its baby-switching dénouement, which is Gilbert's sleight-of-hand way of resolving the action and perhaps ducking the questions he has raised.

The Pirates' tone is clear from the start. There is no notion in *Pinafore* as ludicrous in itself as the idea of a boy being apprenticed to a pirate, or that that should have come about because his nurse misheard the word *pilot*. This is pure absurdity, in the same way as Victorian melodrama and melodramatic operatic plots were absurd. By contrast, *Pinafore* develops quite normally. We meet the ship's crew, Little Buttercup, Ralph and unrequited love. Character and humour there are, but not absurdity.

The distinction is obvious in the two sets of lovers. Frederic is a hilarious prig, 'the slave of duty' to the exclusion of anything else. He has no other character. It is his obsession, plus his leap-year birthday, that carries the plot. He and Mabel are made for each other. She too, in her way, is enslaved to duty, though, as her sisters shrewdly remark, her sense of duty is inspired by Frederic's beauty. (The duty/beauty rhyme rings through the opera like a tinny bell, a little parody in itself.) When the two meet, it is love at first sight; they are eternally united at once—even until 1940—and trouble can only come from outside. By comparison, though Ralph and Josephine are standard lovers, they do have more personality. For one thing, they have much more to go through before they can be joined, and their separation by rank and privilege gives emotional force to Gilbert's satire.

The four all have their love-songs to sing, but those are different too. The critics who found *Pinafore* more spontaneously melodic might well be right. Certainly Ralph and Josephine's tunes seem more genuinely tender and affecting than those Sullivan creates for the *Pirates* couple. The latter's songs have touching moments, but less warmth in general, perhaps because the couple themselves are more artificial. Many times in the operas Sullivan gives a non-Gilbertian slant to a character; he seems less inclined to do so here. But one of his great achievements is Mabel's 'Poor Wandering Ones', which is both parody and show-stopper. It is most slyly effective when performed seriously, as a chance for the soprano to show off her technique—just as we would expect Mabel to do. But Sullivan composed what he called his 'farm-yard effects' tongue-in-cheek, and though the song is rousing enough on its own to close the opera, its take-off of bel canto excesses of the Italian and French opera is a complete triumph. Frederic too has his moments of mock vocal splendour, as do other members of the cast. The whole piece, in every mood, hovers on the edge of caricature.

Richard Temple, who played the Pirate King in London, seems to have caught exactly the right tone. A critic said he 'was a capital representative of the Pirate Chief of old-fashioned melo-drama and gave his music with amusing exaggeration'. The melodramatic Pirate Chief is epitomized by *Treasure Island*'s Long John Silver—cunning, dangerous, larger than life. Gilbert wants to retain that spell but adapt it comically, which he does from the very first line. *The Pirates*' pirates bellow Sullivan's rousing drinking-song with gusto, but it is hard for us to take them seriously when it turns out they are quaffing not grog but sherry. Then, as their sporting regard for the weak is revealed, their unluckiness with the strong and finally their tenderness toward their fellow-orphans, they seem chocolate pirates indeed. Paragons of middle-class values, when they seize the Stanley girls it is marriage, not rape, they have in mind. All this is wonderful broad comedy; satire appears only briefly, in the Pirate King's song, when he compares his profession favourably with the darker side of respectability.

The only really satiric figure in the opera is Major-General Stanley, through whom Gilbert takes a swipe at armchair commanders who know nothing of their real business, as well as parvenus who try to buy themselves a pedigree. But the Major-General is treated much more gently than Sir Joseph Porter. He has none of the First Lord's pretensions, none of his self-congratulating principles. Sir Joseph's patter song is a smug record of opportunism. 'I am the very model of a modern Major-General' is simply a rather whimsical, dithery catalogue of useless knowledge. In fact the Major-General seems the very model of an endearing retired officer, just the sort who would go on a picnic in full uniform. Sir Joseph by contrast is very much on active duty, throwing his rank and opinions about and trying to force his unwelcome affections on Josephine. His military counterpart has no romantic intentions; instead he is rather a be-medalled version of the old woman who lived in a shoe. It is hard to dislike a man with so many daughters. Despite the mild satire, we are fond of him, for his quick wits in becoming an orphan for the pirates and his tender conscience in regretting it for his would-be ancestors. We are even willing to forgive his part in the 'orphan/often' exchange with the buccaneers, which is one of Gilbert's most dubious bits of dialogue (though the 1979 New

York *Pirates* actually repeated it in Act II, with triumphant panache). Equally strained is the 'sat a gee/strategy' rhyme in his patter song. Perhaps the word 'gee', a children's term for horse, was once current enough to be easily recognized, but it has been much more obscure for a couple of generations at least. When any stage Major-General comes to this passage, he looks hopefully at the audience and mounts his sword, as the only way of getting the point across. (Some performers, repeating this stanza as an encore, solve the whole problem by blithely singing 'rode a horse' instead of Gilbert's laboured line.)

The Major-General makes his contribution to the operatic burlesque too. His ballad just before the opera's climax, 'Sighing softly to the river', is a delicious absurdity, having nothing to do with the plot. The nightshirted old man sings a quavering celebration of natural peace, tenderly supported by two hidden bands of warriors armed to the teeth and bent on mutual destruction. The ballad is one of Sullivan's gems of burlesque, with a hopelessly cloying melody and a crooning, twittering accompaniment. G & S knew very well the effect of giving such a song to the comic baritone; part of the joke in the original production was seeing how the vocally limited George Grossmith would cope with a sustained melody.

The most unfortunate character in *The Pirates*, who has no relevance to either burlesque or satire, is poor Ruth. She is one of the most savagely treated of Gilbert's middle-aged women, and almost nothing can make up for what he does to her. Her opening song, 'When Frederic was a little lad . . .', confessing the error that brought him to the pirates, is funny and effective, showing what Sullivan meant when he said Gilbert's lyrics were 'beautifully written for music'. But after this we must sit through her amorous yearning for Frederic, the pirates' heavy irony—'Yes, there are the remains of a fine woman about Ruth'—and finally Frederic's fierce rejection. Beyond stating that he was simply a man of his time, no one has quite explained Gilbert's rage at the waning of girlish charm. Why is it a crime to be forty-seven, to be less than winsome and yet still have feelings? Gilbert's spleen mars several of the operas, and this one in particular.

If anything could redeem Gilbert's coarseness, it would be the entrance of the police. Their baggy-pants charm comes across before they have said a word, in Sullivan's lumbering accompaniment in the lower strings. They are not the stuff heroes are made of, as their classic 'When the foeman bares his steel' tells us, but their simple good nature is enormously appealing. Sullivan gives them superbly appropriate music, martial but modest, interspersed with the bleating 'tarantaras' that keep their courage up. It is all the more effective when the Stanley girls, true soldier's daughters, descend on them like Valkyries, declaiming the glories of death in battle. This is one of the finest moments in Gilbert and Sullivan, as the constables mark time, tooting uneasily, while the sisters, with great teutonic bangs on the harp, ecstatically exhort them to do the last thing they want to do.

The bobbies' second song, 'When a felon's not engaged in his employment', is even more famous and has become a part of modern folklore with its wry sympathy for both policeman and criminal. Certainly the constables themselves are supremely sympathetic, adding a human note to the melodramatic absurdities around them. Part of this effect may be due to the solidarity they convey with their identical uniforms and apprehensions. Their tunes are chorus songs as well, with the men answering their sergeant. (These responses moved a Victorian critic to suspect Gilbert of satirizing the Church.) With their truncheons and lanterns, they are often the highpoint of the opera, even though they come on only in the second half. Their 'policeman's lot' is encored more than any other song in *The Pirates*, which prompted Rutland Barrington, the original sergeant, to suggest that Gilbert write some special verses to use when it was repeated. The librettist, however, had done enough work: 'Encore means "sing it again",' he growled.

Of course the police are no match even for tender-hearted pirates. But in the final melodramatic turn of events they invoke Her Majesty, and, like a goddess descending in a machine, the Queen's image restores order. No one has ever suggested that Gilbert was somehow aiming a dart at Victoria, though from his pen any reference can seem suspect. Certainly his use of the peers is double-edged, a jibe at their assumptions of superiority and privilege. But it is a very mild compared to the 'Hymn to the Nobility' which closed the Paignton *Pirates*:

> 'How doubly blest that glorious land
> Where rank and brains go hand in hand,
> Where wisdom pure and virtue hale
> Obey the law of strict entail.'

Gilbert soft-pedalled his sentiments before the New York and London openings, not out of cowardice but simply because political harangue does not suit *The Pirates'* tone. It is witty, rollicking burlesque, in which satire occurs catch-as-catch-can, without *Pinafore*'s consistency. But, since Gilbert seems to abandon satire in *Pinafore*'s topsy-turvy climax, perhaps *The Pirates* is truer to itself after all.

Nonetheless, just as in *Pinafore*, listeners and performers have not been absolutely clear about what is parody in *The Pirates* and what is not. A New York review pointed to the difficulty: ' . . . the music Mr. Sullivan has written for *The Pirates of Penzance* might have been written for grand opera. The humour of the music lies in fact in its serious imitation of grand opera. . . .' Even when humour was intended, sometimes the composer, perhaps not knowing his own strength, inspired a serious response. One reporter thought that the outlandish a capella hymn in praise of poetry ('Divine Emollient!') at the end of Act I possessed 'the character of a serious prayer', and it can still have an unexpected impact. And, as we have already said, Mabel should launch into 'Poor Wandering One' as if she were singing *Traviata*.

Perhaps some uncertainty is natural. Gilbert, after all, wanted his works played absolutely straight, as if the performer were oblivious to their absurdity. But *The Pirates* is essentially a parody and should be played as one if all its resources are to come alive. This is especially true now, when melodrama is barely a memory, though operatic clichés remain. Unless a 'melo-dramatic opera' is performed in uninhibited style, it can seem simply a rather queer old operatic comedy that does not work. Which is why perhaps the best thing to happen to *The Pirates* since its original New York run was another New York run in 1979. The New York Shakespeare Festival ignored traditions and filled the text with enormous inventive energy. The libretto was little changed, except for some arguably neo-Gilbertian touches; neither was the period setting. It is true that the musical adapter made rather free with Sullivan's orchestration, replacing strings with winds and adding extra percussion, electronics and some broad instrumental gags. The band itself was moved close and sometimes into the action, stationed on a raised pit surrounded by a runway (shades of burlesque!) where the actors cavorted.

Some D'Oyly Cartesians were not amused, and there were moments of questionable taste, but the whole production was freewheelingly faithful to the *Pirates'* spirit. It exemplified both the wide-open American character Carte had taken into account when planning his *Pinafore* campaign, from the beefed-up orchestra to the concealed microphones worn by the singers, and a joyous Broadway instinct for burlesque which is exactly what the show needs. Mable and Frederic were played by pop stars, with voices really too weak for the demands of bel canto, but that disproportion only added to the fun. The sergeant and his force became true Keystone Kops, racing about the stage in a nervous frenzy and executing some dazzling choreography along the way. The Stanley sisters were leather-lunged bathing beauties who responded to Frederic's 'Oh, is there not one maiden here' as if he were Elvis Presley. But the undoubted star of the production was the Pirate King, a swashbuckler of boundless energy and dash, who at one point trounced the orchestra's conductor in a fair fight, rapier against baton. With all this going on, it was possible to forgive the carefree interpolation of two numbers from *Ruddigore* and *Pinafore*, just for a bit of flavouring.

This Yankee vitality rediscovered the real charm of *The Pirates*, as well as proving that Gilbert and Sullivan are still eminently playable. A hundred years after their first visit, G & S became box office on Broadway, the hottest ticket in town, with the show praised by everyone including Bridget D'Oyly Carte, and that success was subsequently repeated in G & S's own London. It may be that it took a return to *The Pirates'* American roots to accomplish the rejuvenation; it may also be that this is the kind of 'unauthorized production' that will keep the old masterpiece alive for its second hundred years.

5

Patience;
or, Bunthorne's Bride

Of all the Savoy operas, Gilbert thought *Patience* had the least chance of surviving its own time. He would have agreed with an American critic who predicted that the piece would be 'popular, though naturally evanescent, just as its subject is the craze of a single winter'. Purely topical, it would undoubtedly fade with the 'aesthetic' fad it satirized. But a writer in the *Illustrated London News* understood the opera's appeal better than its own author. He recognized that *Patience* was 'a satire of a human weakness, more than of a society craze' and prophesied that it would outlast all Gilbert's other productions. Most of the Savoy operas have a claim to immortality, but it is clear by now that *Patience* is indeed a classic of a special kind. Its subject is not simply a phase of Victorian culture, but the eternal recurrence of artistic affectation. Behind the charming period figures of Bunthorne, Grosvenor and the 'love-sick maidens', any age can discern its own cult heroes, its preening rock stars or poetic visionaries, and their followers, hysterical with longing and adulation.

The typically well-turned plot shows that love of art and love of artists may be indistinguishable. Outside Castle Bunthorne linger twenty Rapturous Maidens, garbed in flowing aesthetic gowns. Accompanying themselves on quasi-medieval instruments, they sing of their hopeless love for the poet Bunthorne, who scorns all such attentions. However, the matronly Lady Jane declares that their idol is himself hopelessly enamoured of the village milkmaid, Patience. Innocent and carefree, Patience trips blithely in, wondering at the ladies' distress and affirming happily that she has had no experience of love at all. She informs them that their old fiancés, the 35th Dragoon Guards, have arrived in the village, but the maidens' ethereal poetic passion has scotched affection for mere military men.

The pining chorus trails off to serenade Bunthorne, leaving the stage clear for the rousing entrance of the dragoons. The soldiers express a hearty satisfaction in themselves and the prospect of seeing their sweethearts. But the ladies reappear devotedly following Bunthorne and totally oblivious to them, spurning their claims and even dismissing their brilliant uniforms as garishly unaesthetic. The maidens continue to sigh their love for Bunthorne while the dragoons march off, fuming at this 'ridiculous, preposterous' turn of events.

Left alone, however, Bunthorne confesses that he is an 'aesthetic sham', less concerned with art than with female admiration. Hoping to win Patience over, he confides that his peevish melancholy is a pose, but she firmly declares that she could not love him even if she knew what love was. But when Lady Angela proclaims that love is totally unselfish and the most essential passion in life, Patience decides to fall in love at once. She immediately encounters the handsome Archibald Grosvenor. He identifies himself as her infant playmate of years before, grown physically beautiful and aesthetically pure: he too is a poet, but a poet of mildness, not melancholy. They pledge their undying love, until Patience realizes with horror that loving a being as perfect as Grosvenor cannot be unselfish, and therefore cannot be love.

Meanwhile, Bunthorne, in despair, has decided to raffle himself off, to the delight of the maidens and the fury of the dragoons. But Patience interrupts the proceedings to announce that she will accept his suit after all, since loving *him* can certainly not be selfish. Officers and ladies are on the point of reconciliation when Grosvenor suddenly appears. As soon as they learn that the handsome lad is 'aesthetic and poetic', the ladies forsake their suitors yet again and fall at the newcomer's feet, to his horror and everyone else's.

The maidens pursue their new idol through Act II as they did Bunthorne in Act I, though Grosvenor, yearning for Patience, tells them that their quest is hopeless. Only Lady Jane is faithful to Bunthorne, while he, cut to the quick by his rival's popularity, snubs the unhappy but dutiful Patience. With Lady Jane's encouragement, he resolves to force the intruder to become thoroughly ordinary. Bunthorne himself will become more good-humoured while still retaining his poetic charisma. When the confrontation occurs, Grosvenor resists at first, then submits, glad to be free of adulation. The dragoons have submitted to a new image too, adopting aesthetic costume and attitudes as best they can. They are rewarded by the approval of their former fiancées, who agree at least to consider taking them back.

Bunthorne informs a delighted Patience that he is a changed man, having abandoned his old biliousness. Loving him, she says, will now be a pleasure. But the remorseless logic of aesthetic love intervenes again. Since Bunthorne has reformed, he is now perfect, and loving him cannot be unselfish, as it must be. The poet's protests are drowned out by the entrance of the cheerily commonplace Grosvenor, followed by the maidens and dragoons. The ladies have imitated their hero in discarding aestheticism and have renewed their alliances with the cavalry. Initially shocked, Patience soon realizes she is free to love the run-of-the-mill Grosvenor. Lady Jane's arms are Bunthorne's last resort, but she makes a noble match with the dragoons' Duke of Dunstable. Happiness reigns at last, normality is restored, and only Bunthorne is left without a bride.

Love is obviously central to *Patience* as it is to every other Savoy opera. The eternal force is framed by the distinctive terms of aestheticism, but Gilbert is more concerned with the pangs of desire than with theories of art. What amuses him and us are the outlandish affectation and bizarre code of behaviour which can dictate success in matters of the heart. He has been criticized for portraying only the surface of aestheticism and not treating the movement respectfully. But the fact is that aestheticism was a vague and complex phenomenon at the best of times, containing elements both serious and silly. Gilbert's manner of dealing with it was certainly legitimate and supported by the movement's curious history. Without being aesthetes themselves, his audience would have been aware that what had begun as a crusade had become a fad, even while it had brought beneficial changes to Victorian life.

Aestheticism's forefathers were the Pre-Raphaelite Brotherhood, a band of young painters and poets united in their loathing for the ponderous materialism of Victorian culture. Their chief members eventually included the poet and painter Dante Gabriel Rossetti, the painter Edward Burne-Jones, the poet Algernon Swinburne and the writer and artist William Morris. They were supported by the powerful critic John Ruskin. The Brotherhood came together in 1848, around a programme based on 'Truth to Nature', though such a broad motto quickly inspired a variety of interpretations. The brethren preached a faithful recording of natural objects as an antidote to the corruption of industrial society. But they also sought the purity and spirituality with which nature had been depicted in earlier, untainted ages. Their Pre-Raphaelite title was meant to evoke an era of freshness and innocence in art, before the formulas and conventions of the Renaissance style, which Ruskin denounced as 'indolence, infidelity, sensuality and shallow pride'. The myths and miracles of the Middle Ages offered them a haven and perspective outside their own time. Their poems and paintings presented richly detailed scenes from Dante, King Arthur and the life of Christ, employing vivid colours and the ancient symbols of flowers and birds to create a radiant, passionate alternative to Victorian dullness.

By the 1860s the public were at least taking Pre-Raphaelites seriously, though still somewhat uneasily. The leaders of the movement had evolved their own distinctive styles. Critics were aware of the characteristic Rossetti woman, with her full, pouting lips, long white neck and mass of dark hair, dressed in flowing robes and captured in a moment of ecstasy. Burne-Jones specialized in religious settings, angelic women depicted in visionary stillness, surrounded by swirling drapery. Swinburne shocked Britain with his *Poems and Ballads* of 1866, which praised sensual experience and yearned for escape from the torpor of society.

But it was Morris's individual view of the Pre-Raphaelite cause that would have the most far-reaching effects. Practical as well as idealistic, he believed that culture could only be transformed by fundamental change in the conditions of people's lives. Politically this attitude made him a socialist. But it also convinced him of the essential value of craft and design. These basic skills gave individuals the means to improve their own environment and break free from the sterile shoddiness of the machine age. In 1861, disgusted at the ugly alternatives he had to choose from in setting up his home, he designed and manufactured all his own furnishings—tables and chairs, curtains, even wallpaper. The experience encouraged him to form his own company, which would produce handmade furniture and decorative furnishings of simplicity, beauty and value. The enterprise was a success, introducing the Morris chair among other benefits but chiefly bringing about a considerable reform in what Victorians were prepared to regard as attractive. Morris's fabrics and wallpaper featured the cherished motifs of the Pre-Raphaelite Brotherhood—graceful designs taken from nature in bright and tasteful colours. Victorian gloom did not vanish overnight. For some time murky browns and maroons would continue to enshrine monolithic furniture and thick velvet plush. But in places at least some lightening of the atmosphere could be discerned.

Thus the earnest brothers had made a certain impact. Some change in consciousness had been initiated. A few younger Victorians could perceive other values than a leaden stability and a hodgepodge of mass-produced possessions. If not exactly ripe to throw convention to the winds, they were occasionally able to imagine other possibilities of personal style and attitude.

One of those possibilities came from the Orient, signalling yet another variation in the complicated Pre-Raphaelite impulse. By 1867 blue-and-white Chinese pottery was popular enough to deserve a special sale at Christie's. 'Blue', as it was called, had been introduced to Britain from France. Two of its earliest and most avid collectors had been the Pre-Raphaelite Rossetti and his friend the young American painter James McNeill Whistler. For Rossetti, Chinese pottery was one more form of beautiful exotica, another means of spiritual access to a world remote from contemporary squalor. But Whistler loved 'blue' simply for its aesthetic qualities. He shared none of the Pre-Raphaelites' social concerns and thought their medieval preoccupations quaintly amusing. Educated in France, he had drunk deep of the Bohemian notion of *l'art pour l'art*, art for art's sake. On the Left Bank, the artist was aloof, aristocratic, living by and for the exquisite sensitivity he expressed in paint or words. What he produced had nothing to do with politics, economics or function. It was separate from and even superior to nature itself.

This was a novel and unsettling doctrine, and older Victorians found it absurd and slightly subversive. The Brotherhood may have been radical reformers, but they were at the same time wholly British, full of energy, zeal and a laudable if peculiar sense of responsibility. But the attitude that Whistler represented turned away from society altogether and seemed to encourage a languid self-absorption, infatuation with one's own special personality. Beauty became a private, not a healthily public domain. Whistler, his curly locks set off by a remarkable white streak, wearing a monocle and wide-brimmed hat, an all-white suit or velvet jacket and sporting dancing shoes, proclaimed himself an artist, a unique spirit beholden to no one. And he backed up his outrageous claim with a deadly and devastating wit.

Of course, Whistler was a genuine artist and would have scoffed at anyone who aped his manner without possessing his talent. But other influences appeared preaching a similar gospel of exquisite individual refinement. An Oxford don, Walter Pater, won a legion of young devotees with his book of essays, *The Renaissance*. It counselled them to 'burn with a hard, gem-like flame', to cultivate sensations and seek to live beautifully. Such a message alarmed their elders, who in 1871 had already been warned of grave decadent tendencies in the works of Rossetti and Swinburne, by a little book called *The Fleshly School of Poetry*.

It all seemed a strange perversion of the noble ideals of the Pre-Raphaelites, though the trappings of the Brotherhood were still very much in evidence. Medieval and natural references were a kind of spiritual code among the advanced young, part of an ostentatious worship of the beautiful. But the original impulse had changed direction, turning inward instead of outward. The good old cause had become the latest craze. The Brotherhood, in effect, had given way to the Aesthetic Movement, and style had replaced substance.

The division burst into public view when Whistler sued the old Pre-Raphaelite prophet John Ruskin for libel. Ruskin was as dedicated as William Morris to wedding art and morality. At Oxford, while Walter Pater had been writing his introverted essays praising the Renaissance spirit Ruskin loathed, the older man had been trying to establish a quasi-medieval guild, a model community combining a sense of beauty with practical self-sufficiency. His vision of inspired utility even prompted him to lead a group of undergraduates out to mend a local road.

In 1877 Ruskin, still the leading art critic of the day, attended the opening of London's newest avant-garde art gallery, the Grosvenor. He saw and approved the neo-medieval productions of Burne-Jones, but Whistler's moody impressionist works, like 'Nocturne in Black and Gold: The Falling Rocket', appalled him. These exorbitantly priced smudges were not art. They presented no transcendent image. No one was the better for seeing them. Seizing his pen, Ruskin accused Whistler of 'wilful imposture', called him 'a coxcomb' and denounced the 'Cockney impudence' that could 'ask two hundred guineas for flinging a pot of paint in the public's face'. Whistler consulted his attorney and, at his witty best, triumphed in the ensuing trial. He won only a farthing, but never again could anyone profess to be an absolute judge of what was valuable in art. It certainly had nothing to do with morality. As the aesthetes maintained, it was all a question of special sensitivity.

By the late '70s Victorian culture was a bewildering conglomeration of strains and tendencies. Some households displayed traditional Victorian sobriety, others flaunted aesthetic convictions, many wavered between the two. Morris-style floral wallpaper and hangings were fashionable, as were pastel colour schemes. Contemporary furniture reflected a more delicate eighteenth-century taste, just as architectural style veered towards the age of Queen Anne rather than Victoria. Neo-medieval knick-knacks like brass candleholders and lanterns jostled with Japanese fans and screens. Lilies and sunflowers loomed from blue-and-white vases. Aesthetic women modelled their dress on the women of Rossetti, Burne-Jones and Whistler, eschewing bustles and corsets in favour of naturally flowing gowns. Men adopted broad-brimmed hats or berets and lounged in soft jackets.

But behaviour identified the committed aesthete as much as apparel or possessions. An expression of soulful yearning, of ecstasy or frustrated melancholy, was essential. True initiates always conveyed intensity, that special receptivity that distinguished the sensitive soul. The ugly and earthly pained them; the beautiful and spiritual sent them into raptures. They were very careful judges of what was acceptable or not, and their approval was couched in a weird new jargon. It was unhappily adopted from Ruskin, whose prose was always passionate and sincere, if sometimes purple. He was fond of ultimate adjectives like 'consummate', 'utter' and 'supreme', and these terms, in eccentric combinations, peppered the gushing appreciation of aesthetic devotees.

These self-conscious antics did not go unnoticed by Victorian commentators. One of the most pungent chroniclers of the movement was George du Maurier, the cartoonist of *Punch*. From 1873 he created a whole gallery of aesthetic characters, defining types and attitudes with hilarious accuracy. His people exhibit all the classic traits of the avant-garde. His interiors catch exactly their decorative fetishes. Brasenose Boniface, an aesthetic youth in quilted jacket, flowing tie and knee-breeches shows off his prize fifteenth-century painting to an unimpressed mother and daughter. With all the tremulous spirituality of a Rossetti model, Mrs Cimabue Brown holds forth in her aesthetic salon. A similar young lady unnerves her conventional escort by sighing, 'Are you intense?' A young couple vie with each other to caress their new 'blue' teapot.

The Victorians chuckled at du Maurier's puppets, when all at once, in 1878, they came to life. Oscar Wilde arrived in London from Oxford and immediately became the public embodiment of aestheticism. Above all, the movement was a matter of style, and Wilde had perfected his performance to the point of genius. He had all the right credentials. A genuinely brilliant talker, he had studied with Pater, as well as helping Ruskin repair his road. His college rooms were famous for their artful décor, including a fine collection of 'blue'. His heartfelt cry of 'Oh, would that I could live up to my blue china!' was so definitely aesthetic that du Maurier borrowed it for one of his captions. But this was only fair since Wilde had modelled his dress on the young men in du Maurier's cartoons.

Wilde took full advantage of his talent for publicity. In London he soon presented himself to Whistler and Burne-Jones, who were charmed and fascinated. He eulogized the beauties of the past, the exquisiteness of flowers, and wrote poetry, as well as constantly enhancing his conversational reputation. Designating himself the 'Professor of Aesthetics', he inspired anecdotes and acquired disciples. He became the focal point of the Aesthetic Movement, a grandly, outrageously self-confident media event that seemed to sum up all its tendencies. Interest in aestheticism boomed. In 1880 du Maurier introduced two new characters, the poet Jellaby Postlethwaite and his painter-friend Maudle, both given to making Wildean pronouncements. Later that year F. C. Burnand, editor of *Punch* and Sullivan's first librettist, staged *The Colonel*, a French comedy rather thinly reworked to feature an aesthetic villain. And finally, in April 1881, came *Patience*.

Given the opera's immediate success, it is surprising to realize that Gilbert and Sullivan had not originally intended to write an aesthetic satire. Gilbert had toyed with the idea but abandoned it partly for technical reasons and partly because the ground seemed so thoroughly covered already. Instead, his never-resting nose for humbug sent him after clergymen. He had long been suspicious of the clerical profession. With their air of special sanctity, its members could be just as affected

As befits the original Mabel in *The Pirates of Penzance*, the beautiful Blanche Roosevelt actually was a general's daughter. Later she was the mistress of Guy de Maupassant

Walter Passmore as the lovable Sergeant of Police in a later production of *The Pirates*

In a contemporary drawing, the Pirate King unfurls the skull-and-crossbones

Gilbertian drawings of two subjects from *The Pirates*: a whimsical Modern Major-General and a tearful constable showing why 'a policeman's lot is not a happy one'

Two drawings from 'The Rival Curates', the Bab Ballad which inspired *Patience*, showing the Rev. Hopley Porter's happy fall from mildness to worldliness

Alice Barnett, the original Lady Jane: 'No, not pretty. *Massive*'

The arch-aesthete Oscar Wilde, at the height of his conquest of New York

THE SIX-MARK TEA-POT.

Æsthetic Bridegroom. "It is quite consummate, is it not?"
Intense Bride. "It is, indeed! Oh, Algernon, let us live up to it!"

One of George du Maurier's *Punch* cartoons, with a typical aesthetic couple voicing a typical aesthetic sentiment

From the first production of *Patience*, the dragoons (Richard Temple, Frank Thornton and Durward Lely) struggle to become acceptably Early English

Two sides of the Victorian coin: the 'haggard and lank' Bunthorne and the 'matter-of-fact' Grosvenor

as any aesthete. (Once, by horrible mischance, Gilbert had found himself the only frockless guest at a hotel otherwise completely filled by ecclesiastics. One of the pious brethren observed mildly that the dramatist must feel somewhat out of place. 'I feel like a lion in a den of Daniels,' growled W. S. G.)

Gilbert was particularly irritated by the spectacle of female parishioners worshipping a saintly curate, which seemed a fraud on both sides. Already in *The Sorcerer* Dr Daly had recalled a time

'. . . when maidens of the noblest station,
Forsaking even military men,
Would gaze upon me, rapt in adoration—
Ah me, I was a fair young curate then.'

In the first version of *Patience* Gilbert resurrected the topsy-turvy notion of eligible ladies preferring holiness to manliness. Then he added to it the basic plot of one of his *Bab Ballads*, 'The Rival Curates', in which two winsome churchmen compete for eminence in piety. The conflict is resolved only when one sends his sexton and beadle to pay a call on the other, offering him a choice between becoming more worldly or leaving the world altogether. His rival immediately takes the soft option: for years he has been looking for an excuse to 'play croquet, smoke and dance' like a normal chap and he can now 'do it on compulsion'.

Combining the two stories, the new opera would feature competing curates who would dominate the affections of village maidens, utterly overshadowing a detachment of dragoons. As a final stroke Gilbert even proposed that the despairing troopers would take holy orders. By November 1880 two-thirds of the libretto was finished. But its author was increasingly worried about taking such liberties with the cloth. He found his invention 'crippled at every turn by the necessity of protecting myself from a charge of irreverence'. At last he returned to the less controversial subject of aestheticism, making his churchmen poets but retaining the country setting, maidens and dragoons.

The transformation was not so far-fetched. What interested Gilbert in both versions of *Patience* was the general vice of affectation, rather than any particular pose. He was no more concerned with the aesthetic credo *per se* than he would have been with Church doctrine. He simply saw that each could be carried too far into airy-fairy posturing. It was bad enough when such anti-social doctrines were sincere. But when they concealed a secret desire for the very social rewards they seemed publicly to scorn, that was too much. It was obvious to Gilbert that curates and poets must crave feminine attention just as much as their more earthy brothers, but were too hypocritical to admit it. Instead they tried to achieve it by dishonest means—playing on the female weakness for emotional novelty and representing love as a mysterious and exalted force.

Above all, Gilbert turns aesthetic folly into first-rate theatre. His audience would have recognized from the very beginning of *Patience* all the precious trappings of the movement. The Castle Bunthorne set evokes its nostalgic medievalism. The Rapturous Maidens, in their flowing gowns, sorrowful intensity and stained-glass poses, seem to have stepped from a Burne-Jones painting. The difficulty of 'getting the chorus to dress and make up aesthetically' had been a main reason for Gilbert's hesitation in attempting an aesthetic opera. He had hoped to enlist the noted aesthete-watcher du Maurier to help in the staging but decided that Burne-Jones's paintings would offer ample guidance. As for costumes, Gilbert himself went to Liberty's, the newly opened shop in Regent Street that specialized in aesthetic furnishings and Orientalia. There he chose the authentic patterns and pastel fabrics his maidens required.

The ladies' emotions are as aesthetic as their appearance. When Patience appears, to music as cheerfully resilient as theirs is genteely lugubrious, they chide her for never having loved. To them, love is a spiritual duty, the soul's yearning for an object of perfection. Therefore, it is not only marvellous that the tender agony has passed her by but 'deplorable' as well. To the milkmaid the ladies merely represent 'mad infatuation'. But Lady Jane, a true if ageing aesthetic devotee, calls it a 'transcendentality of delirium', awakened by the ecstasy of art.

Patience is as baffled by such bizarre jargon as she is by the ladies' commitment to their misery. She herself is a sort of Gilbertian paragon, innocent, sensible, untouched by artificial fashions. As we have seen before, her creator distrusted super-charged emotions: love should be a natural social force, made up of affection and good sense. Patience may seem slightly unreal in an age of liberated women, but she does stand for an uncomplicated ideal of Victorian feminity. And such women were not merely stage types; Gilbert's own wife possessed similar qualities. Pretty and self-effacing, Mrs Gilbert—'Kitten'—was a demure seventeen when he married her at the age of thirty-one.

The etherealized maidens of course want nothing to do with the magnificent but mundane dragoons. The officers' splendid entrance is one more demonstration of how skilfully Gilbert plans his effects and how masterfully Sullivan accomplishes them. The opera's first fifteen minutes is a characteristic study in contrasts—first the languor of the ladies, then the blithe gaiety of Patience and finally the strapping martial authority of the dragoons. Moods change, colours change and Sullivan makes the most of every nuance.

The dragoons are unquestionably appealing. Gilbert often showed sham and pomposity in uniform, but he endears these soldiers to us at once when they admit they are only a 'second-class cavalry regiment'. They remind us of the policemen in *The Pirates of Penzance*—good-natured fellows, a trifle thick, men's men who make a good deal of jolly noise. Aestheticism catches them quite out of their depth, which to Gilbert is definitely a mark in their favour. Their straightforward vigour is a pointed contrast to the movement's melancholy excesses.

The colonel's song provides them with a perfect introduction. One of Gilbert's best patter numbers, it demands a nimble tongue and displays yet again the master's virtuosity at spinning out line after line of precise and hilarious verse. But it also affords a wonderful free-assocation celebration of what a formidable and complex creature the heavy dragoon is. Critics have called it a ludicrous potpourri, existing only for the sake of clever rhythm and rhyme. But all its components are, as the colonel says, remarkable, and so are the dragoons.

Very likely few members of the original audience of *Patience* understood every one of the song's flurry of references, but even today most people will recognize a good many. The general sense is clear. We can tell at least that a figure is attached to a particular field—literary, military, political, religious—or that he is a fictional character, like Perveril, Don Roderick, Paddy, Manfred and 'the Stranger'. A few allusions repay closer scrutiny as examples of Gilbert's attention to out-of-the-way references that are still to the point, and his wizardry at fitting them into the demanding format of his composition. In the second verse, for instance, 'Richardson's show' was a popular travelling theatre and circus. 'Beadle of Burlington' has been identified as the brass-buttoned officer in charge of peace-keeping at London's fashionable Burlington Arcade. But, more divertingly, it may refer to Erasmus T. Beadle, an American publisher from Burlington, New York. He became well known to some segments of both American and British society for thrilling boys' books like *The Shawnees' Foe* that came out in 'Beadle's Dime Novels'. One of the most esoteric allusions is 'Paddington Pollaky', who was Ignatius Paul Pollaky, a noted private detective with offices in London's Paddington Green.

Despite this colourful, many-sided appeal, the dragoons find themselves totally ignored when the maidens return, following Bunthorne. To an aesthete, physical vitality is a liability, and the moment of revelation, when the dumbfounded troopers confront the bilious poet and his doleful entourage, is another theatrical coup. Gilbert's presentation of the conflicting parties is superbly matched by Sullivan, with the ladies intoning lachrymose homage to their Reginald while the dragoons bluster their indignation.

In the midst of the confusion, at last we meet its cause. There has been considerable speculation as to who provided the original model for Bunthorne. Whistler, Swinburne and, most often, Wilde have been proposed. But it seems clear that Gilbert had them all in general and no one in particular in mind. Again, he was after a type, a fictional epitome of the arch-aesthete, and he gathered whatever traits would suit his intentions. As with the colonel's song, specific allusions can be traced, but it is the overall effect that matters.

When Bunthorne appears in a modern production of *Patience*, we perceive a preoccupied figure, rather birdlike and emaciated, bizarrely clad and ostentatiously aloof from his surroundings. We think 'an arty fake', which is precisely what the original audience would have registered. Their contemporary experience would simply have permitted them to identify more closely the sources of the Bunthornian image.

The poet's dress—velvet jacket and knickerbockers, knee-stockings and flowing tie—would have reminded them of du Maurier's cartoons and their incarnation in the person of Oscar Wilde. Like any aesthete, Wilde wore his hair long, but Bunthorne's mass of dark curls—especially with its single white streak—would have made alert viewers think of James McNeill Whistler, as would Bunthorne's monocle. In stature Wilde was generously built (at Oxford he had once thrown a marauding Philistine downstairs), but both Whistler and Gilbert's poet were small men. Whistler was well known for the kind of verbal facility that Bunthorne turns to opportunistic ends. Gilbert, in fact, was a friend of the painter and breakfasted with him the very morning his celebrated suit against Ruskin began.

That other diminutive aesthete Algernon Swinburne undoubtedly also contributed to Gilbert's creation. He was a poet of just the 'fleshly' stamp that marks Bunthorne. The wounded world-weariness Gilbert's bard pours out unmistakably echoes Swinburne's tone. His 'bitter-hearted' quatrain

'Oh, to be wafted away
From this black Aceldama of sorrow,
Where the dust of an earthy today
Is the earth of a dusty tomorrow!'

could only be a wicked Gilbertian variation on a standard Swinburnian theme:

'I am weary of days and hours,
Blown buds of barren flowers,
Desires and dreams and powers,
And everything but sleep.'
(*The Garden of Proserpine)*

In fact, the stage direction at Bunthorne's first appearance originally read 'Algernon enters'. But to prove how undogmatic Gilbert's reaction to aestheticism was, at one point he had intended to call Grosvenor Algernon instead of Archibald.

Even with elements added from other sources, however, Oscar Wilde was central to Gilbert's conception of the artist-poseur. The newcomer seemed to be *all* surface, and it is easy to imagine the crusty, suspicious Gilbert thinking the worst of his intentions. The two men once met, and the resulting exchange was mutually characteristic. As always, Wilde was glibly effervescent. Gilbert grated, 'I wish I could talk like you. I'd keep my mouth shut and claim it as a virtue.' Never topped, Oscar crooned back, 'Ah, that would be selfish! I could deny myself the pleasure of talking but not to others the pleasure of listening.'

Of course Bunthorne reveals immediately that despite his supposed concentration on his art he is every bit as aware of his audience as Wilde was. We know he is a fraud from the moment he enters, but in fact Gilbert treats him quite good-humouredly, presenting him as more scamp than scoundrel. At least Bunthorne knows exactly what he is about, which is more than can be said for the Rapturous Maidens. One of the most delicious bits of dialogue in the opera occurs when they dismiss the helpless dragoons, swept out of favour by the aesthetic tide. The improvements Lady Jane suggests in the hapless horsemen's uniforms convey just what extremes of nonsense the movement could inspire: ' . . . there *is* a cobwebby grey velvet, with a tender bloom like cold gravy, which made Florentine fourteenth-century, trimmed with Venetian leather and Spanish altar lace, and surmounted with something Japanese—it matters not what—would at least be Early English!'

This is pure silliness, and Bunthorne, confessing that he is 'an aesthetic sham', shows how to take advantage of it. His famous recipe for success, 'if you're anxious for to shine in the high aesthetic line', is a catalogue of arty pretensions. It is also very neat lyrics set to a disarmingly amiable melody. Bunthorne's advice might have come from Wilde himself: astonish ordinary people by espousing eccentric tastes and appearing dauntingly deep, cultivated and pure. The most familiar line in the song, encouraging the would-be aesthete to 'walk down Piccadilly with a poppy or a lily in your medieval hand' has been associated with Wilde's own habits. But he denied such flowery perambulations, while typically going the claim one better: 'The great and difficult thing was . . . to make the whole world *believe* that I had done it.'

Unfortunately for Bunthorne, the only maiden he wants is the one he can't have. Patience is not taken in for an instant by aesthetic perversions of either love or taste. She is immune to Bunthorne because, since she is not 'etherealized', she sees he is merely peevish and unattractive. Gilbert applauds her clear-sightedness. She is temporarily confused by Lady Angela's soulful vision of love as necessary suffering, but her natural partner is the handsome, uncomplicated Grosvenor, her childhood swain and Bunthorne's poetic rival.

Grosvenor is not as interesting a character as Bunthorne because his version of aestheticism is so blandly healthy and self-satisfied. Gilbert probably modelled him after the earlier, more earnest Pre-Raphaelites and borrowed his name from the Grosvenor Gallery. His insipid virtue and cloying verse may have been influenced by another Victorian poet, Coventry Patmore, who praised homely domesticity. But Archibald's real function is providing a foil for Bunthorne. Part of the contrast between the two reflects the original casting. The rather weedy, angular George Grossmith created the part of Bunthorne, while Gilbert wrote Grosvenor for the 'staid, stolid' Rutland Barrington.

Bunthorne's rival is benign instead of waspish, the 'Apostle of Simplicity' instead of spleen, but Gilbert's point is that the disparity between their views makes no difference whatever to the maidens. Deprived of Bunthorne, they transfer their ecstasies to Grosvenor on the spot simply because he seems sorrowful, solitary and aesthetic. His instant popularity proves that the ladies are most in love with their own emotional state and whatever exotic object they can attach it to. In spite of their intellectual and spiritual pretensions, their real character is adolescent self-indulgence. Again Gilbert's people display timeless attributes: the Rapturous Maidens could be the great-great-grandmothers of stricken groupies shrieking outside any rock star's dressing-room.

The irrational spell is only broken when, as in 'The Rival Curates', the jealous Bunthorne forces Grosvenor to become commonplace. Act II moves smoothly and inevitably to its happily ironic resolution. Bunthorne is undone by aestheticism's own dotty logic. Since he is now willing to be mildly cheerful as well as severely aesthetic, he is perfect—which means that Patience can no longer love him unselfishly. Grosvenor, having renounced art and truth, has become imperfect—that is, normal—and can be loved freely. But since 'Archibald the All-Right' has forsaken the movement, the maidens, now eternally faithful, decide they should too. All then embrace everyday life and each other, except for Bunthorne, who is left alone with his lily.

The climax of the opera is Bunthorne and Grosvenor's confrontation. The encounter is amusing because physical coercion is out of the question for either of them; the idyllic poet surrenders to Bunthorne's threat to—*curse* him. In the duet that follows, Gilbert wittily compares the values of the aesthete with those of the plain chap. In a way, he satirizes both positions, reducing them to contrasting stereotypes.

Bunthorne will remain the spiritual high priest, collecting 'blue' and praising aesthetic colour combinations like green and yellow (the walls of the Grosvenor Gallery were painted green and gold). Grosvenor will become the happy Philistine, eating well, walking his dog—'a half-bred black-and-tan'—and preferring dances in the suburbs to concerts of classical music. He will have a regular job in an office, or in a department store where he will encourage customers with 'What's the next article?'

Gilbert's words in the duet are another *tour de force*, apt, funny, unerringly placed. *Patience* is unquestionably one of his finest achievements—so much so in fact that some critics have lauded his contribution at the expense of Sullivan's. It is true that the composer wrote his music under the usual pressure, brought on for once more by idleness than illness. During the winter he had been engaged on his oratorio *The Martyr of Antioch*. Then he had gone off to his beloved south of France for rest, recuperation and roulette until February. Three days before opening night he was still finishing the score while entertaining one of his royal friends, the Duke of Edinburgh.

Under such circumstances it would be understandable if the music had its perfunctory moments, but it is very difficult to point to any place in the score where Sullivan could be accused of letting his partner down. The tunes he supplies for the Bunthorne-Grosvenor duet, the quintet of the reunited maidens and dragoons and the conspiratorial exchanges of Lady Jane and Bunthorne are as high-spirited as anything he ever wrote. And there are several of those tender moments that are Sullivan's particular glory, where he creates moods of real emotion where Gilbert on his own is unconvincing. The Duke's 'Your maiden hearts, ah, do not steel' is intended to be half-humorous, but Sullivan gives it real feeling, and Patience's 'Love is a plaintive song' aptly conveys her perplexed unhappiness.

But Sullivan's most remarkable achievement is his transformation of Lady Jane's solo at the beginning of Act II. Gilbert's lyrics are deliberately unkind, the candid picture of a woman's physical decline as she ages. However, Sullivan adorns them with a melody regretful, dignified and genuinely touching. The song manages to evoke both humour and emotion and makes Lady Jane a distinctly sympathetic character. Later, Sullivan's publisher took novel advantage of his client's tune, transferring it to a more conventional context. With new words—not, needless to say, by Gilbert—it became 'In the Twilight of our Love', a treacly ballad for the Victorian drawing-room. But, somehow predictably, without Gilbert's barbed and contrary verses its magic was lost.

To the opera's first audience, on 23 April 1881, *Patience* was an unequivocal triumph for both its creators. Its songs and satire gave pleasure from beginning to end. As one paper reported, the fashionable crowd's reaction even at the interval was 'a chorus of delight. Everyone goes about saying "Hey, willow-waly,O". Nobody knows what this means, but all say "Aesthetic, don't cher know".' There were numerous encores and showers of critical praise. *Patience* was obviously set for a very long run, and its begetters relaxed characteristically. Shortly after opening night Sullivan was off on a royal vacation aboard a warship with the Duke of Edinburgh, calling on crowned heads in Denmark, Germany and Russia; Gilbert stayed quietly at home.

The opera was immediately recognized as 'the most subtle and incisive of all the contributions to the exhaustive satire of aestheticism'. There was no doubt that it was unique. The programme had specified carefully that it was 'an entirely New and Original Aesthetic Opera', and a note certified that Gilbert's libretto had predated Burnand's comedy *The Colonel*. But the piece's freshness and ingenuity spoke for itself. To spike criticism from the avant-garde, D'Oyly Carte prepared a statement distinguishing the 'pure and healthy teaching' of the Pre-Raphaelites from 'the gospel of morbid languor and sickly sensuousness' which had become fashionable among the young. He concluded: 'In satirizing the excesses of these (so-called) aesthetes, the authors of *Patience* have not desired to cast ridicule on the true aesthetic spirit, but only to attack the unmanly oddities which masquerade in its likeness. . . .'

And yet the shoe did not seem to fit very many people. *Patience* was nowhere more popular than among its likeliest targets. Even before opening night Oscar Wilde had written to George Grossmith, his supposed stage persona, to request a three-guinea box be reserved for him. 'With Gilbert and Sullivan,' he added, 'I am looking forward to being greatly amused.' Whether he was present at the first night is not absolutely certain, though it is likely. Newspaper reports did not mention him by name, though one referred to the apparition of 'HIMSELF . . . the apostle of uncut hair!' complete with daffodil. Whistler certainly attended with pleasure, his dry, slightly sinister laugh prominent in the stalls. Afterwards he sent a wrily appreciative note to Grossmith. 'My dear Bunthorne,' it read, 'I knew you [were] amazing!—but I did not know you were more amazing than I.' Sadly, the ill and ageing Dante Gabriel Rossetti had to be reassured by friends that Bunthorne was not a caricature of him.

In the summer of 1881 the American response to *Patience* proved that the acclaim was more than a local phenomenon. Performed by the inevitable pirate companies, it opened on 28 July in St Louis and subsequently spread east and west. American critics conceded that native audiences had only a vague grasp of the intricacies of aestheticism, and yet the opera was a great and growing sensation. A San Francisco reporter overheard a theatre-goer musing, 'People seem to understand this sort of thing a great deal better than I expected they would.' They certainly understood it well enough. Some notion of the movement had penetrated the hinterland, but *Patience* established its own terms in any case, and Sullivan's music was universally hailed as irresistible. Indeed, one extravagant critic felt obliged to warn his audience not to be so captivated by the score that they might 'go away unconscious they have been hearing a libretto worthy of Horace. . .'.

Patience owed its existence in some degree to the notoriety of Oscar Wilde, and it repaid the debt by making him even more notorious. Their fortunes continued to intertwine in America, where Wilde arrived, by no means coincidentally, for a lecture tour in January 1882. The tour was arranged by his agent—Gilbert and Sullivan's own D'Oyly Carte. Carte has been accused of sending Wilde to the States as an advance man for the official version of the opera, to show the colonials what a real aesthete looked like. But of course the pirated *Patience* was already an American hit, and the advantage worked both ways. The impresario was well aware of this and told Wilde he must not mind Carte's employing 'a little bunkum to push him in America'.

As it turned out, the lecture tour was a great success. Wilde created a stir from the moment he arrived, announcing at customs that he had nothing to declare but his genius, and telling reporters that the Atlantic had not lived up to his expectations. As always with Oscar, it was hard to tell whether this was pure sham or brilliance. But he charmed his audiences from New York to the Wild West with his wit and a quiet manliness they had not expected. He and *Patience* did promote each other. As Carte later reported from America, '*Patience* is still playing to fair business. Wilde has given it a fresh spirit and it has simply made him. His business is *enormous*.'

Meanwhile, in London the opera had been part of an historic development in the partnership of Gilbert, Sullivan and Carte. On 10 October 1881, after 170 performances at the Opera Comique, it transferred to Carte's just-completed Savoy Theatre. Spacious but intimate, with superb acoustics, the new house was widely praised. It was decorated in simple but impeccable taste, with a colour scheme of white, pale yellow and gold. Mindful of the lessons of *Patience*, Carte specifically denied that the Aesthetic Movement had had any influence on his choice of décor. It was, he said, neither Queen Anne nor Early English, free equally from gingerbread and cherubim. And yet in its subtle delicacy, so different from the ponderous confusion of much Victorian design, the new Savoy expressed just those principles that the forebears of aestheticism had preached. Modern in this, it was even more up to date in its lighting. On 28 December it became the first London theatre to be illuminated completely by electricity. Ever the showman, Carte gave a dramatic stage demonstration of the new system, breaking a lighted bulb under a muslin cloth to show that no fire would result.

Patience thus became the first true Savoy opera and ran continuously until 22 November 1882. Despite its success—it had 578 performances, second only to *The Mikado*—it was not revived until the autumn of 1900. Gilbert was still afraid that its popularity depended on the topicality of aestheticism. But the work stood firmly on its own, as it has ever since. The second Savoy production was an undeniable hit, running for another 150 performances without the benefit of the disgraced and self-exiled Wilde, the old Pre-Raphaelites or the dimly remembered cartoons in *Punch*.

The first night of the revival was an emotional occasion. All three members of the Savoy triumvirate were in poor health, and Carte and Sullivan were prematurely aged. The chronically strained relations between Gilbert and Sullivan had been eased through the intercession of Carte's wife, and the author, only half-facetiously, proposed that the three old men take a curtain call in wheelchairs. The ailing Sullivan good-naturedly agreed, writing to Mrs Carte that 'three such frightful wrecks . . . would create something of a sensation.' But on the night he was far too ill to appear. Gilbert and Carte acknowledged the warm applause leaning on their walking sticks and looking, someone said, like Chelsea pensioners.

Gilbert wrote to Sullivan that 'the old opera woke up splendidly,' but it was the last opening the three great Savoyards would share. Sullivan died two weeks later, and Carte followed him in the early spring of 1901. Between them, a month after the revival of *Patience* opened, Oscar Wilde died in Paris.

6

Iolanthe;
or The Peer and the Peri

Iolanthe may not be the most widely known of the Savoy operas, but it can rightly be called the connoisseur's favourite. Gilbert said it was a 'fairy opera'; it has also been described as 'political', 'very pretty yet somewhat cynical', 'tender and pathetic' and 'subtle'. In fact, it is a delicate combination of all these things. In *Iolanthe,* satire and nonsense do not conflict as they do in some of the other operas. It offers fantasy instead of absurdity, delightful contrasts and, best of all, genuine emotion. Since, as a critic observed, emotion was Arthur Sullivan's 'true field of action', *Iolanthe* gave him a rare opportunity, and he did not waste it. Full of charm, the fairy piece may be his best score; certainly it has few rivals. Together, he and Gilbert create a perfect if improbable balance between Parliament, Arcady and Fairyland. The result is the only really *romantic* Savoy opera, lyrical and touching in spite of its satiric edge. It is also one of the small number of G & S works to make its way into 'grand opera' circles, which would have amazed both partners and immensely gratified at least one of them.

It was conceived in an atmosphere of buoyant success. *Patience* was a huge hit, and different enough from *Pinafore* and *Pirates*—which many people still regarded as a matched set—to show that the Savoy team were not limited in subject. They were definitely a thriving institution, with financial rewards to match. Both Gilbert and Sullivan moved into splendid new households, which of course, were completely different in style. Sullivan's was a handsome bachelor flat, furnished in comfortably eclectic Victorian taste. It would be his home for the rest of his life, the site of elegant parties for his royal, artistocratic and artistic friends. Gilbert's house was a family mansion, built to his specifications in a very desirable neighbourhood. Its luxury blended the richly traditional and the absolutely up-to-date. There were moulded ceilings, panelled walls and stained-glass windows, as well as electricity, central heating and bathrooms on all four floors.

The librettist entertained too, but his visitor's book was less grand than his partner's. Indeed, his favourite guests were children, and his parties for them were frolicsome affairs, with Gilbert (who had no offspring of his own) a whole-hearted participant. The small fry had priority even on more sedate occasions. The country place Gilbert later owned contained a menagerie of domestic animals, which were there at least partly for the pleasure of visiting children. Once a gathering of adults was diverted by the spectacle of their host, the scourge of Victorian theatre, being led away by a fair-haired toddler. 'The little girl', he explained seriously, 'wants to look at the chickens'.

One appliance both households possessed was a telephone, a considerable novelty at the time. Gilbert ordered his first and recommended the contraption to his partner. The ever-vigilant author had already ordered a phone for the stage of the Savoy, as he told Sullivan, 'so that I shall be able to hear the performance from my study—so will you, from your house, if you decide to have one. . . .' It seems quite clear that what Gilbert had in mind was not an idle evening's entertainment but monitoring the cast's fidelity to his script. By contrast it was Sullivan who took advantage of the instrument's social possibilities. On his forty-first birthday, during *Iolanthe*'s run, he gave a glittering soirée attended by the first guest of the realm, the Prince of Wales. Gilbert was there as well. At the decisive moment, Sullivan casually rang the Savoy where the company had gathered at his expense for a special performance of selections from the opera. Taking turns at the telephone, the party-goers marvelled at this new wonder of the age, broadcasting peers and peris to them live across London.

But Sullivan's fortieth birthday, the year before in 1882, had been followed almost immediately by a shattering blow. His mother, the last member of his precious family, died after a short illness, leaving him, as he said in his diary, 'feeling dreadfully lonely'. He formed a new family by adopting his nephew Herbert, son of his late brother Fred. Feminine companionship came from the renowned socialite Mrs Ronalds, a beautiful American long separated from her husband. Her circle, like Sullivan's, included royal acquaintances. The Prince and Princess of Wales visited her regularly, taking particular pleasure in the musical afternoons at which she herself performed. The Prince declared, 'I would travel the length of my kingdom to hear Mrs. Ronalds sing "The Lost Chord",' and Sullivan wept at her rendering of the song he had written in grief for his brother. For the rest of the composer's life she gave him affection and support. In London they saw each other every day; when either of them travelled, they exchanged letters and telegrams.

Sullivan began work on *Iolanthe* early in June 1882, shortly after his mother's funeral, and the opera's lyric qualities gave him a welcome outlet for his feelings of tenderness and loss. Gilbert, meanwhile, had been working diligently for months, following his usual pattern—

writing and rewriting the plot, then turning to the songs before finally framing the dialogue. Since total control of the production rested with him, he was also filling his notebooks with sketches for costumes and sets. He had enhanced the realism of *H.M.S. Pinafore* by having the crew's uniforms made by a naval tailor. He took the same measures with the magnificently gaudy peers in *Iolanthe*, commissioning replicas of the state robes of each knightly order from Queen Victoria's own robe-maker. At some stage he decided to model the Fairy Queen after Richard Wagner's Teutonic heroine Brünnhilde, complete with winged helmet and armour. Wagner's *Ring* operas were the talk of at least some of the town, having received their London première earlier in 1882.

By the time he came to rehearsal, Gilbert as always had every stage movement blocked out, every gesture planned, every vocal inflection calculated. As always his particular concern was the chorus's part in action. In his notes he had worked out phrase by phrase and movement by movement how they should respond to the speeches of the main characters. There would be no dull or dead spots anywhere in the production. 'Remember, ladies and gentlemen,' he would exhort the company, 'you've got to do your damnedest in this passage, or it'll go flat!' His insistence on *pace* makes him the great-grandfather of modern musical comedy direction.

Gilbert's domination of his ensemble in the theatre was famous, but he also occasionally influenced their private lives. During a performance of *Patience* he had intercepted what he considered to be an improper note to one of his actresses. In a fine Gilbertian rage, he confronted the four young men who had sent it and demanded they leave the theatre at once. The incident prompted journalistic quips about the 'Savoy Boarding School', but during *Iolanthe* Gilbert gave assistance in two more pressing matters of honour. A cavalry officer had boasted at his club that he had spent a night with an attractive lady of the Savoy chorus. The claim was untrue, and Gilbert tracked the offender down and forced him to sign a statement admitting it. Months later the same girl so bewitched a young nobleman that he proposed marriage—rashly, as it turned out, because his family forced him to break off the engagement soon after it was announced. Gilbert immediately took up the jilted actress's cause and won her an out-of-court settlement of £10,000. Such intervention was clearly above and beyond the call of theatrical duty. But whatever the jibes of the newspapers, the Savoy company returned their chief's devotion, and its effects showed in their energy on stage.

Sullivan did a good deal of his work on *Iolanthe* far from the intrigues of London. An aristocratic friend had offered him creative peace in Cornwall, as one of a party at her country estate. Sullivan spent a happy summer alternating between composition and sociability. He came and went as he pleased, holding up his end at cards and conversation but never letting his fellow guests in on his professional activities. He, Gilbert and Carte were all determined to maintain as much secrecy as possible to thwart leaks foreign and domestic. Though *Patience* had been plagued by American pirates, the trio's attempts to stop them in the courts had been overruled. Sullivan remarked bitterly that US judges seemed to think 'a free and independent American citizen ought not to be robbed of his rights of robbing somebody else.' It had already been decided that the new opera would open in New York and London on the same day, with Gilbert rehearsing the second company in secret before their transatlantic crossing. Security was vital, and when the composer and the vacationing librettist met at a hotel restaurant to rework Act I, they whispered like conspirators.

The hard grind of rehearsals was well under way in September. For the D'Oyly Carte company it meant continuing to play one opera while they learned a new one. For Gilbert it meant putting two casts through their paces, and for Sullivan rehearsing while finishing the actual composition of the piece. Once again he was behind, due to illness and indolence. But, once again, when he buckled down, his efforts were prodigious. He worked until the early hours and one night composed five songs in a single sitting. The normal pressure was increased because he had to have the score ready for the early departure of the American company. He met his deadline successfully except for the overture, and the conductor of the New York production, his friend Alfred Cellier, had to provide one himself.

The cast learned the music as it trickled in, song by song, the choral numbers first, then the small ensembles and solos. Gilbert sat poised in the stalls. He always rather proudly claimed he had no ear for music—'I know only two tunes: one is "God Save the Queen" and the other isn't'—but when his words were not crystal clear, he would pounce. Not only was his author's pride provoked, but his hatred of shoddiness in any aspect of the production. On stage he railed at the men's chorus, ordinary chaps who were supposed to be impersonating the British nobility, attired in gorgeous robes and crowns. 'For Heaven's sake,' he thundered, 'wear your coronets as if you were used to them!' Every detail of appearance counted. When the peers were supposed to kneel in supplication, he made sure they only went down part way, to avoid smudging their white silk tights.

Gilbert did have his playful moments, even though they were bound to be Gilbertian. At one rehearsal he horrified the ample Alice Barnett, who played the Fairy Queen, by having the dancing master demonstrate some intricate dance steps he had just decided she should add to her part. At length he assured her it was all a joke. But he was quite serious when he told the male chorus that he wanted the peers clean-shaven. For the good of the play they must sacrifice the luxuriant moustaches in which they took considerable manly pride. Their first response was blunt refusal, but Gilbert demanded and persuaded until almost all gave way. Only one held fast to his principles and whiskers, with the inevitable result. 'In his case,' George Grossmith recalled, 'the moustache stayed on, but he did not.'

With opening night almost upon them, the whole cast received a shock. Throughout the rehearsals, they had been told that the opera and its fairy heroine were called *Perola*. Even Gilbert's stage diagrams had carried that name. Now it was suddenly decided that the opera's title would be *Iolanthe*, and that they must substitute that word whenever 'Perola' occurred. G & S historians have suggested various reasons for the switch. One has said that Gilbert selected Perola originally to carry on the lucky sequence of operas whose names began with P, but changed his mind at the last minute. Others maintain that Perola was a ruse all along, part of the anti-piracy campaign. But the eminent Savoyard Reginald Allen believes that, though Gilbert preferred Iolanthe from the outset, he feared legal difficulties in using it, since the noted actor Henry Irving had written and produced a one-act play by that name in 1880. Gilbert was no fan of the great man, and it was left to D'Oyly Carte to ensure he would not object. Irving was agreeable, but Gilbert had already substituted Perola just in case. When Iolanthe was installed at last, the whole company was thunderstruck. After so long, they complained to Sullivan, how could they be sure of remembering to use the new name on opening night? Their maestro was suavely reassuring, somewhat at his partner's expense. 'Never mind, so long as you sing the music,' he said. 'Use any name that happens to come first to you. Nobody in the audience will be any the wiser, except Mr. Gilbert, and he won't be there.' He knew very well that, after the curtain went up, the Savoy was the last place Gilbert would be.

As it turned out, *Iolanthe*'s première, on 25 November 1882, was a brilliant event with or without Gilbert. The Savoy trio's first nights had become gala occasions, highlights of the social calendar. The stalls and boxes were filled with luminaries—aristocrats, men about town, men of affairs and their stunning consorts. D'Oyly Carte's sumptuous theatre was a worthy setting for their elegance, and from up in the gallery less splendid patrons made their contributions to the atmosphere by singing tunes from the earlier Savoy operas in chorus. Many play-goers leafed through copies of the libretto, which Gilbert had printed so that no one would miss a word. Entering the orchestra to conduct the fairy opera's first performance, Sullivan received a hero's welcome, which he acknowledged with his customary geniality. He gave no hint that on leaving his flat he had learned that his financial brokers were bankrupt and that his savings had been wiped out. But even the rapturous cheers for himself and Gilbert at the show's conclusion could not prevent him from feeling 'very low'.

However, the next day all the signs indicated that his lost fortune would be speedily recouped. The opera was acclaimed for its wit, beauty and remarkable staging. The response to the peers' entrance made Gilbert's pains worthwhile. One critic said their dress was 'correct to a ribbon end' and called them 'a procession of the most gorgeous beings that ever trod the boards of the Savoy or any other theatre'. Gilbert had heightened the effect by borrowing the band of the Grenadier Guards to lead the procession. The fairies delighted everyone, especially in the second act, when electric lights, powered by unseen batteries, twinkled in their hair. The audience applauded the realism of Gilbert's Act II set of Westminster Palace Yard. The papers praised the 'excellent fooling' in his libretto, though some of his political jibes were considered too near the bone. Several critics thought they noticed Wagnerian references in Sullivan's music as well as in the Fairy Queen's costume. But, Wagner or no, most would have agreed with *The Theatre*'s critic who declared that 'In every respect *Iolanthe* sustains Dr. Sullivan's reputation as the most spontaneous, fertile and scholarly composer of comic opera this country has ever produced.'

Further praise came from the highest office in the land. The Prime Minister, Mr Gladstone, wrote to Sullivan from Downing Street that 'nothing . . . could be happier than the manner in which the comic strain of the piece was blended with its harmonies of sight and sound, so good in taste and so admirable in execution from beginning to end.' Five months later he would write again, to offer the composer a knighthood in recognition of his 'distinguished talents' and his 'services to the Art of Music'. The honour crowned Sullivan's soaring reputation, but it would also make him and others question once more whether trifles like *Iolanthe* were a fit medium for his talents and an adequate service to his art.

Even a superficial look at the plot of *Iolanthe* conveys its romantic flavour and artful construction. Gilbert confessed to Sullivan that he had 'infinite difficulty' whipping it into shape, but the story, though complex, shows no sign of strain.

The curtain opens on 'An Arcadian Landscape', a charming rural scene with a running brook. In trip a band of 'dainty little fairies', whose carefree singing and dancing are marred by sorrow for their sister Iolanthe, banished for marrying a mortal. Though her punishment should have been death, the Fairy Queen 'commuted her sentence to penal servitude for life, on condition that she left her husband and never communicated with him again'. Inexplicably, the guilty fairy chose to serve her sentence at the bottom of a stream, where she has been for twenty-five years. The other fairies plead for her return, and at last the Queen agrees. The abject Iolanthe is overjoyed at her pardon and explains that she lived in the stream to be near her son; Strephon, born shortly after she left her husband. Now he is twenty-four, which is amusing because, since fairies never age, Iolanthe looks like a teenager herself.

Strephon, an Arcadian shepherd, enters piping happily. Today he is to marry his sweetheart, Phyllis, a ward of the court of Chancery, even though the Lord Chancellor has refused his permission. His fiancée knows nothing of his fairy connections, but the Queen thinks his fairy brain would be an ideal qualification for Parliament and offers him one of the seats at her disposal. She also promises him assistance whenever he needs it, as the fairies trip away.

Phyllis joins Strephon. She is uneasy about defying the Lord Chancellor, but he refuses to alter their plans: before she comes of age, she might fall in love with someone else. As it is, half the House of Lords is pursuing her. The lovers pledge eternal devotion and wander off, leaving the stage clear for the tremendous entrance of the haughty peers. The Lord Chancellor follows them, complaining that his role as guardian to the Wards of Chancery is frustrating because he is susceptible to their charms himself. In particular he is 'singularly attracted' to Phyllis, as are the peers, who want her to choose one of them as a husband. But Phyllis declares her heart is already given. The Lord Chancellor demands to know who has disobeyed him, and Strephon proudly steps forward, announcing their imminent wedding. The peers march off in confusion, trying to conceal their distress with bravado.

Interrogated by the Chancellor, Strephon appeals to the law of nature against the statues of Parliament, but the old judge dismisses his case for lack of evidence. Iolanthe finds her son alone and in tears. Mention of the Lord Chancellor has an odd effect on her, but she tells Strephon she will invoke the Fairy Queen's aid on his behalf. As mother and son embrace, the peers enter with Phyllis. Because of Iolanthe's girlish appearance, they assume that Strephon is betraying his fiancée, and they ridicule his explanation that 'this lady's my mother.' Veiled, Iolanthe slips away in the confusion. The broken-hearted Phyllis rejects her faithless shepherd and agrees to accept any of the peers instead.

Desperate, Strephon summons the Fairy Queen, who marches in with her little band, denounces the mocking peers and unleashes her mystic powers. She decrees Strephon *will* go to Parliament. He will pass any measure he likes and overturn all traditions and privileges. The peers are horrified, and, though they try to put on a bold front, the act ends with the fairies firmly in control.

Act II takes place in the Palace Yard, Westminster, at night. Standing guard, Private Willis meditates on the queer nature of the party system. Then the fairies and peers describe the havoc Strephon has created in Parliament. Both parties are powerless; the old order is in chaos. The fairies dismiss the lords' protests but find themselves attracted to the manly mortals all the same. Their Queen scolds her yearning sisters. Fairy law demands that they subdue temptation, though she admits that Private Willis has an equally disturbing effect on her. The peris withdraw in distress.

Phyllis is distressed too. She is engaged to both Lord Tolloler and Lord Mountararat but really still loves Strephon though she swears she hates him. However, when her two noble suitors try to decide which of them will marry her, they conclude that their friendship is really more important. Equally confused, the Lord Chancellor recounts the nightmares his longing for Phyllis has caused. Mountararat and Tolloler comfort him, and he confesses that he has just had a most discouraging interview between himself as Phyllis's suitor and himself as her guardian. But the lords buck him up, and he dances off to try again.

Strephon appears, as unhappy as everyone else. His Parliamentary triumphs give him no satisfaction because he still yearns for Phyllis. His ex-fiancée comes in opportunely, and at last Strephon convinces her of the truth about Iolanthe and his half-fairy nature. She renounces her aristocratic admirers, and the two agree to marry at once. The only obstacle remains the Lord Chancellor. They appeal to Iolanthe to intercede for them, but she reveals that the judge is her long-abandoned husband and Strephon's father. The discovery should simplify everything, except for the Fairy Queen's decree that, under pain of death, Iolanthe must not make contact with her mortal mate.

When the Chancellor comes into view, Iolanthe veils herself, and the lovers tiptoe away. The clever judge has successfully petitioned himself for Phyllis's hand, and he rejects Iolanthe's appeal for Strephon. But when she learns that *he* plans to marry Phyllis, the horrified fairy is forced to reveal herself as his wife, while, offstage, her sisters lament piteously. Straightaway the grim Queen appears to carry out her execution. But she is checked when the other fairies suddenly announce that death for Iolanthe means death for them as well—they have all married peers. The Queen's unexpected dilemma is resolved by the Lord Chancellor, who changes the Fairy Statutes to read that it is death *not* to marry a mortal. The Queen saves herself by proposing to Private Willis, wings sprout magically from the mortals' shoulders, and the newly-weds all fly away to fairyland.

To a modern audience *Iolanthe* seems innocent enough. Despite its legislative setting, it is primarily about love and pretension, just as *Patience* is. Gilbert's political criticisms are no more specific than his criticism of art. Still, it was one thing to expose the foibles of trendy poets and their followers and quite another to poke fun at Parliament. Some people, indeed, thought *Iolanthe* confirmed the dangerous anti-social tendencies of the Savoyards. One distraught reviewer spoke for them all: 'Where is this topsy-turvydom, this musical and dramatic turning of ideas wrong side out, to end? . . . It seems to me that Gilbert starts out primarily with the object of bringing Truth and Love and Friendship into contempt, just as we are taught the devil does. Mr. Gilbert tries to prove that there is no such thing as virtue, but that we are all lying, selfish, vain, and unworthy. In the Gilbertian world there are no martyrs, no patriots, and no lovers. . . . As a moral lesson I prefer Punch and Judy to *Iolanthe*.'

Even Sullivan was attacked for his 'sacred harmonies gone wrong'. This seems a classic case of over-reacting, but of course, Gilbert had been accused of iconoclasm before, particularly of a political kind. His 1873 play *The Happy Land* had featured actors clearly impersonating Prime Minister Gladstone and two of his Cabinet. The Lord Chamberlain compelled the removal of the caricatures, but the piece had a healthy run, and Mr Gladstone himself was once seen laughing in the stalls. Of the earlier operas, *Pinafore* had seemed daring in its treatment of Sir Joseph, but its popularity proved that the satiric bits only added spice. Gilbert did indeed have serious views on public vice and virtue, but he also knew what was appropriate for a Savoy opera and a Savoy audience. As with many humorists, it bothered him that his earnest plays, which he did intend as 'moral lessons', had little success. At the end of his life he complained that he had been 'scribbling twaddle for thirty-five years'. But whatever his personal feelings, his professional instinct at least would keep him from truly playing the devil in a comic opera.

In fact, *Iolanthe*'s treatment of the House of Lords was only a mild, comic version of some of the discussions taking place in radical political circles. Some of Mr Gladstone's Liberals wanted the House abolished because it was so patently undemocratic, such a private club for rank and privilege. Gilbert's peers take some knocks, but on the whole he treats them with good humour, like the dragoons in *Patience* or his Penzance bobbies and pirates. Their entrance is one of the stellar moments in G & S, with the two partners creating a mood of lofty arrogance. The flower of British nobility stride in to a ringing fanfare and march, brilliant in their robes and crowns, disdainfully crying 'Bow, bow, ye lower middle classes.' The crowns of course were a great joke, a piece of pseudo-regalia that no real peer ever wore. During rehearsals, Gilbert wondered if American audiences would believe that British lords went about like that.

But despite their haughty bearing, the poor lords are unable to command Phyllis's affection, which is the thing that means the most to them. For Gilbert, love is again the great leveller. The simple shepherdess is as unimpressed by rank as Patience was by aestheticism. As a matter of fact, like any pure romantic she steadfastly maintains that poverty is true nobility: 'in lowly cot,/Alone is virtue found.' With all their wealth and position, the mighty peers are on the defensive. Lord Tolloler pleads that she 'spurn not the nobly born', and Sullivan gives him a genuinely touching melody. The helplessness of the crowned heads is both comic and somewhat pathetic.

The next blow to their pride and pre-eminence is even more unexpected, as the Fairy Queen, with influence in places even higher than theirs, vows to eradicate their Parliamentary customs and prerogatives. Some of her specific targets have become unfamiliar since the opera's heyday, such as the 'cherished rights . . . on Friday nights', when individual members could introduce their own bills for Parliamentary consideration, or the question of whether a widower could marry the sister of his deceased wife, which has long since been settled. Naturally the nobility, with their passion for hunting and fishing, would detest having to remain in the House during 'the grouse and salmon season'. But what worries them most is the threat of an end to their own distinctiveness—the thought of titles being given to 'all the Common Councilmen' and, even worse, dukedoms being awarded by competitive examination. In spite of their attempts at bravado—and their ostentatious use of quotes from French, Latin and Greek to show they are men of the world—the peers end Act I quaking under the fairies' wands.

Thoroughly vanquished, they look like the 'great geese' the fairies say they are. But Gilbert has attacked their pretensions, not their politics. Besides, the peers are manly fellows, even if, like Captain Corcoran, they are 'very far from clever'. They recover some of their lost ground when their fairy adversaries cannot help finding them attractive. And they are resolute, even if absurd. Lord Mountararat defiantly maintains that 'if there is an institution in Great Britain which is not susceptible of any improvement at all, it is the House of Peers!' His song 'When Britain really ruled the waves' claims that historically the House's great strengths have been knowing when to do nothing and how not to interfere in matters beyond its comprehension. This is as wicked as Gilbert's satire gets, but the song's effect is curiously muted, first of all by Sullivan's stirring melody. His noble setting, recalling 'He is an Englishman' from *Pinafore* in character, makes the Handelian anthem sound like a hymn to all the traditions that have made Britain great. In spite of its obvious edge, it became a drawing-room favourite, a prime example of how ambiguous the operas' appeal can be. (Gilbert himself seems to have had second thoughts about it and its subject. Twenty-five years after *Iolanthe* he refused to let the song be used as part of another assault on the House of Lords. 'The lyrics,' he said, 'do not at all express my own views. They are supposed to be those of the wrong-headed donkey who sings them.')

But the song's barb is also blunted because, like the fairies, we have discovered that these wrong-headed donkeys are quite likeable. Their dubious political value seems less important after Private Willis's song, which suggests that politicians as a whole, whether peers or commons, are a dull lot and that the value of politics itself is dubious. If the flaw is simply in the system, we feel more kindly towards its members, particularly in these trying circumstances. Harassed by love and the supernatural, there is not much anyone can do.

The original production of Iolanthe did contain two second-act numbers that considerably sharpened its satire, but they were both cut soon after the opening. One concerned the talented Mr de Belville, renowned as poet, painter and inventor, who is given no official recognition or support until he inherits a fortune. Only then is he made a peer. Strephon's deleted solo 'Fold your flapping wings' accuses the 'soaring Legislature'—*both* Houses of Parliament—of forgetting that its members' lofty rank is largely the result of luck. 'Force of circumstances; might have made any of them 'a wretched thief/Through the city sneaking'. Commentators have supposed that Gilbert removed these numbers because their satire was too bold. But his real reason was probably only that it was out of place in a comic opera. Whatever your political views, Strephon's lyric does jar the mood of the piece. Since he felt that the second act was too long as well, Gilbert no doubt had little difficulty deciding what ought to go.

Gilbert's plays and verses frequently combine fairies and social comment. He produced a series of 'fairy comedies' in which supernatural whimsy exposes earthly folly. Like *Iolanthe, The Happy Land* employed both politicians and peris. One of the *Bab Ballads*, 'The Fairy Curate', presented a clergyman who, like Strephon, had an immortal mother and who got into trouble with his bishop because of it.

The great advantage of introducing the fairies is that Gilbert can have both his nonsense and his satire. Since the ladies are not 'normal', they can turn normality on its head without straining the audience's credulity. Their topsy-turvy feats are charming and consistent, and their creator can puncture pomposity just as he does in *Pinafore* without resorting to a *Pinafore*-ish trick to make the plot come out.

As we have already seen, Gilbert gave his fairy visitors an extra comic dimension by references to Richard Wagner's mythic women.

The Queen traditionally resembles the Ring's formidable Brünnhilde, and her sisters remind us of the Rhinemaidens, especially when Iolanthe confronts the Lord Chancellor. Then their offstage cries of 'Aiaiah, willaloo' specifically recall the Rhinemaidens' 'Wallala weiala weia'. The joke is increased because Gilbert's maidens are such proper English girls, despite their magical powers. And Sullivan gives them, generally, most unteutonic music. They always enter to a dainty pizzicato melody which contrasts winningly with the peers' grandiose strains.

The Fairy Queen is obviously one of Gilbert's dragons, but, like everything else in *Iolanthe*, she is free from the heavy-handed caricature that similar ladies endure in other operas. The librettist does poke a bit of fun at her matronly figure. The Queen recollects fondly that Iolanthe taught her, among other things, to 'dive into a dewdrop' and nestle in a nutshell', to which her attendant Leila responds wryly that Iolanthe 'certainly did surprising things'.

The Queen's mighty intervention on her nephew's behalf leaves Parliament at her mercy, but she and the other fairies are at the mercy of love like everyone else. Her 'tendency to fall in love' and her determination to resist it produce one of the best-known songs in the opera. In 'Oh, foolish fay' Sullivan once again gives a rich and heartfelt setting to outlandish lyrics. It may not be hard to conjure up feeling in the first stanza, where the Queen compares herself to one of the doves of Ovid ('Ovidius Naso'). But to create a mood of passionate longing in the second, as she proposes to turn 'the hose of common sense' on her emotion, like Captain Shaw of London's Fire Brigade dousing a blaze, is the mark of an exceptional composer. (Captain Shaw, an important figure in the history of fire-fighting, loved the theatre and was actually present at *Iolanthe*'s first performance. Happy coincidence or clever planning put him right in the centre of the stalls, where he could receive the full impact of the Fairy Queen's appeal, to the great amusement of his friends.)

The fairies and the peers meet first in Arcadia, where Phyllis and Strephon reside. Gilbert chose the location not just because it is 'the country' but because Arcadia has traditional literary overtones. It is a place of perfect innocence and untroubled happiness, where simple swains and simple maidens lead simple lives in harmony with nature. To Gilbert this image seemed ridiculous, and he had mocked the whole pastoral idea in a play called *Happy Arcadia*. But the only sign of Arcadian satire in *Iolanthe* is Strephon's open-hearted appeal to the Lord Chancellor, that his love for Phyllis needs no permission from the court because it is sanctioned by 'Nature's Acts of Parliament': 'The bees—the breeze—the seas—the rooks—the brooks—the gales—the vales—the fountains and the mountains cry, "You love this maiden—

take her, we command you!"' Gilbert always said he hated 'gush', and this kind of posturing made him especially ill. It reminds us of Ralph Rackstraw's 'simple eloquence' in courting Josephine. In turn Phyllis reminds us of that other simple country maid, Patience, though the shepherdess is more aware of her charms. In fact, though she and Strephon are supposedly idyllic, they seem to have a sophisticated view of marital relations. Reunited after their separation, they decide to marry at once, before they change their minds. Instead they'll change their minds *after* they marry, which, Strephon says, is 'the usual course'. The remark shows that Gilbert was sceptical about more than politics and privilege. However, throughout the opera Sullivan gives the Arcadian couple sweet pastoral tunes, full of delicate piping (*Iolanthe* contains some of his most attractive writing for the winds). Librettist and composer combine in producing the lovely Act I duet, 'None shall part us from each other.'

A key ingredient in Gilbert's beautifully worked-out blend of plot and character is the Lord Chancellor. He is one of the most appealing of all G & S comic figures—honest, self-aware and merrily eccentric all at once. Sullivan brings him on with a sober fugue that epitomizes the convolutions of the legal mind, and he does take his legal obligations seriously. The unusual integrity he describes in 'When I went to the bar as a very young man' gives a much more favourable impression than the career of the judge in *Trial by Jury*. But the lively old gentleman is still susceptible to romance. His amorous affliction produces another of the great moments in Gilbert and Sullivan, the brilliant patter song 'When you're lying awake with a dismal headache'. When Gilbert is represented in verse anthologies, it is usually by this *tour de force*, a supreme test of endurance and enunciation. It gallops along in true nightmare fashion, weaving a narrative that is a surreal, psychoanalytic delight, veering from the English Channel to Salisbury Plain, from steamers to bicycles. Sullivan's see-sawing minor-key accompaniment to Gilbert's wild details heightens the anxiety. The sudden switch to major as morning comes is like a sigh of relief, followed by a cheery, scampering conclusion. Equally cheery is the Lord Chancellor's trio with Lord Mountararat and Tolloler after they have encouraged him to ask himself once more for Phyllis's hand. The sight of the learned judge kicking up his heels in robe and full wig is one of the opera's high points.

Another of its high points—and a moment unique in G & S—is the climactic recognition scene between Iolanthe and the Lord Chancellor. Until now the opera's title character has had relatively little part in the action. Her return from the stream where she has been doing her penal servitude—'on her head', which is just Victorian slang for 'without difficulty'—gets the play under way. Later, her moment of maternal comfort brings about the crisis between peers and peris. But she herself is not involved in the topsy-turvy results. In fact her only appearance in Act II comes at the very end, when her son appeals to her to intercede with the husband she has not been seen for twenty-five years and whom she has been forbidden to see on pain of death.

Pathos is the rarest quality in the Savoy operas, since it is customarily outside their emotional scope. And yet, when Iolanthe reveals herself to the Lord Chancellor, in spite of certain doom, and he gasps, 'Iolanthe! Thou livest?', audiences can be moved to tears. Here, as everywhere else in this most integrated opera, both its creators share in the effect. Gilbert brings the dramatic elements to bear, and Sullivan refines and intensifies them. The fairy's plea to her unsuspecting husband is set to a sweeping, poignant melody. The anguished offstage cries concentrate the tension. And then, as the Queen inexorably raises her spear, it turns out that love has defeated law once again. Since all the fairies have succumbed to mortals' charms, their Queen can only join them, assisted by the Lord Chancellor's legal advice and the gallant Private Willis. Tears change to laughter as everyone miraculously sprouts wings and dances away to fairydom, leaving courts and Parliament behind.

It is a rollicking and somehow touching conclusion. In *Iolanthe*, for once, the topsy-turvy wins. There is no return to solid Victorian values. The good-hearted, thick-headed peers happily leave the House to the complications of intelligence; someone else will give away the Lord Chancellor's wards. The atmosphere may not actually be mythic, but there is a feeling of fantasy about it found in few of the other operas. Finally it really is a fairy-tale, light, bright and romantic, with dreary reality defeated at the end.

Iolanthe's special qualities, and the particular harmony of its text and music, have taken it to places the more earth-bound Savoy operas cannot reach. When the copyright on Gilbert's words expired in 1961, it was the first G & S work produced by the Sadlers Wells Opera, and it has frequently been revived since by that distinguished group, now the English National Opera. It will undoubtedly continue its dual life, being gleefully performed by G & S amateurs and operatic professionals alike—quite appropriate for a piece in which different worlds so successfully meet.

7

Princess Ida;
or Castle Adamant

Princess Ida is generally considered one of Gilbert's least effective productions, which is awkward because a number of Savoyards—among them George Grossmith—have thought it Sullivan's best. In fact Act II contains a sequence of tunes so good it is sometimes known as 'Sullivan's string of pearls', and throughout the piece the composer is certainly close to the peak of his powers. Gilbert's libretto, however, was adapted from one of his old burlesques, complete with painful puns and stilted blank verse. Today the opera's subject seems even more unfortunate, a heavy-handed, patronizing satire on women's right to be taken seriously, especially in regard to higher education. Ever since its opening, this mixed pedigree has kept *Princess Ida* from being the whole-hearted favourite that, for its songs alone, it deserves to be.

The burlesque that inspired the opera had received only a lukewarm reception in 1870, though Gilbert defiantly remembered it as a 'signal success'. Called *The Princess,* it was based on a long poem of the same name published in 1847 by Alfred Tennyson, a sensitive work that suggested women might want to be more than domestic and decorative. Gilbert's 'Respectful Perversion' retained its model's general plot and characters, and even its blank verse form. Gilbert's lines, however, have none of the Poet Laureate's fluency. As his biographer Hesketh Pearson remarked, the Savoy wit 'liked being mistaken for a poet', but clever rhyming was generally his limit. Also limited was his capacity to sympathize with Tennyson's noble vision. To Gilbert the idea of frustrated women rejecting male society to found their own college was merely a golden chance for merry-making. He handled it in true burlesque fashion, interpolating several jolly songs with melodies borrowed from well-known operas. At one point, with characteristic economy, he even employed his early translation of the 'Laughing Song' from *Manon Lescaut*. Of course the piece abounded in breath-taking puns, and, though Gilbert disapproved of the burlesque custom of 'breeches parts'—women dressed form-fittingly as men—the princes in *The Princess* were played by six girls.

Adapting his perversion fourteen years after its original production, Gilbert performed his usual workmanlike job of cutting and trimming. He reshaped *The Princess*'s five scenes into three acts and rearranged and condensed the action. He tightened up the dialogue, though almost all the opera's speeches are still drawn verbatim from the play. But in spite of the reworking, the atmosphere of vintage burlesque still permeates the piece all too clearly.

The opera opens in King Hildebrand's court, with attendants scanning the horizon for King Gama. Twenty years ago Gama's infant daughter Ida and Hildebrand's baby son Hilarion were betrothed, and the match is to be confirmed today. If Gama does not appear with his daughter, the consequences will be grave. As Hildebrand uneasily describes Gama's peevish nature, the little monarch hoves into sight. But his entourage seems to be exclusively male, and Hilarion has heard that Ida has 'forsworn the world' to devote herself to study.

Gama's three sons stamp in fiercely, proclaiming that 'fighting is their trade', followed by their father, whose trade is clearly being disagreeable. But the hunchbacked King has to confess that his daughter has indeed founded a university for women only. Hilarion and his friends Cyril and Florian immediately declare they will go and charm the ladies back to their senses. Hildebrand takes Gama and his sons hostage, to be slain if the expedition fails.

Act II opens in Castle Adamant, Princess Ida's academy. The 'girl graduates' sing of their mutual zeal for learning, though Lady Psyche recommends they read bowdlerized versions of the classics. She decrees that 'man is Nature's sole mistake', and her colleague Lady Blanche disciplines those girls who have shown *any* sign of male interest—even to possessing chessmen.

Hailed by all, Princess Ida enters and invokes the goddess Minerva's bid in their great cause: replacing men as society's rulers. But it appears that Lady Blanche is also eager to replace Princess Ida as head of the college. Ida warns her against ambition, the ladies withdraw, and over the garden wall creep Hilarion, Cyril and Florian. The intruders snicker at the ladies' aspirations—'A woman's college! maddest folly going!'—and merrily disguise themselves in academic gowns. Surprised by the Princess, the three 'well-born maids' ask admission to the university, which Ida grants after they earnestly swear to love their fellow students and 'never marry any man'. When she departs, the lads congratulate themselves on their good fortune, unaware that Lady Psyche is watching with suspicion. When they do notice her, Florian suddenly realizes that the lady is his sister. Trapped, they confess who they are. Psyche warns them of their danger, which is increased when it turns out that Melissa, the daughter of Lady Blanche, has overheard everything.

But Melissa is more intrigued than scandalized. Her mother has told her that 'Man, sprung from an Ape, is Ape at heart', but she has never actually encountered the male of the species before. Now she finds them not at all 'hideous, idiotic, and deformed' but infinitely more beautiful than women! The happy group celebrate this new truth and dance off. Though the irate Lady Blanche is not fooled for a minute by the young men's costumes, Melissa wins her over by pointing out that, if Hilarion claims Princess Ida, Lady Blanche will rule the university.

But the reprieve is only temporary. Cyril gets tipsy at a picnic lunch, shocks the Princess with familiar references to her supposedly far-off husband and then launches into a kissing song. The furious Hilarion strikes him, and Cyril, surprised, calls him by name. In the ensuing confusion, Ida falls into a nearby stream, and Hilarion plunges in and saves her. Despite his heroism and everyone's pleas for mercy, she commands the intruders be imprisoned. No sooner have they been led away than King Hildebrand and his men burst through the castle gates. Hildebrand declares his patience is exhausted. Either Ida honours her baby bridal vows or her father-in-law will level her college and kill her brothers. The act ends with the Princess still defiant, though everyone else tries to persuade her that it might not be 'so dreadful, after all' to be Hilarion's wife.

Castle Adamant is ready for war in Act III, but Ida's women soon turn timid, and she vows to 'meet these men alone'. Then King Gama proposes that the issue be decided by a combat between her brothers and Hilarion, Florian and Cyril. Out of pity for her father, Ida agrees. Poor Gama is at his wit's end because the cunning Hildebrand gives him 'nothing whatever to grumble at'. Still in their gowns, Hilarion and his friends are led in to Gama's sneers. While they retire to change, Gama's sons prepare for combat by stripping *off* their armour. In the fight that follows, Hilarion and company triumph. Ida accepts her fate grudgingly, until Hildebrand and Gama remind her that without men there would be no posterity to carry on her work. The Princess admits her error, everyone pairs up in happy obedience to nature, and the play ends with an uplifting quote from Tennyson's *Princess*.

With typical diligence, Gilbert had set to work recycling his old play soon after *Iolanthe*'s sparkling first night. He read the Prologue, which later became Act I, to Sullivan on 8 February 1883, after the two partners had signed a new five-year contract with Carte. The composer seems to have had misgivings about the renovated *Princess*. It was not until almost six months later, after a good deal of modification, that his diary records he did 'like the piece as now shaped out, very much'.

Sullivan's part of the task proceeded in typical fits and starts. On the very day he began it, he turned out two songs and two choruses. But in the autumn he took charge once more of the Leeds Festival, where his performance of Beethoven's *Missa Solemnis* aroused enormous enthusiasm. After he resumed work on *Princess Ida,* his old physical complaint began to trouble him, aggravated as usual by overwork. None of this shows in the music, and little of it appeared in rehearsal, even when Sullivan was sorely tried. When one of the Savoy soloists persistently misinterpreted a melody, the composer protested good-naturedly that either he or the singer did not understand it. The star huffily retorted that he thought *he* understood it. Sullivan fixed him with his glinting monocle. 'Perhaps you do,' he said quietly. 'That's the worst of being a composer. One always begins at the wrong end of the stick. In future, I shall start at the other end. I'll get you to sing my songs first, then I'll compose them afterwards.'

Verbal thrusts like that were usually Gilbert's property. The *Princess Ida* rehearsals produced several tart exchanges, perhaps because the cast found the blank verse dialogue hard to fathom. One actor rebelled against the author's inexorable demands with, 'Look here, sir, I will not be bullied! I know my lines!' 'That may be so,' rejoined Gilbert, 'but you don't know mine.' Playing King Gama, George Grossmith later recalled he had 'a pretty easy time of it', since the part was meaty but small. But he still got his share of disciplinary attention from his chief. At one troublesome spot, thinking he had heard Gilbert insulting as well as correcting him, Grossmith said hotly, 'I beg your pardon!' To which Gilbert innocently replied, 'I accept the apology. Let's get on with the rehearsal.'

In another oft-quoted episode Grossmith fumed at having to repeat one sequence again and again and again. At last he burst out, 'I've rehearsed this confounded business until I feel a perfect fool!' 'Ah,' Gilbert shot back. 'Now we can talk on equal terms.' Though all G & S historians agree this is witty, none seems to mention that the librettist was plagiarizing his own opera. In Act I Hildebrand threatens to cut off Gama's 'monkey head', to which the waspish King retorts, 'Bravo! Your King deprives me of my head/That he and I may meet on equal terms.' Gilbert's line should have sounded oddly familiar to Gama/Grossmith.

The new opera was scheduled to open shortly after New Year 1884, and as the pace of rehearsals intensified, Sullivan found himself yet again under severe pressure. There was still music to compose, he was unwell, and at Christmas he sustained two personal blows. The first was the departure from England of his late brother's widow, who had remarried and was going with her children to settle in California. The second, more serious, occurred soon after, when his dear friend Fred Clay, who had introduced him to Gilbert years before, suffered two crippling strokes. Even with the première less than ten days away, Sullivan was for a time too upset to work.

Professional that he was, he pulled himself together and plunged back into composing, rewriting and rehearsing. He finished *Princess Ida*'s score by working straight through New Year's Eve, oblivious to Big Ben a short distance away, chiming in 1884. He rehearsed all the next day and into the night, walked home through a snowstorm and then composed two new songs for Act III. The strain was too much for anyone, and after the final dress rehearsal went on until 2.30 a.m., Sullivan's body simply gave way. Prostrate, unable to sleep, in pain that even morphine could not relieve, he could barely move, let alone think of going to the Savoy. And yet as curtain-time approached, as his diary records, he 'resolved to conduct the first performance of the new Opera'. Carte had already made up new programmes listing Frank Cellier as Sullivan's substitute. But, after black coffee and another injection of morphine, the composer drove to the theatre 'more dead than alive'. In a repetition of his feat at the première of *The Pirates of Penzance*, he got through the performance and enjoyed a brilliant call with Gilbert. However, he collapsed immediately afterwards.

One writer has suggested that Sullivan's precarious condition during the first performance induced Gilbert, for once, to remain at the theatre. Whatever the cause, remain he did, browsing through a newspaper in the green room with grim nonchalance. His sang-froid was too much for the Frenchman who had supplied the armour for the show, and who was more and more excited by the waves of applause and laughter filling the theatre. He rushed in to Gilbert in Gallic rapture. '*Mais, monsieur,*' he cried, '*savez-vous que vous avez là un succès solide*?' The Englishman responded coolly, 'It seems to be going very well,' provoking the Frenchman to exclaim, '*Mais vous êtes si calme*!' 'I suppose,' Gilbert sniffed later, 'he expected to see me kissing all the carpenters.'

In fact, the armourer had had a worthy share in the production's considerable glamour. *Princess Ida* capped all its predecessors in splendid costumes, opulent staging and general expense. Nevertheless, as the newspapers reported gleefully, more time should have been spent in checking the drop for the Princess's second-act plunge into the stream. From the stalls she seemed to disappear convincingly, but up in the gallery delighted ticket-holders could still clearly see her 'floundering on a feather mattress'.

Despite its solid success with the audience, the papers' verdict on the new opera was very mixed. Almost all thought it was too long, with its three acts and two lengthy intervals. One drama critic called it 'a desperately dull performance', and other spoke of it as 'clumsy' and 'tedious'. Gilbert's wit and staging did receive the customary plaudits from many quarters, and Sullivan's contribution was especially praised. The critic from the *Sunday Times* called the new score 'the best in every way that Sir Arthur Sullivan has produced, apart from his serious works. . .'. But it was not too long before it became clear that *Princess Ida*'s days were numbered. The opera ended its run after nine months, a relative failure after the previous triumphs of the series, and it was not revived until 1919.

Though it fared better in subsequent American and Australian versions, *Princess Ida* has never attained the general popularity of many of the other Savoy classics. The opera's trouble was and is not simply that it satirizes women's rights. Though Gilbert's heavy-handedness is likely to make a modern audience squirm, most Victorians were not at all sure equality for women was a good thing. It is true that Tennyson's *The Princess* had treated the question seriously and lyrically. It is also true that his lofty poem presaged the founding of several women's colleges in Cambridge and London in the 1870s, which should have proved that such institutions were not the 'maddest folly going'. But Hesketh Pearson believed the opera failed because its audience still did not 'regard the independent woman as pleasant or natural'. Some, perhaps many, would have shared Gilbert's scorn for such abnormal behaviour. Years later, when a band of suffragettes—militant granddaughters of *The Princess*—chained themselves outside 10 Downing Street to cry 'Votes for women', the cantankerous playwright threatened to make a similar scene outside Queen Charlotte's Maternity Hospital to demand 'Beds for men!' In fact, playgoers who were offended by Gilbert's satire might, Reginald Allen has suggested, have objected more to his disrespect toward Lord Tennyson than to his crude treatment of women.

No, the trouble with *Princess Ida* is that it is basically a one-joke play, with that joke at best unsubtle and badly, repetitiously told. Even early critics, who could still praise Gilbert's blank verse dialogue and 'pungent puns', admitted the story was 'very slight'. Its bareness is due to its origins. In 1870 Gilbert's 'respectful perversion' might have got by with a simple caricature for a subject; that was what burlesque was about. Its girls, puns and high spirits were not meant to encourage discrimination. But a revolution had taken place since burlesque's heyday, in which Gilbert himself had played a significant part. At the Savoy in 1884 the audience demanded more than his clanking vehicle had to give.

Perhaps the mushrooming puns are its most obvious sign of age. Even in his later works Gilbert often found a pun hard to resist, but in his early days they were evidently his favourite form of humour. Some of them are mild enough. When Gama describes how exclusively female Ida's college is, he says, 'She'll scarcely suffer Dr. Watt's hymns—And all the animals she owns are "hers"!' A more extreme example was newly coined for the opera. Referring to Gama's stinging tongue, Hildebrand observes, 'his "sting" is present, though his "stung" is past.' Gilbert did eliminate an intolerable section in which singing gentlemen plan to attack the castle, with high tenors acting as scouts because they can 'go up to see'. But he retained an absolutely vintage '60s pun, which should be treasured simply as an historical curiosity. Relating how her mother found out Hilarion and his friends, Melissa explains:

> ' . . . It was my fault—
> I blushed and stammered so that she exclaimed
> 'Can these be men?' Then, seeing this, 'Why, these'—
> '*Are men*', she would have added, but '*are men*'
> Stuck in her throat!'

The magnificently contorted sequence refers to the moment in Shakespeare's *Macbeth* when the ill-fated thane has just murdered Duncan. 'I had most need of blessing,' he says, 'and "Amen" stuck in my throat.'

Unfortunately, the puns are tiresome even before their period flavour has worn off, and Gilbert's blank verse, the other distinctive feature of his dialogue, only increases his occasional tendency to pomposity. But more serious flaws lie in *Princess Ida*'s form. It is the only Savoy opera with three acts, not two, the result of Gilbert's following the plot of Tennyson's poem. Act I, at Hildebrand's castle, must establish Hilarion's and Ida's betrothal, her rejection, his campaign and the seizure of Gama and his sons. The main action takes place in Act II, presenting Castle Adamant and the ladies, the entrance of Hilarion and friends, their exposure and Hildebrand's attack. Act III winds things up with ritual combat and reconciliation. A three-act structure is not awkward in itself, but these three acts have awkward proportions. Acts I and III together are half as long as Act II. Act I is lively enough as the plot is set in motion, but Act III feels distinctly anti-climactic, consisting of one central episode and a lot of laboured talk. Even at the opening night one critic labelled it 'from every point of view the weakest.'

The structure also splits up the characters. King Gama, one of Gilbert's liveliest creations, does not appear in Act II at all. Hildebrand and Gama's sons only sneak in for its finale. In fact, the opera has so many leading roles that they are never really explored. (Rutland

Barrington, for instance, claimed *Princess Ida* failed because Hildebrand was such a small part—played, of course, by Rutland Barrington.) This is all right for burlesque where caricature is what counts, but an opera audience would expect more dramatic interest—particularly after the subtle, beautifully integrated *Iolanthe*. Indeed, comparison with *Iolanthe* only emphasizes the weaknesses of *Princess Ida*. The preceding opera's light touch, its carefully worked-out structure and characters made fantasy believable. *Ida*'s dated material and hand-me-down form make satire embarrassing.

The second-hand flaws are the more unfortunate because of the opera's real virtues. Gilbert's lyrics show him very much the master of the '80s, not the novice of the '60s. They have bite and occasionally even tenderness. Both of Gama's patter songs were widely admired and quoted, which must have pleased their author since he told Grossmith that the tetchy King was a self-portrait: 'I meant it for myself: I thought it my duty to live up to my reputation!' (Years later, at a commemorative dinner in his honour, Gilbert capped his reminiscenses of the Savoy years with Gama's catch-line, 'Yet everybody says I'm such a disagreeable man! And I can't think why!') Gama's persecutor, the no-nonsense Hildebrand, firmly establishes himself as 'a peppery kind of king', and Hilarion's lilting love ballad 'Whom thou hast chained' is a welcome diversion from the mocking battle of the sexes. Though Gilbert sides with the masculine status quo, Melissa's Darwinian fable, 'The Maiden and the Ape', shows that men have their ridiculous aspects too.

Perhaps *Princess Ida*'s fundamental flaw is simply that it is two productions stitched not very convincingly together. One is the silly old play of the dialogue, the other the quite brilliant comic opera of the songs. The gap between them makes the piece seem like a revue more than a musical drama. Characters pop out of the dialogue and sing; the tunes seem not to grow out of the text but to be inserted in it.

This curious state of affairs is most obvious in Gilbert's handling of Gama's sons. In the 1870s play they exist solely for the climactic fight with Hilarion's band. Until then they don't appear at all; throughout the play Hildebrand's only hostage is Gama. In framing the opera, Gilbert increased the importance of the three warriors, bringing them on rousingly in Act I. In all, they have four musical numbers, each one a gem of gruff, baggy-pants (or rusty-armour) humour. But they have only two lines of dialogue in the whole piece, delivered by Arac. The lines, like the scene that contains them, are taken verbatim from the 1870 *Princess*. Essentially the brothers exist only in songs and action, but even in that limited context Gilbert-of-the-'80s manages to make them more intriguing figures than many of the burlesque types that surround them. How amusing, for instance, that these blood-and-thunder knights, after their first crashing entrance, spend the rest of the opera as prisoners, and when they are at last released to fight, they lose. Gilbert's ambivalence toward the military mind (his own mind, after all, was very military) is shown in their first battle song:

'Bold, and fierce, and strong, ha! ha!
    For a war we burn,
With its right or wrong, ha! ha!
    We have no concern.'

By the end, this rough-tough amorality has slackened somewhat. Perhaps the dungeon has reduced the brothers' taste for martial glory; in one of the best loved G & S numbers, 'This helmet, I suppose', set to vigorous mock-Handelian music, they gird themselves for combat by a ritual *dis*arming. Gilbert has made them kinsmen of the *Penzance* bobbies and the dragoons of *Patience* (three of whom, after all, also abandoned their uniforms). This secondary satire on militarism is much more deft than the opera's feeble carping at women, and it is achieved without benefit of dialogue.

If the best part of *Princess Ida* is the songs, the best part of the songs is Sullivan's music. Almost all of it is so good that it makes even more obvious the shortcomings of the plot and dialogue. The purest example of the discrepancy is Princess Ida's invocation to Minerva, goddess of wisdom, near the beginning of Act II. The act has opened with the 'girl graduates' extolling learning and unity, but their reading turns out to be watered-down classics and their views on man simply name-calling: 'Man is of no kind of use—Man's a donkey—Man's a goose. . . .' These lyrics are weak because they are insubstantial; Gilbert makes the women's cause seem merely childish. But Ida's 'Oh, goddess wise' momentarily changes everything. On the page it seems graceful and sincere though rather slight, with eight short and two longer lines. Sullivan, however, transforms it into a passionate appeal, a real address to the heavens, full of all the ardour and idealism that Gilbert's image of the women lacks. The composer reshapes the lyric, intensifying it by repetition and building to a climax of operatic grandeur. Sullivan reveals himself as a worthy member of the line of Mozart and Verdi, and this is the one moment in *Princess Ida* when the nobility of Tennyson's *Princess* is restored.

But as soon as it is over, Gilbert's *Princess* returns. Ida's long speech is monumentally silly, a resumé of situation-comedy clichés about women, their wiles, illogicality and obsession with fashion. It makes us glad there is so much music in Act II and sorry there is any dialogue at all. As a whole, the act is surely one of Sullivan's zeniths, full of extraordinary variety, warmth and humour. His settings contribute another badly needed dimension to the characters as well. When Hilarion, Cyril and Florian climb over the castle wall, the music conveys all their boyish delight in the enterprise. Sullivan treats the orchestra almost as a separate participant, a chorus of onlookers bubbling away with amusement as the young men relate the hazards they have overcome to get inside. Their trio scoffing at the ladies' academic pretensions—Florian has already said any girl will learn 'twice as much in half-an-hour outside' with him—is redeemed by the sheer high spirits of the melody and setting. Sullivan's orchestration in the song's refrain is especially artful, creating another little duet between the stage and the pit.

'I am a maiden, cold and stately', in which the jolly intruders prance about in their feminine robes, displays the same innocent gusto. Gilbert thought as little of 'men in women's clothes' as Princess Ida does; it was one of the ribald traditions of burlesque he vowed the Savoy would have nothing to do with. (It is, of course, still a tradition of English pantomime.) But his old plot required the concession, and the musical setting removes any hint of scandal: the lads remain hearty and masculine even in their frolics. Like several others in the opera, the song derives much of its energy from a spirited, quasi-baroque bass line, provided here by the bassoon. Each verse is introduced by a joyously rhythmic orchestral figure, which Sullivan, with typical ingenuity, then employs to accompany the climactic final chorus.

A beautiful and unexpectedly poignant moment follows in the madrigal-like quartet 'The world is but a broken toy', in which Hilarion, Cyril and Florian pretend to agree with Ida's belief in the vanity of human wishes. The melancholy little song illustrates again the distance between plot and lyrics. The eager youths are supposedly just humouring Ida in order to join the ladies, but such cynicism is only in the play. In the opera both Gilbert and Sullivan—and particularly the latter—seem serious about the song's quiet resignation.

It is a great temptation to go on itemizing the many lovely achievements in the score of *Princess Ida*, but listeners can make detailed discoveries for themselves. Briefly, other treats in Act II include the jovial quintet, when nature prevails against Ida's regulations, and which reminds us of similar celebrations in *Patience* and *Iolanthe*. Melissa and Lady Blanche have an elegantly dead-pan duet, 'Now wouldn't you like to rule the roast?' almost Lady Blanche's only musical appearance since her rather leaden solo, 'Come, Mighty Must', is usually omitted. Indeed, one could happily do without Melissa's mother and her ponderous philosophizing altogether. 'Would you know the kind of maid', Cyril's tipsy solo just before the finale, is a light-hearted gem, and the finale itself a masterful sequence of moods and musical combinations.

The rest of the opera has abundant delights too, like the warlike music Sullivan provides for the clattering entrances of Gama's sons and his snappish accompaniments for their sour father. (As a happy example of Sullivan's art it is worth noting the transition from the sons' strong-armed first number, which ends like an Indian war-dance, to Gama's mincing introduction which immediately succeeds it.) Hildebrand's first song 'Now hearken to my strict command', is a classic display of knowing what not to do in a setting. The whole humour of the ditty lies in the King's perfect willingness to give Gama good cheer or to string him up 'in the old familiar way' depending on whether or not he brings Ida with him. For the second possibility, Sullivan could have created a mood of menace, for instance, by switching to a minor key. But the music remains exactly as it was for the prospect of a sunny welcome. The effect of suddenly grim lyrics and unswervingly jolly melody is very funny and no doubt just what Gilbert wanted. It illustrates what the librettist meant when he said, 'Sullivan and I have the same sense of humour. When I tell him a joke he understands it immediately. I never have to tell it twice, which is fatal.'

The musical numbers in *Princess Ida* demonstrate that artistic unity of lyricist and composer at their best, and the composer's contributions have an excellence all their own. But the opera cannot help being divided against itself. The play will always give viewers a sinking sensation, though it is worth trying to transcend for the sake of the riches interspersed in it. The opera probably responds best to a blithe operetta style, accepting its conventions without taking them seriously, opting for innocence rather than satire. But it is possible that *Princess Ida* is one Savoy classic best enjoyed on records. In any case, its virtues are much too substantial to be neglected.

On the same diary page where Sullivan had recorded his ordeal on *Princess Ida*'s opening night, he entered a single potent sentence on 29 January: 'Told Carte of my decision not to write any more Savoy operas.' The impresario responded with the same tactic that had brought George Grossmith around in wage-bargaining for *The Sorcerer*: he and Sullivan had a friendly meal together. But though their friendship remained unshaken, so did Sullivan's resolve.

With the composer vacationing in Europe and *Princess Ida* doing its best at the Savoy, there was no more discussion for the moment. Carte could hope that he would return with a more reasonable attitude. But in March *Ida*'s attendance definitely began to sag. According to the terms of their agreement, Carte formally notified his partners that a new opera would be needed in six months. In reply, however, Sullivan insisted: 'It is impossible for me to do another piece of the character of those already written by Gilbert and myself.' Now genuinely alarmed,

Carte brought Gilbert into play. The librettist wrote to the composer of his 'unbounded surprise' at his decision and, like a good lawyer, reminded him of the terms of their contract—they must produce a new work on six months' notice or be liable for Carte's losses. Gilbert closed more in sorrow than in anger. He had already begun another libretto. He had 'invariably subordinated' his views to Sullivan's. Sullivan had often mentioned 'the thorough good feeling with which we have worked together for so many years'. He knew of no reason why Sullivan's opinion might have changed and was, 'therefore, absolutely at a loss to account for the decision'.

But Sullivan had views that Gilbert, with a basically secure sense of his life and craft, knew nothing of. The composer was under completely different pressures. It was enough that Gilbert was a successful West End—and international—author, but Sullivan was still supposed to be Britain's musical messiah. His status, and his dilemma had been increased by his knighthood in 1883. The high-toned *Musical Review* had exhorted him in no uncertain terms: ' . . . some things that Mr. Arthur Sullivan may do, Sir Arthur Sullivan ought not to do . . . it will look rather more than odd to see announced in the papers that a new comic opera is in preparation, the book by Mr. W. S. Gilbert and the music by Sir Arthur Sullivan . . . he must not dare to soil his hands with anything less than an anthem or a madrigal; oratorio . . . and symphony must now be his line. Here is not only an opportunity, but a positive obligation for him to return to the sphere from which he has too long descended . . . to do battle for the honour of English art.' (The writer's final, amazing appeal that 'our musical daze be broken by our musical knight' makes Gilbert's weakness for punning more understandable.)

Sullivan never ceased to be vulnerable to this kind of accusation. His success at Leeds reminded him that he was being applauded as a conductor, not a composer. A new Sullivan symphony had been proposed for the festival, but *Princess Ida* had taken all his time. Even during *Patience* he and Carte, who was still devoted to the cause of English opera, had discussed a full-scale operatic work on Mary, Queen of Scots, for Covent Garden, but nothing had come of it. And Sullivan did feel an obligation to English art. In early 1884 national music received a snub on its own ground when Hans Richter, a German, was appointed conductor of the prestigious Birmingham Festival. Sir Arthur was less disappointed as a candidate than offended as a patriot; the committee, he declared, should have chosen someone British.

All these events played a part in Sullivan's rejection of the Savoy. His sense of personal crisis was intensified by the departure of his sister-in-law and her children, Fred Clay's grave illness and his own fragile health. Everything seemed to tell him it was time to stop wasting his substance, betraying his gifts and undermining British music.

But there was a contract to be honoured. Sullivan may have wished ideally to be quits of comic opera altogether, but he wrote to Gilbert that what he found 'most difficult, most fatiguing and I may say most disheartening' was writing music for stories that lacked 'human interest and probability'. *Princess Ida*, he said, had brought him to the end of his tether 'in that class of piece'. He had so far devoted himself to 'keeping down the music' to the advantage of the words, with the same skill that had prompted a critic of his very first effort, *Cox and Box*, to praise the way he matched 'exquisite melodies' to 'ludicrous sentiments'. But now he had had enough of ludicrous sentiments and topsy-turvy situations. He wanted 'the music to act in its own sphere . . . to arise and speak for itself', which required a story with 'a feeling of reality about it'. Nonetheless, he still concluded, 'I hope with all my heart that there may be no break in our chain of joint workmanship.'

Gilbert reacted with hurt astonishment and accused Sullivan of 'trying to teach me the ABC of my profession'. But when the composer returned to London, the librettist presented him with an idea for a new opera that confirmed everything Sullivan had said and showed that Gilbert truly did not understand his objections. The 'new plot' was one that had already been proposed and refused two years before. As Sullivan reported in his diary, it was 'based on the notion that by means of a charm (formerly a coin, now a lozenge) a person would really become the character he or she represented themselves to be'. It was pure Gilbert. Despite its satiric possibilities, Sullivan rejected it again as 'unreal and artificial', though his discussions with Gilbert were friendly.

However, it soon became obvious that the partners were at an impasse, even with Carte acting as an increasingly anxious go-between. Gilbert generously suggested that, this once, he would step aside for another librettist, but Sullivan would not hear of it, praising his collaborator's 'matchless skill and genius'. Gilbert tried making changes in the lozenge plot 'to give it a very serious and tender interest', but the lozenge principle remained, which was what Sullivan objected to. The composer also pointed out its resemblance to *The Sorcerer*. Finally he wrote Gilbert begging for another plot altogether, saying it was impossible for him to do justice to a piece for which he felt neither interest nor enthusiasm. The librettist now dug in his heels. Earlier he had confessed, 'I am absolutely at a loss to know what it is you want from me.' Now he declared he would stand or fall by the lozenge: 'Anxious as I am, and have always been, to give due weight to your suggestions, the time has arrived when I must state—and I do so with great reluctance—that I cannot consent to construct another plot for the next Opera.' Sullivan replied that, though he regretted it very much, Gilbert's tone appeared to make further discussion useless.

Outwardly, it seemed incredible that this brilliant and innovative team should come apart over such a trifle, but the lozenge crisis revealed absolute differences between the two allies, which were as basic as the difference between Gilbert's *Princess* and Gilbert and Sullivan's *Princess Ida*. This time, as G & S mythology has it, the deadlock was broken and the partnership saved when a Japanese sword suddenly fell from the wall of Gilbert's study. A great comic opera resulted, but the breach between its creators would remain, and widen.

8

The Mikado;
or, The Town of Titipu

By almost every standard, *The Mikado* has been the most popular of all the Gilbert and Sullivan operas. It had the longest original run at the Savoy, 672 performances. It is the only one of the duo's productions to achieve a reputation outside the English-speaking world. It is still the great favourite of most G & S fans and familiar as well to non-Savoyards. Unlike many masterpieces, its special status was clear from the beginning. Recalling its ecstatic première on 14 March 1885, Rutland Barrington declared, 'Never during the whole of my experience have I assisted at such an enthusiastic first night as greeted this delightful work.' One enthusiastic first-nighter bubbled, 'The whole thing is like a glass of champagne.' A similarly intoxicated critic compared it to Dante's *Divine Comedy*, an unquestionable first for any comic opera. To this day *The Mikado* is quintessential Gilbert and Sullivan, not only because it displays its creators' gifts in such brilliant profusion but because, despite its familiarity, it remains a somewhat baffling if sparkling mixture of pantomime, satire, fairy-tale, romance and oriental spectacle. A modern critic has referred to it as 'this very odd opera', but it is this oddity that makes it most typically G & S.

The Mikado's high spirits might be due partly to its begetters' simple relief that they were still working together. The crisis that followed *Princess Ida*, initiated by Sullivan's refusal to turn out more of the Savoy product and stiffened by Gilbert's devotion to his lozenge plot, was just barely resolved. It is hard to say how it came about, but it did happen quickly. The two men exchanged what seemed to be parting shots on 3 and 4 May 1884, Gilbert insisting on the lozenge and Sullivan concluding that further discussion was useless. But on 8 May the composer happily acknowledged the librettist's suggestion that they do a Japanese opera and agreed 'to set it without further discussing the matter, or asking what the subject is to be', as long as it was free from 'supernatural and improbable elements'.

Gilbert later attributed his change of heart to a lucky stroke of inspiration. As he fumed and fretted about Sullivan's intransigence, a decorative Japanese sword suddenly came crashing off the wall of his study, sparking a new train of ideas. This makes a good story, but Gilbert was more matter-of-fact in other accounts, leaving the sword on the wall or confessing that he did not have 'a good reason for our forthcoming piece being laid in Japan'. Certainly the best reason—the same one that had produced *Patience*—was topicality. In 1884 the Land of the Rising Sun was very much in the public eye. It had not been many years since Perry and the American Navy had ended Japan's lordly isolation, opening the way for undreamed-of trade and *Madame Butterfly*. In Britain, the real-life models for *Patience*, aesthetes like Wilde, Whistler and Rossetti, had played a part in increasing public awareness of the mysterious East by their taste in prints and pottery. In the years preceding *The Mikado*, 'all one sees that's Japanese' had become more and more abundant. Gilbert's sword (which showed that even he was not immune to the fashion) may have been a catalyst, but these influences were certainly already hovering in his mind. An even more immediate influence came from only a little way east of his Kensington home. A Japanese Exhibition had just opened in Knightsbridge, including a full-scale native village complete with inhabitants. Londoners flocked to the event, intrigued by the exotic visitors, their novel dress, customs and ceremonies.

Gilbert thus had ready-made publicity for a Japanese show of his own, as well as technical advice on how to mount it, and he took advantage of both. A first-night reviewer correctly linked *The Mikado* to the wave of Oriental interest: 'We are all being more or less Japanned. Advertisements tell us every morning that we have Japan in London. . . .' The native staff at the Exhibition helped Gilbert's version of Japan in London attain the required realism by coaching the D'Oyly Carte company. The women learned how to dress, make up and move with the quick, shuffling step appropriate to ladies in kimonos. Both men and women practised manipulating the large, ornate fans that became a particularly gorgeous feature of the opera, adding authentic flair to every mood and gesture.

The Mikado's programme acknowledged this 'valuable assistance afforded by the directors and native inhabitants of the Japanese Village, Knightsbridge', and the opera drew further assistance from their home country itself. The strikingly colourful costumes were made from Japanese silk purchased at Liberty's, the modish department store which had also supplied the aesthetic prints for *Patience*. Other of the costumes were originals of real value and antiquity. Katisha's formidable presence was enhanced by a gown two hundred years old. The Mikado's robe was a replica of the Emperor's official dress, and the grotesque mask worn by his guard were exact copies as well. Gilbert and D'Oyly Carte had also purchased some ancient armour direct from

Japan, but it turned out to be both too small and too heavy for any member of the Savoy cast to wear.

The librettist, of course, had been refining his conception of how all these elements would hang together, from the moment the sword fell in his study (or did not). Once he had decided that costumes, make-up and scenery were feasible, he began mulling over specific characters and incidents. He told an interviewer that the idea of the three little maids, one of the opera's great hits, came about simply because the actresses who played them were all the same height. They would make an effective group throughout, and schoolgirls seemed likely casting for the purpose. He was equally analytical about setting the scenes. What locales would provide maximum spectacle and interest? He considered 'the respective advantages of a street in Nagasaki, a Japanese market-place, wharf with shipping, a Japanese garden, a seaside beach and the courtyard of a Japanese palace' before opting for courtyard and garden.

Gilbert's recollections sound a little too well-organized and methodical to be true, but he was a very well-organized, methodical man. He went at the story and scenario with the same diligence, going through twelve drafts before it satisfied him. In November Sullivan came to dine and hear the final version, making suggestions for more effective musical possibilities but approving highly of his partner's work. He did have one small query. Why, when traditional Japanese titles were so resounding, had he avoided working them into his libretto? Gilbert replied he had been inclined to do just that, especially to take advantage of possible 'excruciating rhymes', but the aristocratic 'samurais' had made him drop the whole idea. He was afraid he would not be able to resist the obvious pairing with 'damn your eyes', which would have scandalized Japanese and Savoyards alike. The only alternative would have been to have Sullivan drown out the shocking phrase with 'tympani fortissimo'.

With that waggish temptation out of the way, the happily reunited collaborators set to work on the songs, to be followed as usual by the dialogue. Their painstaking efforts paid off handsomely, for the new piece combined the verve of the earliest operas with the concision of *Patience*, the satire and subtlety of *Iolanthe* and the musical wealth of *Princess Ida*. But its Oriental fascination was all its own.

The opera establishes itself as a Victorian-Anglicized view of Japan from the outset. The curtain opens on a collection of stunningly garbed Oriental figures who announce they are 'gentlemen of Japan' and refer the audience for comparison to the images on the vases and jars in any stylish British drawing-room. Then a young man enters and introduces himself as a wandering minstrel. He is Nanki-poo and is seeking Yum-

Yum, the ward of Ko-Ko, a cheap tailor. They met and fell in love a year ago, when Nanki-poo was Second Trombone with the Titipu Town Band, but Yum-Yum was already engaged to her guardian. After a year wandering in despair, he has heard that Ko-Ko, under the Mikado's bizarre and stringent law, has 'been condemned to death for flirting!' But his new hopes are dashed when the nobleman Pish-tush tells him that Ko-Ko has not only been reprieved but has been appointed Lord High Executioner, 'the highest rank a citizen can attain'. The startling turn of events is Titipu's canny response to the Mikado's severity. If their executioner is the man next due for decapitation, executions must cease, since the responsible official cannot perform on himself.

For the price of a small bribe to the enormously august Pooh-Bah, who occupies *all* civic offices except the post of executioner, Nanki-Poo learns Yum-Yum and Ko-Ko are to wed that very day. Then the Lord High Executioner himself makes a grand entrance, to reflect on his miraculous escape and elevation and go through his 'little list' of society offenders'—ripe candidates for execution if he ever needs one. He consults Pooh-Bah about how much money the city might provide for his imminent wedding but receives wildly conflicting advice depending on which one of his many official hats Pooh-Bah is wearing. As usual, however, a large bribe will settle everything.

In scamper a group of pretty schoolgirls, one of whom is Yum-Yum. She gives Ko-Ko a grudging kiss, but she and her friends Pitti-Sing and Peep-Bo are much more excited at the sight of Nanki-Poo. He blurts out his love for her; Ko-Ko thanks him for the compliment and has him removed. But when they are alone, the minstrel reveals to her that he is none other than the son of the Mikado, having fled in disguise to avoid a forced marriage to an elderly harridan at the imperial court. Dramatic as it is, the announcement makes no difference to their dreary prospects, and the unhappy couple part.

Meanwhile a letter has arrived from the Emperor himself, noting the dearth of executions in Titipu and decreeing that someone's head must roll within a month or the executioner's post 'shall be abolished and the city reduced to the rank of a village'. A voluntary victim is obviously needed, but neither Pish-Tush, Pooh-Bah or Ko-Ko will accept the honour. Then Ko-Ko comes upon the lovelorn Nanki-Poo preparing to dispatch himself and proposes that his suicide be conducted by the state. Nanki-Poo agrees but demands Yum-Yum's hand in return, even if it is only for a month.

The Lord High Executioner proclaims their bargain to the rapturous citizens, but their celebrations are interrupted by the furious figure of Katisha, the woman Nanki-Poo absconded to avoid. She claims her 'perjured lover', but Pitti-Sing blithely informs her that 'he's going to marry Yum-Yum.' Enraged, the elderly maid attempts to expose the minstrel's true identity, only to be thwarted once more when Yum-Yum leads the assembly in drowning her out. Katisha rushes off to tell her tale to the Mikado, and the Titipuans defiantly return to their festivities.

Act II finds Yum-Yum preparing for her wedding though her imminent widowhood somewhat dampens the proceedings. Then Ko-Ko arrives with the astounding information that 'by the Mikado's law, when a married man is beheaded his wife is buried alive.' This thunderbolt makes Yum-Yum think twice about Nanki-Poo, who declares that, if she will not marry him, he will kill himself at once and deprive Ko-Ko of his victim. When Ko-Ko objects, Nanki-Poo demands to be beheaded at once. But that suggestion totally unnerves the Lord High Executioner, who has never killed anything. He proposes that they resolve the dilemma by swearing the execution has taken place even though it hasn't. A bribe to Pooh-Bah wins the support of all his official positions, and Nanki-Poo and Yum-Yum trip away to be married.

With much ado, in come the Mikado and his entourage with Katisha. Ko-Ko proudly informs him of the execution, which he, Pooh-Bah and Pitti-Sing describe in lurid detail. But the Mikado is less interested in executions than in his vagrant son. To the trio's horror, the imperial heir turns out to be the very Nanki-Poo they have supposedly just killed. The Mikado is very sympathetic, but he can do nothing to alter the law which prescribes a hideous punishment—'something lingering, with boiling oil in it, I fancy'—for 'compassing the death of the Heir Apparent'.

Obviously Nanki-Poo must come to life at once. But he points out that, if he does, Katisha will certainly insist he be beheaded for marrying Yum-Yum, which will mean in turn Yum-Yum's burial alive. The only possible solution is for Ko-Ko to marry Katisha himself. Aghast at the idea, Ko-Ko nevertheless contrives a heartfelt appeal that at length wins over the blood-thirsty old maid. When the Mikado reappears, benignly ready to punish his son's assassins, she sues for mercy on their behalf. Then Nanki-Poo himself appears, and all difficulties vanish, except for Katisha's rage at Ko-Ko's deception, which the Mikado requires him to explain. The resourceful executioner replies that, since the Emperor's will is law, a gentleman commanded to be executed is as good as dead already, 'and if he is dead, why not say so?' This satisfies the Mikado, if not Katisha, and the opera ends with the prospect of life-long happiness—at least for Yum-Yum and Nanki-Poo.

Sullivan began his part of *The Mikado* shortly before Christmas 1884. Auspiciously, as it turned out, his first production was 'Three little maids from school', which he wrote in one day, along with another piece. As usual, his rate of composition varied. Perhaps his speediest performance was completing 'The flowers that bloom in the spring' in one sitting between teatime and supper. He had most of Act I's music in hand by 18 February, when Gilbert read the finished libretto to the Savoy company, and he spent the rest of February and March wholly absorbed in his task. On 2 March he recorded that for the last ten days he had had 'no drives, parties, or recreations of any kind'. The next night he turned in a classic Sullivan feat, staying up until 5 a.m. scoring the great Act I finale, a total of sixty-three pages at one go. (His speed at scoring was legendary. Once, watching Sullivan's pen flashing over the staves, George Grossmith marvelled, 'It's like shorthand.' 'Yes,' replied the composer nonchalantly, 'only much faster.')

Act II was finished on 6 March and rushed into rehearsal. The atmosphere at the Savoy was more than usually tense, because Gilbert was determined that the new piece would not meet the same unsatisfactory reception as *Princess Ida*. Rumours about the impending 'Japanese opera' had titillated the public, but one critic had opined that it would merely prove that its author's 'vein of topsyturvydom is exhausted'.

The pressure told on everyone, including Gilbert himself. At the final dress rehearsal, he was seized by an almost disastrous fit of bad judgement. Within hours of the overture, he decided that the Mikado's song 'My object all sublime' had to be cut. Only a concerted appeal from the men's chorus saved what would turn out to be one of the most famous G & S numbers.

When opening night did arrive, the finely polished Savoy troupe were as nervous as amateurs. George Grossmith, highly strung at the best of times, was particularly on edge, and, as Sullivan reported, his 'nervousness nearly upset the piece'. To the audience as well he seemed uncomfortable and constricted, especially in his Japanese robes. But at last, in the second act, he kicked up his heels, and the first-nighters cheered lustily.

Cheers, loud and prolonged, were the story of the evening, and the anxieties of most of the cast were allayed long before Act II. Awaiting their entrance, the three little maids trembled in the wings like real-life schoolgirls, but their trio was a stunning success, encored three times. Even allowing for a few lapses of memory, the whole performance's effect was remarkable, indeed unprecedented. Sullivan noted that the house was 'most brilliant' and the reception 'tremendous', giving 'every sign of real success'. He and Gilbert took triumphant bows, hand in hand, to tumultuous acclaim.

The Press echoed the triumphal note, with praise for the sets and

The Act II set of *Iolanthe*, with the electrically lit fairies dancing in Westminster Palace Yard. Above them, Private Willis, Iolanthe summoned by the Fairy Queen, and Iolanthe's bucolic son Strephon

Two of *Iolanthe's* love-struck mortals: the noble Lords Mountararat and Tolloler, played by Rutland Barrington (in evening dress for Act II) and Durward Lely (in robes and coronet for Act I)

A page of scenes from the original production of *Princess Ida*. In the centre Hilarion, Cyril and Florian confront the Princess. King Gama sneers in the lower left corner; his sons stand four-square at the top

This page of sketches from the original production of *The Mikado* conveys the quasi-Oriental charm of its characters and costumes

The indispensable George Grossmith, who had his problems as Ko-Ko

The original Three Little Maids: Sybil Grey, Leonora Braham and Jessie Bond

Gilbertian illustrations for two songs from *The Mikado*'s second act: 'Braid the raven hair' and Ko-Ko's ballad of the heart-broken tomtit

Rutland Barrington and Jessie Bond cut a sober caper in *Ruddigore*, as the reformed Despard Murgatroyd and Mad Margaret

Scenes and characters from *Ruddigore* with the procession of ghostly ancestors in the centre, the bridesmaids of Rederring at the top and Sir Roderic's reappearance (as originally written, from below) at the bottom costumes and a prediction that Japanese fashions might become the new London rage. But they saved their warmest compliments for Messrs Gilbert and Sullivan, with the honours richly divided. 'The text,' said one reviewer, 'sparkles with countless gems of wit,' 'its author's rhyming and rhythmic gifts have never been more splendidly displayed,' the dialogue 'is positively . . . full of points and hits'. And Sullivan's score was full of 'musical jewels of great price, all aglow with the lustre of a pure and luminous genius'.

Such accolades summed up the general critical reaction, but their author, *The Theatre*'s Mr Beatty-Kingston, had some unexpected reservations as well. They recalled the tormented objections of an earlier reviewer to *Iolanthe*'s supposedly devilish qualities. In a similar vein Beatty-Kingston pointed to 'things grave and even horrible invested with a ridiculous aspect—all the motives prompting our actions traced back to inexhaustible sources of selfishness and cowardice. . .'. He was equally uneasy about the opera's persistent concern with violent death: 'decapitation, disembowelment, immersion in boiling oil or molten lead. . .'.

Gilbert was disgusted at this ponderous misreading of his intention, though he was undoubtedly pleased at Beatty-Kingston's praise for the way he had carried it off. He made no attempt at a rejoinder, being more interested in further practical means for ensuring *The Mikado*'s success. Those memory slips had upset him, and he and Sullivan also had plans for altering the sequence of the text to make it flow more effectively. Therefore, Saturday's traumatic but triumphant opening was followed by a Sunday morning rehearsal. Ko-Ko's 'little list' was moved from later in Act I to immediately after his entrance—an ideal place for it. Then Yum-Yum's superb aria 'The sun whose rays are all ablaze' was transferred from its original position following the three little maids' trio and their quartet with Pooh-Bah to its present location as part of the wedding preparations in Act II. The change came about because the soprano singing Yum-Yum complained the first arrangement left her no breath to do justice to the song. But its present effect as a kind of soliloquy for the bride-to-be is perfect. Other small changes occurred in Katisha's catalogue of her dubious physical charms. Thus in short order the official text was set, and *The Mikado* became the 'Japanese opera' we know today.

Since its opening, however, there has been a certain amount of controversy as to how 'Japanese' it really is. G. K. Chesterton stated one position forthrightly when he declared: 'There is not, the whole length of *The Mikado*, a single joke that is a joke against Japan. They are all . . . jokes against England, or that Western civilization which an Englishman knows best in England.' And more pithily, '*The Mikado* is not a picture of Japan; but it is a Japanese picture.'

All the same, the Japanese were worried enough by Gilbert's barbs to protest, albeit briefly, during the opera's first run. And twenty years later, in 1907, when Japan was becoming a power to be reckoned with, the Lord Chamberlain withdrew *The Mikado*'s licence during a state visit by a Japanese prince. For six weeks the play was officially banned, though Helen D'Oyly Carte went ahead with her planned performances all the same. Of course Gilbert was irate. No one was sure whether the Lord Chamberlain was taking precautionary action or whether the ban had been requested by the Japanese government (Gilbert believed it was).

Public opinion found it absurd, a turn of events in itself Gilbertian. A correspondent to a newspaper revealed that *The Mikado* had already been performed in Japan, under the title *Three Little Maids*. Members of Parliament asked the Home Secretary if he was aware that Japanese military bands regularly played the opera's music, though British bands were forbidden to. Something like a last word came from a Japanese journalist, in England to cover the Prince's visit. He attended the proscribed performance and confessed himself 'deeply and pleasingly disappointed'. Expecting 'real insults' to his country, he had found only 'bright music and much fun'.

However, a few years later Gilbert published his libretto as a children's book called *The Story of the Mikado*. His outlook may have been coloured by the licensing controversy, but his first paragraph does paint a rather acid picture of Japan. Gilbert drily agrees that Japan is now known as 'a great and glorious country', mainly because of its victory in the Russo-Japanese war, but asserts that its people 'attained their present condition of civilization very gradually, and at the date of my story they had peculiar tastes, ideas and fashions of their own, many of which they discarded when they found that they did not coincide with the ideas of the more enlightened countries of Europe. So if my readers are of opinion (as they very likely will be) that some of their customs, as they are revealed in this story, are curious, odd or ridiculous, they must bear in mind that the Japan of that time was unlike the Japan of to-day.'

To an extent the librettist treats Japan as a caricature country, though he does not really satirize it. Gilbert depends on his operatic audience having a vague conception of the empire (formerly, if not presently) as a decidedly odd place, with highly ritualized conduct, strange views on suicide and capital punishment and an arbitrary and autocratic ruler. It is a stereotyped view to which certain Japanese citizens might indeed object, but it gives Gilbert a colourful, mythic world with conventions he can exploit for his topsy-turvy purposes. In certain ways it resembles the fairyland of *Iolanthe*, but without the definitely English locale of Westminster. *The Mikado*'s world is 'real' enough to be recognizable, but 'unreal' enough for its wit and satire to be timeless and universal.

At the time of the 1907 ban, Gilbert protested that *his* Mikado had 'no more actuality than a pantomime king', and this remark catches the flavour of the piece exactly. Its setting is a kind of extravaganza Japan, a rather comic, mythic place whose stage reality is maintained throughout. Its characters are pseudo-Japanese, but with more or less obviously Western personalities, and its humour, songs and music are essentially English. (The Japanese reporter who saw the D'Oyly Carte production said, 'I envy the nation possessing such music.') The result is a unique balance between reality and fantasy, creating an exotic country of its own, which is why *The Mikado* has been enjoyed in countries where the other, plainly 'English' operas have not.

The same balance disarms dour criticisms of the opera's moral tone, like those levelled by Beatty-Kingston. Gilbert's violence is innocent mayhem, like that of Punch and Judy. The framework and mood are so carefully established that it never occurs to us—or most of us—to consider these bogeys as real. It *is* pantomime, piquant but harmless, and the references to decapitation are no more frightening (probably less) than Lewis Carroll's Queen of Hearts screeching 'Off with his head' in *Alice in Wonderland*. In the same way, though Katisha is the most forbidding of Gilbert's dragons, we resent his jokes at her expense less because she is such a Japanese-pantomime dragon. We may be touched by her distress at the loss of Nanki-Poo, but she does not seem as helplessly human as Ruth or Lady Jane. Every one of Gilbert's puppets exists in the grandiose, richly eccentric stage world he has created for them. We respond to them with laughter and tenderness, but never with dread.

The two collaborators set the tone of their Savoy Japan from the very first note. Their achievement is unfailingly mutual. Each man has a precise and hilarious sense of how far to go with the Orientalism, and just what its character should be. When the curtain goes up, we are confronted by a magnificent gathering of colourful males. They certainly look Japanese. Up to a point they rather sound Japanese, too: Sullivan introduces them with two declamatory chords followed by a long, whirling unison passage through the orchestra. Unaccompanied, it seems vaguely eastern, but in fact it consists purely of a good old G major scale.

When the august personages burst into song, the same flavour persists—a unison melody, simple and impressive, that might be at home in the imperial court. But the mood quickly becomes gaily European, the music almost a can-can. Gilbert establishes the same tongue-in-cheek, painted-eyebrows duality. His creations declare that they *are* creations—'gentlemen of Japan', all right, but only as Japanese as the gentlemen the audience has seen 'on many a vase and jar, on many a screen and fan'. They are painted figures that Gilbert has brought to life, 'queer and quaint' without a doubt, real and not real. Though they deny it, they are marionettes—Gilbert's puppets in a new, spectacular guise. They claim their stiffness is 'simply court etiquette', which the audience would also accept as particularly Japanese; but Gilbert uses these rigid manners to satirize the rigidity of all courtly codes. Having defined their divided nature, Gilbert can play his puppets any way he likes; conditions are ripe for topsy-turvyness. The Japanified figures finish their chorus grandly intoning an Oriental-sounding 'Oh', while the orchestra capers beneath them with Sullivan's can-can strains.

Nanki-Poo's song, 'A wandering minstrel I', illustrates another of the opera's special traits, its ability to change moods from mirth to melancholy and back again. Often in previous works Sullivan gave an unexpected emotional turn to Gilbert's words. In *The Mikado* the two of them provide the touching moments in absolute harmony.

Nanki-Poo's demonstration of his minstrel's wares gives both of his creators a chance to show off their own. Though he supposedly accompanies himself on 'a native guitar', Sullivan gives him strumming music no more foreign than Edwin's solo accompaniment in *Trial by Jury*. His description of himself as 'a thing of shreds and patches' is a restrained Gilbertian pun drawn from Shakespeare's *Hamlet*, where the Prince describes his perfidious uncle as 'a king of shreds and patches'. As promised, his song does range 'through every passion', or at least three of them, from the tender, dreaming first verse to rousing military and nautical choruses. Gilbert's astuteness at staging appears in this series of set pieces. The Japanese gentlemen throw themselves whole-heartedly into Nanki-Poo's catalogue, especially his 'song of the sea', and for a memorable moment these lacquered grandees disport themselves like jolly tars. (One of the more mysterious references in the nautical section is the word 'rumblelow', which has nothing to do with demon drink but is simply a traditional refrain in shanties. In his *Mikado* for children, Gilbert admitted he did not know what it meant but that it seemed 'to hold the same place in a sea-song that the "old plantation" does in Negro minstrelsy'.)

Nanki-Poo ends in the same touching mood with which he began. It is almost immediately succeeded by Pish-Tush's scintillating account of how Titipu out-manoeuvred 'Our Great Mikado, virtuous man' in the matter of executions. The excellent number should be better known and certainly would be if its purpose was not simply to advance the plot. Gilbert's rhymes are masterfully brisk, Sullivan's pizzicato accompaniment buoyantly delightful. It is worth noting that almost all of the opera's opening action takes place in song rather than dialogue.

This might be Gilbert's attempt to give Sullivan an opportunity to 'let the music arise and speak for itself', but it is very effective in any case and brings out the best in Gilbert too.

The first solid bit of dialogue comes, quite appropriately, with the entrance of Pooh-Bah. You might think that one of Gilbert's great male characters would deserve a self-introductory song, but the ditties for Ko-Ko and the Mikado take up the available space. Perhaps the spoken word, delivered with unspeakable condescension, is Pooh-Bah's natural medium anyway. In his vast self-regarding pomposity, his devotion to his family heritage, he represents one image of Japan a British audience would think they recognized. But they would also recognize that Britain, and every other country, had its Pooh-Bahs too.

With great deftness, Gilbert gets considerable satiric mileage out of this single, albeit many-sided character. Of course Pooh-Bah's inflated speech and manner are Gilbert's standard targets. In addition, the Lord High Everything Else represents a kind of astounding one-man bureaucratic tangle, calmly spinning out yards of multi-ministerial red tape. Inordinately fond of his ancestry, he can trace his origins—like anybody else—'to a protoplasmal primordial atomic globule'. He is also a snob, in the spirit of the *Iolanthe* peers, patronizing the lower orders, though not too proud to rent his presence to them for a fee. Bribes, indeed, are his major preoccupation. He may be old—even prehistoric—money, but he is not above accepting new money whenever he can. And opportunities for easy graft abound, since he occupies all Titipu's administrative positions. It is as this wonderful one-man governing body that Pooh-Bah passed into Victorian slang, carrying the concepts of 'jobs for the boys' and centralized government to unimagined heights.

His song, 'Young man, despair', like Pish-Tush's, serves mainly to advance the plot, but both Gilbert and Sullivan fit it perfectly to his character. The librettist uses the occasion to spin out a series of outrageous rhymes on 'executioner' of which 'you very imperfect ablutioner' is the most far-fetched. (Gilbert explained to his youthful readers that 'the Japanese are an extremely clean people, and . . . Pooh-Bah was honestly shocked to find that Nanki-Poo's long march had left its traces on his person.') Sullivan does his part with a puffed-up little march interspersed with dignified but stirring fanfares.

Everything in Gilbert's remarkably streamlined libretto supports everything else: Pooh-Bah's grandiloquence brings on another of Gilbert's great characters, Ko-Ko, who comes in to a superbly martial male chorus which Sullivan, with delicious irony, based on a traditional air called 'A Fine Old English Gentleman'. The effect is merrily mock-heroic, because the little ex-tailor represents himself stumbling under the weight of a sword of office which, like the office itself, is much too big for him. (In the original production Grossmith carried the very blade from Gilbert's wall.) The chorus's commands to 'bow down' to this pipsqueak parvenu increase the fun. In its comic suavity, the music to his first short solo, 'Taken from a county jail', reminds us of that other parvenu, Sir Joseph Porter in *Pinafore*. But the two men are really nothing alike. Ko-Ko is rather full of himself, but his progress from tailor to condemned man to Lord High Executioner has been so meteoric he has not forgotten who he is. We like him because he is plucky, not really impressed with himself, and, as it happens, much too tender-hearted to execute anything. He also turns out to be slyly resourceful, though his tale of Nanki-Poo's demise is almost too fatally clever. And he is sensible, finally not hesitating a moment to give up his ill-advised match with Yum-Yum. (Gilbert seems to approve no more of older men pursuing younger women than the reverse, though he is more lenient toward the men.) The same good sense, plus resignation and a resilient constitution, helps him accept Katisha.

He does remind us somewhat of the Lord Chancellor, who also wanted to marry his ward. This is appropriate because Pooh-Bah says the Mikado has combined the offices of judge and executioner, which seems to mean that Ko-Ko must be a judge too. Certainly the notion of making the two positions one is vintage Gilbert. The man who sentences a criminal to death is as directly involved in his execution as the functionary who makes the fatal stroke. More subtle is the idea that Lord High Executioner is the highest office in the land—a grim comment on where a government's ultimate authority lies.

Ko-Ko's 'I've got a little list' is one of everybody's favourite items in the G & S canon. Its lyrics have been altered from time to time, according to whoever the 'society offenders' of a particular moment are. With the course of events, 'the lady novelist' has become 'the red-hot socialist' or 'suffragist' or 'motorist' or 'prohibitionist'. During D'Oyly Carte's 1981 London season, after the company's application for government support had been rejected, 'Arts Councilist' duly appeared on the list. One permanent change was made in 1948. Gilbert's unfortunate Victorian reference to 'nigger serenader' was altered to 'banjo serenader' after complaints on an American tour. The Mikado's song was similarly amended, 'blacked like a nigger' being replaced by 'painted with vigour'. But the majority of Ko-Ko's indictments have stayed the same because the offences have. His learned allusion to 'Nisi Prius' simply means a civil court. His 'lady from the provinces who dresses like a guy' is not a transvestite but someone so peculiarly garbed she looks like a Guy Fawkes dummy.

The Mikado's men have the stage to themselves for almost half the first act, but the delay in the schoolgirls' entrance only makes it more attractive. Sullivan brings them on with coyly skipping strings that catch their personalities before they have said or sung a word. But the song they do sing, 'Comes a train of little ladies', is a gem, one of the opera's moments of delicate ambivalence. Their opening lines express their delight at being free 'from scholastic trammels'. But, no more than eighteen and on the threshold of adulthood, they also wonder 'what the world can be'. The lyrics suddenly become reflective, without being any less girlish, and Sullivan's melody ceases to skip and rises in yearning uncertainty.

'Is it but a world of trouble
Sadness set to song?
Is its beauty but a bubble
Bound to break ere long?'

The moods alternate and complement each other, presenting a quietly complex and appealing picture of adolescence.

No such ambiguity underlies the 'Three little maids' trio, which is pure giggling delight both in the lyrics and in Sullivan's accompaniment. Gilbert's girls are themselves delightful, and pure English. They offer a complete contrast to the mock-Japanese aura of Pooh-Bah and the male chorus. Even if they are fetchingly gowned in kimonos and obis, they are authentic teenagers, particularly in the giddy speeches which Gilbert has the little maids chatter out simultaneously.

One of the funniest moments in the opera is the maids' encounter with Pooh-Bah. Pitti-Sing's inquiry of Ko-Ko, 'I beg your pardon, but what is this? Customer come to try on?' painfully pricks the great man's *amour-propre*, and Ko-Ko continues the damage by identifying him as 'a Tremendous Swell'. The sport leads to the irresistible quartet 'So please you, sir, we much regret', in which the Lord High Everything Else, declining to sing and dance with the girls, at last does sing and dance, with as much abandon as someone of pre-Adamite ancestry can muster. The concept is Gilbert's but the realization is Sullivan's, with first the maids, then the Tremendous Swell, required to deliver rapid-fire tra-la-las in support of the song's zestful melody.

Yum-Yum, being Ko-Ko's fiancée, then Nanki-poo's wife, is very much head girl, but she has the same kind of unsentimental wit as Pitti-Sing and Peep-Bo. When Nanki-Poo broaches the secret of his true identity, he suggests he might not really be a musician. He gets no further because Yum-Yum flashes back, 'There! I was certain of it, directly I heard you play!' Gilbert's humour can be inflated and strained, sometimes even when he is apparently trying to be inflated and strained, but the girls are genuinely funny.

A famous example of Gilbert's ability to take humour where he finds it occurs when Yum-Yum confesses to Nanki-poo that she does not love Ko-Ko. His response in Gilbert's original text was simply 'Rapture!' but in rehearsal Durward Lely, playing Nanki-Poo, overstressed the word, and Gilbert, ever-vigilant in the stalls, snapped 'Modified rapture!' 'Modified rapture!' Lely dutifully repeated, and that is how the line has stayed ever since.

Perhaps the most opaque line in the whole opera—and one of the most obsure references in all of Gilbert and Sullivan—is also given to the lovers. Their duet imagines, perhaps with a trifle too much Victorian cuteness, their happiness 'were you not to Ko-Ko plighted'. They embrace fondly and kiss, till Yum-Yum remembers how things are:

> 'But as I'm engaged to Ko-Ko
> To embrace you thus, *con fuoco,*
> Would distinctly be no *gioco*
> And for yam I should get toko. . . . '

The quatrain as a whole shows Gilbert working hard for clever rhymes. *Con fuoco* and *gioco* are straightforward Italian snippets meaning respectively 'with passion' and 'joke', but 'yam for toko' seems to be nonsense. Nevertheless, simply put, it is arcane Victorian slang meaning to be punished for doing something enjoyable.

Infinitely more accessible, and one of the surest show-stoppers in the piece, is the 'short sharp shock' trio by Ko-Ko, Push-Tush and Pooh-Bah. When Gilbert sent the lyrics to his partner on 9 December 1884, he noted he had 'put the three verses side by side for convenience' sake, but, of course, they will be sung separately'. He also fancied that, because he had given each verse a different metre, each one could be set differently, but left it to the composer's discretion.

Little did he know what Sullivan's discretion would produce. The composer does indeed give each singer his own characteristic melody—Pooh-Bah stately and 'Japanese', Ko-Ko rather whining and apprehensive, Pish-Tush brisk and hearty—and then combines them as well, in a marvellous fugue that leads to their famous three-men-on-a-horse patter refrain:

> 'To sit in solemn silence in a dull, dark dock,
> In a pestilential prison, with a life-long lock,
> Awaiting the sensation of a short, sharp shock,
> From a cheap and chippy chopper on a big black block!'

The trio hurtle through this tongue-twister three times, each with different settings, building to a superlative climax.

But the opera's most superlative climax—and, not a few critics believe, Sullivan's finest moment in the whole G & S collaboration—is Act I's dazzling finale. It demonstrates all his virtues—invention, gusto, variety, taste and consummate musicianship. It begins as Ko-Ko announces his pact with Nanki-Poo (which the English chorus-in-disguise greets with 'the Japanese equivalent for Hear, Hear, Hear!'), and the lovers strike up a tune of real celebration. The melody is appealing by itself, but Sullivan's treatment makes it splendid. Nanki-Poo and Yum-Yum alternate phrases, then Pooh-Bah, Pish-Tush, Peep-Bo and Pitti-Sing join them in a little sextet. Gilbert's bright quatrain

'Then let the throng
Our joy advance,
With laughing song
And merry dance,'

gains quick momentum through Sullivan's energetic variations on the last two lines. Then the six deliver 'song' with a powerful crescendo, the orchestra's strings rise ecstatically beneath them and the full chorus thunders in 'with joyous shout and ringing cheer'. It is a jubilant moment, with Sullivan realizing all the unmodified rapture the words and scene suggest. He divides the chorus beautifully, with soaring sopranos taking up where the strings left off. And his bandmaster father would no doubt be proud of his boy's thrilling use of bass drum and cymbals to drive home the accents.

Thankfully, the section is repeated; once is definitely not enough. Then Pooh-Bah offers typically unctuous though heartfelt congratulations, and the choral transport begins again. But this time the menacing Katisha intrudes. Sullivan conjures up a dark, furious mood, with ominous tremolos in the orchestra. As always, the words he chooses to stress give maximum dramatic effect. As she addresses Nanki-Poo, the full weight of the wronged maid's wrath falls on

'Thy *heart* unbind,
Oh fool, oh blind!
Give *me* my place,
Oh rash, oh base!'

'Doom' and 'knell' have similar emphasis when she turns on Yum-Yum. But it is too late, as Pitti-Sing breezily tells her, since 'He's going to marry Yum-Yum.' Sullivan asserts the happy fact in a droll, impish little march. The contrast with what has gone before could not be greater, and another contrast occurs immediately after, with Katisha's lament, 'The hour of gladness is dead and gone.' But her grief becomes vengeance, and the mood of crisis returns as she tries to expose Nanki-Poo's real, royal identity. The choral interjection that drowns her ('Oni! bikkuri shakkuri to!') is Gilbertian mock-Japanese, though it has been translated literally as having something to do with hiccups!

Finally, celebration sweeps away discord in an ensemble that is again completely different from what has preceded it. Katisha's rage has no chance against the triumphant serenity of 'We do not heed their dismal sound/For joy rings everywhere around.'

Thomas Dunhill has suggested that the finale is somewhat improbable dramatically: why doesn't the crowd want to hear who Nanki-Poo really is? But there is no denying its musical authenticity. It is the kind of achievement that makes clear how ideally suited Sullivan was for comic opera. The 'serious' works he felt obliged to turn out rarely attain such freshness and emotional vitality. After *The Mikado* he composed *The Golden Legend*, a massive cantata which was hailed as a great and worthy success. But when Sullivan remarked hopefully to a discerning musical friend that he thought it was the best thing he had done, she disappointed him by replying that that honour went to *The Mikado*, and she was quite right.

The musical and verbal riches continue in Act II. Gilbert is as adept as Sullivan at mood and pace, and the act is noteworthy for several light-hearted songs that relieve the uneasy atmosphere of beheading, live burial and boiling in oil. They include the trio 'Here's a how-de-do', the quintet 'See how the fates their gifts allot' and the supremely sprightly duet for Nanki-Poo and Ko-Ko, 'The flowers that bloom in the spring'. Performing this last number in the original run, Grossmith accidentally tripped and fell. The audience howled, and Gilbert, despite his habitual distaste for gagging, told him to leave the tumble in. But Grossmith was less lucky on his own initiative. In the scene where they and Pooh-Bah kneel trembling before the Mikado, he arranged for Pitti-Sing to give him a great push, rolling him over. Gilbert heard about it and curtly told him to stop. Grossmith objected that he got 'a great laugh by it'. Gilbert was unimpressed. 'So you would if you sat on a pork-pie,' he said with finality.

Some of the act's—and opera's—most compelling numbers are those that, like Nanki-Poo's minstrel solo and the girls' 'Comes a train of little ladies' in Act I, present more than one emotional face. In a way, ambivalence is natural to Act II, where nuptial bliss and the prospect of fatal separation go hand in hand. At the beginning of the act, as the girls prepare Yum-Yum for her wedding, Gilbert emphasizes their self-conscious, even calculating awareness of womanly allure. But Sullivan takes the idea and makes it an exquisite expression of the Eternal Feminine, particularly in Yum-Yum's luminous solo 'The sun whose rays are all ablaze'. His setting has an eastern flavour, with a gracefully flowing, rising and falling melody over hushed orchestral chords, and the result is one of his very finest songs.

The madrigal that follows ('Brightly dawns our wedding day') is beautifully touching as well, an attempt to raise the wedding party's spirits that continually falls back into sombre reflection. It is quite convincing quasi-Elizabethan—just what you would expect in a 'Japanese opera'—and contains unexpectedly moving lines from Gilbert:

> 'Yet until the shadows fall
> Over one and over all,
> Sing a merry madrigal. . . .'

Sullivan's counterpoint is rich but transparent, a treat for singers and listeners alike, as he weaves in his sonorous 'ding dongs'. But despite the pleasure in the music and the quartet's good intentions to herald the bright dawn of the wedding day, their last fal-las turn into tears. (As originally planned, the quartet includes Pish-Tush. But in some productions—the first one among them—Pish-Tush, a baritone, has been replaced by a bass from the chorus to handle the madrigal's *profundo* bottom line. For his one appearance he is called—courtesy of Gilbert—Go-To.)

Perhaps the most surprising blend of tenderness and humour occurs in Ko-Ko's wooing song to Katisha, 'On a tree by a river a little tom-tit'. It is surprising as well that it comes from Ko-Ko, but the little executioner displays new resources throughout the opera. Gilbert's words strike a fine balance between an essentially comic idea—a romantic bird ravaged by love—and sympathy for his distress. Sullivan's melody is equally well weighted, simple but touching, letting the words and the oddly compelling, traditional refrain of 'willow, titwillow, titwillow' make their effect.

The effect works on us and on Katisha too. Before Ko-Ko's appeal she has had a moving solo of her own, the keening 'Hearts do not break', which recalls the Fairy Queen's address to Captain Shaw in *Iolanthe*. But here the words speak very genuinely of her grief at the loss of Nanki-Poo; for once Gilbert finds nothing comic about an abandoned old maid. Her feelings turn to rage when Ko-Ko appears, but his poignant tale of the lovesick tom-tit reduces her to whimpering, 'Did he really die of love?' The ex-tailor is master of the situation, and their closing duet, 'There is beauty in the bellow of the blast', is a robust, amusing affair, with Ko-Ko showing he is compatible with his fiancée's fierce, blood-thirsty tastes. Its refrain of 'derry down derry' is another carefree injection of Old English into the 'Japanese' setting.

One of the peculiarities of this 'very odd opera' might seem to be the fact that its title character does not appear until midway through Act II. This is partly just effective staging; Gilbert is very adroit at arranging entrances. But it is also only superficially peculiar. While the Mikado is not presented in person, his impact is everywhere. The consequences of his arbitrary rule hold the whole plot together. His laws create topsy-turvy situations and appropriate responses and are the essence of the 'Japanese' mood even more than the exotic sets, costumes and colours. Without the Emperor's draconic views on flirting and matrimony, Nanki-Poo would never have fled the court and met Yum-Yum, and Ko-Ko would not have been sentenced and then made Lord High Executioner. Without the imperial wish for a quota of executions there would have been no arrangement between Nanki-Poo and Ko-Ko, and no wedding between Nanki-Poo and Yum-Yum. Perhaps Nanki-Poo would have dispatched himself, and Yum-Yum become the unwilling bride of Ko-Ko. The whole plot has a firm if Gilbertian logic, and it is all based on his concept of the totally autocratic Emperor, like a wizard in a fairy tale. (The only illogical circumstance may be Katisha's chance arrival in Titipu at the end of Act I, though it is easy to imagine her tracking Nanki-Poo for over a year.)

The entrance of the Emperor and his 'daughter-in-law elect' is one of the opera's many spectacular strokes, and the accompanying music is the only piece of authentic Japanese melody in the whole work. It and its lyrics were apparently a Japanese army marching song. But Sullivan's skill at mock-Oriental is so deft that the real thing sounds as though it might have come from his pen too.

The great Mikado himself is a supreme Gilbertian achievement, especially considering he is not on stage for very long. But this 'pantomime king' establishes himself at once, helped along by the impression we have already gathered from his legal code. In spirit he is derived from the genial violence of the *Bab Ballads*, like the tale of 'King Borria Bungalee Boo', a cannibal monarch whose court includes 'haughty Pish-Tush-Pooh-Bah'. In modern productions he is played rather too demonically. His real character is hair-raisingly sympathetic and debonair, adding to the horror of his weird edicts. When it comes out that the Titipu trio seem inadvertently to have slain the Crown Prince, the Mikado could not be sorrier or more understanding. But the law is the law, and the punishment—'something humorous, but lingering, with either boiling oil or melted lead'—is the punishment. The sad fact is that 'It's an unjust world and virtue is triumphant only in theatrical performances.' Clearly this is Gilbert pointing up the danger of rigid legalism at the same time as he is using it to concoct his plot.

The Emperor's solo, 'A more humane Mikado', like Ko-Ko's 'little list', is Gilbert getting even with miscellaneous disturbers of the peace. The notion of the punishment fitting the crime caught the public fancy and is still familiar. (Its immediate ancestor could be the cruelly kind way Hildebrand treated King Gama in *Princess Ida*.) As with Ko-Ko's song, most of the references are self-explanatory. The only puzzle may be the allusion to the 'buffer on Parliamentary trains', that is, the front end of the cheap but tedious third-class trains that Parliament had stipulated should serve every station once a day. Since the song's first hearing, musical connoisseurs have delighted in a scholarly joke by Sullivan—a quick quotation from Bach's 'Great' G minor organ fugue when the Mikado mentions the old master in relation to the 'Monday Pops' concert series.

Before revealing the real purpose of his visit, the Emperor shows polite interest in the execution that has cost Ko-Ko such trouble and anxiety. The song describing it ('The criminal cried, as he dropped him down') features gaily grisly details abetted by apt comments from the orchestra—the shriek of the condemned man, his nonchalant whistle, the thump of the severed head. But the horrible mistake is soon revealed, and the guilty trio's attempt to insist that Nanki-Poo has merely gone abroad—to Knightsbridge and the Japanese Exhibition—is unavailing. (With Gilbert's approval, any outlandish location can be substituted, but none can have the appropriateness of the original.) Only quick thinking and Ko-Ko's resoluteness can forestall 'a dreadful fate'. At the opera's conclusion, the little executioner also sums up the absurdity of anyone's will being law. Such topsy-turvy logic means that that same will can prevail over what really happened, a principle to which the Mikado is quite happy to agree.

Since its glorious first night, *The Mikado*'s history has been almost as rich, varied and topsy-turvy as the opera itself. After such an opening, of course, New York producers were eager to present the show, and one of them, Mr Stetson, won D'Oyly Carte's permission. His rival, Mr Duff, a graceless loser, went off to put on his own pirate version. D'Oyly Carte opposed him as best he could, even to buying up all the Japanese costumes in Paris, where one of Duff's representatives had gone after Liberty's had refused to supply him. The ultimate *coup* came after Duff had already scheduled his opening. Carte spirited an entire touring company aboard ship under assumed names, arrived in New York in total secrecy and beat Duff's production onto the stage.

The opera caused an even greater furore in America than *Pinafore* had. 'Mikado rooms' became the rage in the smartest homes, to be filled with Japanese knick-knacks. But as usual very few of the financial returns from the craze came back to the Savoy. Pirates popped up everywhere, and D'Oyly Carte companies could not challenge them all. The impresario did take them on in the courts, with varying results. One learned judge stated flatly that 'no Englishman possesses any rights which a true-born American is bound to respect.'

In the summer of 1885 Arthur Sullivan, true-born Briton, came to America to visit his brother's children in California, their mother having recently died. In the course of his travels he was mistaken for John L. Sullivan, the great bare-knuckle boxer, though the confused welcomers knew *Pinafore* and invited him to have a drink anyway. Sullivan also conducted a gala performance of *The Mikado* in New York and addressed the audience, mentioning that this alone was the authorized production and looking forward to the day when American laws would 'see fit to afford the same protection to a man who employs his brains in Literature and Art as they do to one who invents a new beer-tap'. Though proper financial rewards were rather long in coming, there was no question of *Mikado*'s enduring American fame. At the turn of the century, in his story *The Man That Corrupted Hadleyburg,* Mark Twain could picture a town meeting spontaneously setting new words to the second-act trio describing Nanki-Poo's 'execution' and expect his readers both to believe it and to know exactly what he was referring to.

Later productions have often proved decidedly unauthorized. A Berlin version in the decadent '20s featured Katisha arriving in an automobile, the schoolgirls in short skirts, a Charleston in the first-act finale and Yum-Yum bathing nude at the beginning of the second. Also in the '20s but much more sedate was an Oxford *Mikado* in modern dress. American contributions have included *two* swing or 'hot' *Mikados* that competed with each other on Broadway in 1939, one of them starring the legendary tapdancer, Bill 'Bojangles' Robinson. In the '60s a television abridgement had Groucho Marx as Ko-Ko. In London in the '70s a *Black Mikado* made the whole show beautifully rhythmic and supple, with West Indian touches in the orchestration and a magnificently fulsome, impeccably articulating Pooh-Bah.

Purists may shudder at these inroads on orthodoxy. But the only real orthodoxy is the excellence and potential of *The Mikado* itself. The libretto is too sharp and diverse, the opportunities for stage effects too inviting, and the music too lustrous not to continue to inspire new productions of all kinds. They only show that the premier Gilbert and Sullivan opera retains both its place and its great qualities. And the more exposure those qualities receive, the better.

9

Ruddigore;
or The Witch's Curse

Rutland Barrington, after fondly recalling the unparalleled excitement of the *The Mikado*'s opening, recorded a very different verdict on the première of *Ruddigore*, the Japanese opera's successor. That, he said, was 'a very stormy first night', with the customary cheers tainted by boos and hisses. The new piece's first difficulty was probably just that it was not *The Mikado*: no production could have followed that celebrated hit. But *Ruddigore* did have problems of its own, beginning with its title, which—particularly in its original spelling, 'Ruddygore'—looked shockingly like the rude expletive 'bloody'. Then, too, Gilbert's subject was rather dated, a satire on creaking melodramas whose popularity had waned. Some critics found his libretto both too full of his own mannerisms and too confused: a later commentator winced at 'its crude contrasts, its unbelievable motives and its somewhat harsh character-drawing'. Further confusion came from Sullivan's music, which some listeners thought redeemed the piece, while others felt it smacked too often of grand opera. With all these frailties, *Ruddigore* was not one of the duo's prime successes, and, though its stock has risen a good deal since 1887, it still seems an uncomfortable work, exposing its creators' conflicting points of view. Despite attractive qualities and great moments, it is not quite synchronized and comes across as a much odder work than the 'very odd' *Mikado*.

As its original audience was well aware, Gilbert's starting-point for his 'supernatural opera' was transpontine melodrama, a far-fetched theatrical genre most often seen in the poky houses south of the Thames. Its conventions included the heavy villain, usually a debauched baronet, bent on seducing a pure and virtuous village maid. His machinations were barely foiled by the arrival of a strapping young sailor who then took the maiden as his bride.

Gilbert's village is Rederring, in Cornwall, at the time of the Napoleonic wars. The first inhabitants we meet are a chorus of full-time bridesmaids, endowed by charity, who come every morning to the cottage of Rose Maybud to see if this may be the day she will be married. The girls' last wedding was over six months ago, and Rose is the village's ideal marital candidate. The trouble is she is too ideal. 'Appalled by her beauty and modesty', all the local young men are too tongue-tied to propose.

One of the maidens suggests to the elderly Dame Hannah that she might still wed, but the 'nice old person' reveals she is pledged to eternal maidenhood. Years ago she was wooed unawares by Sir Roderic Murgatroyd, one of the bad Baronets of Ruddigore. When she discovered his identity, she rejected him, wanting no part of the doom placed on the family two hundred years before when Sir Rupert Murgatroyd, a renowned persecutor of witches, was cursed by one of his victims. He and each heir to his title were bound to do an evil deed each day or die in agony. Ever since, the Baronets of Ruddigore have committed their daily sin until, racked by guilt, they have defied the curse and suffered the consequences.

Rose Maybud emerges from her cottage, bent on her curious good deeds, like taking a pound of snuff to an orphan girl. Hannah chides her for not marrying: if she loves someone, she should take the initiative. But Rose's life is governed by the book of etiquette that was left with her as a foundling child, and such forwardness would be impossible. The maiden's problem is illustrated when Robin Oakapple, a very eligible, very shy young farmer, appears. Though they fancy each other, the couple conceal their feelings behind the pretence of seeking advice for lovelorn friends.

After this tender but unsatisfactory exchange, Rose departs. Robin's faithful servant Adam enters and addresses his master by his true name: Sir Ruthven Murgatroyd. Twenty years ago Robin/Ruthven, rightful heir to the Ruddigore baronetcy, tried to evade the title and its curse by flight. Presumed dead, he was replaced by his younger brother, Despard.

Robin's true identity is known only to Adam and to Robin's dashing 'foster-brother and dearest friend', Richard Dauntless, who has just arrived in Rederring after ten years at sea. After Richard describes how he and his shipmates gallantly spared the feeble French, Robin confesses his own feebleness at wooing Rose Maybud. Shyness is no problem for Richard, who always acts according to the dictates of his heart. He offers to speak to Rose on his foster-brother's behalf. But when he sees her, his heart insists he speak for himself, and Rose accepts him, to Robin's consternation. But Rose's heart is erratic too. Aware now of Robin's feelings, recalling his prosperous farm and uncertain about being a sailor's wife, she blithely changes partners.

The confused threesome is followed by another victim of the heart, Mad Margaret, whose hopeless love for the bad Sir Despard has cost her her wits. She has come to Rederring to pinch Rose, out of jealousy, because the wicked Baronet intends to abduct her. Despard arrives, preceded by a rakish crew of 'Bucks and Blades'. They are dangerously handsome in military uniforms, he menacingly ugly as a bad Baronet must be, and all the bridesmaids recoil from him.

Sir Despard laments the Ruddigore curse and the glowering pictures of his ancestors that enforce it. But Richard Dauntless suddenly appears to save him. The sailor's heart requires that he expose Robin as the true Ruddigore heir, and, as Robin, Rose and the bridesmaids prepare for the wedding, Despard dramatically demands that his elder brother assume the title and its doom. Rose, of course, abandons her fiancé at once and turns to Despard, but now he is free to wed Mad Margaret. She finally reaccepts Richard, and the act ends with the new couples dancing gaily, and the new Baronet of Ruddigore falling senseless in their midst.

Act II finds Robin transformed from worthy yeoman to wicked knight. However reluctantly, he and Adam have been partners in crime for a week, and when Richard and Rose come to seek permission to marry, he threatens to cast her into a dungeon. The scheme is foiled only when Richard unfurls a Union Jack. Moved by Rose's appeal, Robin agrees to their marriage. Then he addresses the forbidding pictures of his Ruddigore ancestors. Are the rather mild evil deeds he has committed so far acceptable to them? In a harrowing scene, the pictures come to life and denounce him. He must be more wicked, or they will torment him. Desperate, Robin agrees and dispatches Adam to abduct a village maiden.

Despard and Margaret enters to relate the delights of their new sober respectability. Margaret still occasionally lapses into her old madness, which Despard relieves by means of a secret word: 'Basingstoke'. The former Baronet has come to urge his brother to cease his wickedness and defy the curse, whatever the cost. Robin consents, but Adam rushes in with his kidnapped maiden. She turns out to be the enraged Dame Hannah, who so intimidates Robin that he calls to his ancestors for help. Hannah's old love, Sir Roderic, suddenly comes to life before her. He dismisses his nephew, and the bizarrely reunited couple recall their old love.

They are interrupted when Robin announces that he has hit on an ingenious way around the curse. Since a Baronet can only die by not committing his daily crime, not committing that crime is tantamount to suicide—which is a crime in itself. Therefore defying the curse is actually fulfilling its terms. No longer the bad Baronet, Robin reclaims Rose over Richard's protests (though he quickly pairs up with one of the bridesmaids), the resurrected Sir Roderic stays alive to marry Hannah, and everyone celebrates the end of the curse and the beginning of bliss.

If Gilbert had had his way, *The Mikado*'s successor would have been, as he had written to Sullivan, 'the admirable plot I proposed to you last year', i.e. the stubborn lozenge. But Sir Arthur discouraged him so suavely that he set his pet project aside (temporarily) with no hurt feelings. *Ruddigore* came from several sources. Melodrama supplied the mood and characters, and Gilbert's earlier production, *Ages Ago*—at a rehearsal for which he had first met Sullivan—provided the theatrical coup of ancestral portraits coming to life. A couple of *Bab Ballads* had an influence too, for instance 'Thomas Winterbottom Hance', in which for years a British soldier and his French counterpart scorn and threaten each other, without ever coming to blows. *Ruddigore*'s obvious antecedents among the operas include *The Pirates of Penzance*, another burlesque where the story's basic outline is sung by a matronly lady and where enslavement to duty is a vital theme, and *The Sorcerer*, with its pleasant village setting, marital preoccupation and dealings with the supernatural.

Gilbert read his plot to his partner in January 1886. Sullivan accepted it but did not turn at once to composing the music, first because *The Mikado* seemed likely to go on and on, secondly because he was committed to his cantata, *The Golden Legend*, which was scheduled for performance in the autumn, and finally because of an attack of his 'natural indolence', which for a while made him neglect all his work. He was much more interested in attending race meetings and soirées and playing host to the visiting Franz Lizst. In April, when Gilbert rebuked him for his lethargy, Sullivan 'gave it to him back', as he told his diary, and complained, 'Do they think me a barrel-organ?'

In October *The Golden Legend* had a great success. Sullivan was bombarded with flowers from the audience and choir and with magnificent bouquets from the critics, one of whom dubbed him 'the Mozart of England'. Other performances of the piece were scheduled, as the composition of *Ruddigore* got under way at last. Sullivan went from rehearsing one piece to writing the other, and the grander work might have influenced the lighter one. Gilbert had congratulated his collaborator on the cantata's enthusiastic reception, calling it 'from all accounts . . . the biggest thing you've done'. But he was worried about that bigness distorting the score for his libretto. Midway through *Ruddigore*'s rehearsals he observed to a mutual friend that, 'though to my uninstructed ear, nothing could be better than the music, there is so much of it that I am afraid the audience will lose the thread of the story and forget what it is all about. Perhaps you could suggest to Sullivan that if one or two numbers were cut the piece would move more briskly.'

It is doubtful the friend was willing, but in any case he did not get the chance. When he saw Sullivan, the composer asked, 'How do you think the piece is shaping? It is supposed to be an opera, but it is really becoming a play with a few songs and some concerted music. Don't you think it would be as well to hint to Gilbert that the music is disappearing in the background?'

The very Gilbertian opera was proving something of a strain to the musical instincts of 'the Mozart of England'. But Gilbert had his instincts too and was equally uneasy at seeing them subverted. The friend may have decided just to ignore *Ruddigore* altogether.

Rehearsals went smoothly enough, however, and at one point the two collaborators displayed perfect professional harmony. Gilbert expressed slight dissatisfaction with Sullivan's setting for the bridesmaids' chorus. He could not specify exactly what troubled him; something seemed to lack lift. The composer pondered a moment, changed a note value, and the librettist was delighted.

One of the show's surprises also came about at rehearsal, recalling Gilbert's 'modified rapture' stroke in *The Mikado*. It involved the same performer, the tenor Durward Lely, who was playing Richard Dauntless. At the first run-through of his bragging song against the French, he observed that it sounded as if it ought to be followed by a hornpipe. Gilbert's only response was a grunt, then a few days of silence. But he suddenly came up to Lely and asked him if he could dance a hornpipe. Lely replied he had never tried, and the librettist sent him to the dancing master for a test. Lely passed, and Gilbert said, 'Right. I'll get Arthur to write you one.' On opening night the sight of a tenor not only moving his limbs but using them to dance caused a sensation, earning a double encore.

At another rehearsal, however, Lely got a taste of Gilbert's *idée fixe*. The author appeared from the back of the hall and praised his performance but objected that 'There were one or two words which failed to reach me quite distinctly. Sullivan's music is, of course, very beautiful, and I heard every note without difficulty, but I think my words are not altogether without merit, and ought also to be heard without undue effort. Please pay particular attention to the consonants, the Ms, the Ns, and especially the Ss.'

He was also as attentive as ever to detail and spectacle in the staging. *Ruddigore* may not have been able to boast authentic Japanese fashions, but it did produce some pomp of its own, in the Act I entrance of the Bucks and Blades. Gilbert dressed them in exact replicas of the uniforms twenty different British Army regiments would have worn about 1815. No less a figure than Field Marshal Lord Wolseley agreed to review their authenticity, though at the last moment he sent his Quartermaster-General instead. (Some modern productions have dispensed with the uniforms and deck the men's chorus out as a collection of Regency dandies, à la Beau Brummel.) Uniforms and props cost

£6,000; the two sets were £1,000 each, making *Ruddigore* the most expensive Savoy production yet.

Ruddigore received more advance publicity than the other operas too: interest in how Gilbert and Sullivan would attempt to follow *The Mikado* was considerable. The Savoy campaign to preserve secrecy and foil the inevitable pirates attracted publicity as well, particularly concerning the name of the new piece. Gilbert wrote to one paper that even he would not know the name until just before opening night. Ten days before the event one journal had ascertained that the new work would parody 'old-fashioned melodrama'. Another had got wind of the picture transformation in Act II and promised its readers that the spectacle 'would be the most thrilling thing ever seen on a London stage'.

Such anticipation was good for ticket sales, which were very brisk right up to opening night. But when the première finally arrived, on 22 January 1887, all the speculation only added to the first-nighters' disappointment. They were uneasy before a note or a word had been heard, staring at the repellent title on their programmes. To Gilbert, 'Ruddygore' simply suggested the sanguinary qualities of melodrama; he did not consider it a variation on a term not used in polite society. That, however, was the way everyone else took it. One newspaper said the opera's name was 'not very happily selected', another that it was 'most unfortunate'.

Despite that initial shock, the first act was well received. Critics and audience found it neat, witty and tuneful. But the genial mood at the interval did not last long into the second act. Opinions differed as to where the displeasure began. One reviewer thought the Union Jack episode was too heavy-handed. More objected to the much-touted picture scene that followed. In theory it should have been stunning. Gilbert had made sure the paintings resembled the members of the Savoy chorus playing the Murgatroyd ancestors. The stage would go dark, machinery would silently raise the portraits, and when the lights went up, the eerie transformation would be revealed. (The spectral scene required another innovation, a glass baton with a glowing platinum wire inside so that the orchestra could see Sir Arthur's beat in the dark.)

However, neither audience nor critics were won over by Gilbert's legerdemain. One writer called it 'a very tame affair', especially after the 'preliminary notices and hints . . . which had led one to expect much'. He found the carefully wrought portraits 'a set of ugly daubs' and the stage business primitive, especially since two of the machines raising the pictures misfired. The same critic said Sullivan's music for the scene was 'pitched in the wrong key', entirely too serious, as if the ancestral ghosts 'were a dread reality coming straight from the charnel house'. Another scribe made the same objection and referred directly to the composer's divided loyalties: 'It may be set down to Sir Arthur Sullivan's credit as a musician, but scores against him as a dramatist, that many parts of this "ghost scene" might well be transplanted into serious opera.'

Much worse was to come. If the brilliant Savoy assembly were dissatisfied by the ghost scene, a good number were close to contemptuous of the opera's conclusion. As presented on that first night—but not for very long after—instead of only Sir Roderick receiving a new lease of life, *all* the fated Murgatroyds were resurrected, and in the gay finale the former ghosts and the bridesmaids happily embraced. This astounding turn of events vastly overstrained the audience's indulgence—as Sullivan, in fact, had feared it would. They did not object so much to the slightly grisly aspect of the scene, perhaps, but to such an outlandish resolution of the plot. One paper said it was unworthy of *opéra bouffe*. Of course the many good things about the opera guaranteed a generally warm response, but there was no mistaking the minority strain of boos and hisses clearly directed at the work's authors. There were even cries of 'Bring back *The Mikado*!'

It was too late for that, but Gilbert and Sullivan did what they could with the piece in hand. The very next day they met to recast the second act. Gilbert rewrote one patter song completely and did a good deal of pruning. (In one case the pruning was confusingly incomplete. In the original second act he had changed Adam's name to the melodramatic 'Gideon Crawle' to go with his master's new wicked identity. Revising, he cut the verse where the change was introduced but left one reference to Gideon Crawle in the dialogue, where it remained for many years and many editions.) Above all, except for Roderic, Gilbert returned the Murgatroyds to the dearly departed. He also altered the manner of Roderic's reappearance. On the first night the old Baronet, like John Wellington Wells in reverse, had risen from a trap door, with simulated flames billowing around him. Perhaps Gilbert considered this entrance dated, or thought the suggestion of where Roderic had been spending his afterlife rather too bold. At any rate the old ghost subsequently descended from his picture, as he had earlier.

Gilbert also gave way on the sticky matter of the title. He wanted to change it first to *Kensington Gore; or, Robin and Richard were Two Pretty Men*, but Sullivan and Carte objected. Then, in view of the audience's protests, he peevishly suggested *Kensington Gore; or, Not so Good as The Mikado*. Finally, he simply changed the middle 'y' to 'i' and hoped for the best.

The alterations went into effect in the piece's second week. Sullivan added a new finale, and the Press reported that the changes made for 'greater briskness'. As if the collaborators had not had enough trouble with unfriendly criticism, they also had to contend with a small international incident. Richard Dauntless's solo, in which he describes the encounter between his sloop and a French frigate, was taken as a slur on Gallic honour. The London correspondent of *Le Figaro* attended the opening night performance, and his dispatch to Paris excited several naval and military tempers. The fact that in the song Richard's bragging is intended to cover up a hasty British retreat made no difference to the French. Neither did Lely's hornpipe. So Gilbert and Sullivan composed a placating letter to the newspaper which seemed to have the desired effect. More justifiable chagrin came from certain British patriots, but G & S ignored them.

Ruddigore's opening run was less than half as long as its illustrious predecessor's, 288 performances in all. Its supposed failure always rankled with Gilbert, who was quite proud of his libretto. He defied critics by saying the 'failure' had put £7,000 in his pocket. It also took him a while to admit his choice of title had been unwise, though at length he did. During the work's early days he had tried to insist that those who took offence were simply missing the point. An acquaintance once inquired how 'Bloodygore' was faring. Gilbert protested it was *Ruddigore*, but his friend nonchalantly replied it was the same thing. Gilbert bristled 'Is it? Then I suppose you'll take it that if I say "I admire your ruddy countenance", I mean "I like your bloody cheek!"'

Though he accepted responsibility for the opera's only moderate success, he believed all the same that Sullivan's grandiose music had had a share in it. The reviewers had not helped matters by praising the score, on the whole, and attributing to it more than half the show's appeal. But the disgruntled librettist felt that the effect of the ghost music was like inserting 'fifty lines of *Paradise Lost* into a farcical comedy'. He suggested that his partner 'thought his professional position demanded something grander and more impressive than the words suggested'. And when he considered reviving the opera after Sullivan's death, he had no hesitation in proposing to 'cut a good deal of the heavy music in Act II'.

Present day audiences do not share Gilbert's jaundiced opinion of Sullivan's 'heavy music'. Indeed the score as a whole, particularly in the second act, has done much to secure *Ruddigore*'s modern reputation. The trouble with the opera is that, like *Princess Ida*, it was clearly written by two people. It is tempting to agree with Sullivan's assessment of the work; much of it does seem to be a play with music, and quite a waspish play at that. Critics had often accused Gilbert of being cynical, even in *The Mikado*. But *Ruddigore*'s caustic spirit only emphasizes how comparatively tender and unified the Japanese opera is.

The difference between the two works is due largely to the characters in each, their motivations and Gilbert's satiric treatment of them. Satire is really not predominant in *The Mikado*. The dangers of autocracy are arraigned a little, and Pooh-Bah is a humorous example of opportunism in action, but the play's charm lies in its timeless, fairy-tale fantasy. The characters are simple and human: Nanki-Poo and Yum-Yum want to get married; Ko-Ko wants to save his head. They are all threatened—and the whole action of the play is shaped—by the gigantic whims of the Mikado. His laws may be arbitrary, but they bind all his subjects, and the little creatures' schemes to get around their emperor give the opera its jollity.

But in *Ruddigore* Gilbert is the Mikado. The play is satiric through and through, and the satire is based on his favourite premise—that human beings are purely mechanical, motivated by self-interest and dominated by rigid codes. This bleak prospect makes *Ruddigore*'s humour especially wicked and its action relentlessly dog-eat-dog. (Its background is also darker than *The Mikado*'s, where, despite the talk of decapitation and boiling oil, the only real casualty is Ko-Ko's tom-tit. Dame Hannah's description of Sir Rupert's dying witches is much crueller than anything in the earlier piece.) In a way, Gilbert has succeeded in foisting on Sullivan a version of his lozenge plot, whose basic principle is mechanical self-interest. Years later, when the librettist did stage the lozenge in the opera *The Mountebanks* (without Sullivan), he included a quatrain that applies to much of *Ruddigore* as well:

> 'Clockwork figures may be found
> Everywhere and all around.
> Ten to one, if we but knew,
> You are clockwork figures too.'

Though *Ruddigore* does burlesque hoary melodramas, Gilbert uses the genre's stereotypes as models of the stereotypes human beings live by anyway. Most of *Ruddigore*'s people are locked in a role. The most obvious is that of the doomed Baronet who must adopt the personality and conduct that go with his curse. Sir Despard's song 'Oh, why am I moody and sad?' is a list of villainous clichés, from his tormented disposition to a voice 'husky and hoarse' and an expression 'warped and destroyed'. When the blight passes to Robin (who does not seem to have much personality of his own anyway), he is helplessly transformed from 'pure and blameless peasant' to 'bad Bart' and opens Act II skulking about the stage 'wearing the haggard aspect of a guilty roué' (as Gilbert's directions indicate) and emitting spine-chilling laughter.

The other characters may not be cursed, but they have similarly mechanical motivations, of which Rose Maybud is the most delicious example. She is drawn from the innocent, virtuous heroine of melodrama, but her total allegiance to her book of etiquette is an original Gilbertian stroke. For Gilbert, a slavish devotion to the precepts of 'proper manners' was one of the most ridiculous instances of social unreality. (His *Bab Ballad* simply titled 'Etiquette' told of two castaways on a desert island whose relations were poisoned by their deference to 'good breeding'.)

Constantly dipping into her little tome for instruction on how to behave, Rose is amusing enough, but Gilbert gives the satire another twist through her 'good deeds'—the snuff for the orphan girl, false teeth for a hearty lass and hard candy for an 'old gaffer' who probably has no teeth at all. Her other trait, of course, is self-interest. Her older sisters are Phyllis in *Iolanthe* and Yum-Yum, each the kind of Gilbertian girl who is aware of her effect. Rose knows she is 'sweet Rose Maybud'; knows too that, even though she has pledged herself to Richard, Robin is a riper catch: ' . . . behold, he is but a lowly mariner, and very poor withal, whereas thou art a tiller of the land, and thou hast fat oxen, and many sheep and swine, a considerable dairy farm and much corn and oil!'

It is a funny speech, made funnier by Rose's constant habit of expressing herself in the pious cadences of the King James Bible. What else would you expect from a virtuous village maid? Her conduct in the finale of Act I is utterly consistent. Having linked herself to Robin, she leaves him when he becomes the bad Bart, offering herself on the spot to Despard before winding up back with Richard.

For his part, Richard recalls several other Gilbertian swains in his devotion to duty, conscience, his heart and himself. Frederick, Ralph Rackstraw and Strephon come to mind, but Richard is certainly the purest case of the romantic young man, as bound to his heart as Rose is to her etiquette. But hearts do veer about according to their owners' desires. Richard and Rose are well matched, and in their jolly trio with Robin they agree that,

> 'In sailing o'er life's ocean wide
> No doubt the heart should be your guide,
> But it is awkward when you find
> A heart that does not know its mind!'

Hearts never do, Gilbert would say: they only know what they want. Rather fittingly, the trio is one of the few moments in G & S where a switch in the plot occurs in a musical number instead of in dialogue: Rose's heart carries her from poor Richard to wealthy Robin by the song's end.

Changes of mind and, even more, betrayals run rampant in *Ruddi-*

gore, with characters following the main chance whatever their justification. The first bit of chicanery has occurred before the opera begins, and is perhaps the most understandable: Robin has fled to avoid the doom of the Ruddigores but has thereby doomed his younger brother. Richard betrays Robin by pleading his own suit to Rose, and Rose then throws him over for Robin. Ever dauntless, Richard exposes Robin to Sir Despard to get Rose back, and Rose obligingly leaves Robin when Despard reveals who he is.

The moral atmosphere is not very sunny, and Gilbert darkens it further by making sacred matrimony the butt of the joke. We have seen the librettist's dubious view of love and marriage before. Here it becomes the most mechanical of all desires. His creation of the professional bridesmaids, ready on the spot for any whiff of a wedding, is maliciously perfect. So is using the same melody (which may have been Sullivan's inspiration) for their opening chorus, 'Fair is Rose as the bright May-day', and for the marital hymn 'Hail the Bridegroom—hail the Bride' which is a maddening refrain whenever the girls appear, clutching their bouquets. In this opera, Rose does seem to be the spirit of the marital urge.

Again, the atmosphere is very different from *The Mikado*. There too marriage is important, but the only alliance—leaving aside Ko-Ko's last-ditch bid for Katisha—is that of Nanki-Poo and Yum-Yum. There is none of the wholesale, wind-up, almost manic view of the institution that marks *Ruddigore*. In *The Mikado*'s finale, the marriage of the young lovers is a happy escape from the fate that has dogged them throughout. *Ruddigore* ends with everybody pairing up as they celebrate the joy of 'a lover . . . when he embraces his bride!' But from what the opera has shown us, it appears a pretty hollow, even cynical gesture, and it must have been infinitely worse—an outright sneer—in Gilbert's rather ghoulish original version, with each resuscitated Murgatroyd taking a bridesmaid to have and to hold.

Obviously a mood like this would make the song-writing side of the opera somewhat difficult. Act I is full of peppery numbers, narrative and patter songs, and bright ensembles, but, predictably, there is not much lyricism around. Sullivan gives Rose a romantic, quite Viennese strain as the second half of her solo 'If somebody there chanced to be', but the number's main interest is Gilbert's discussion of the problems of encouraging swains while obeying the laws of good manners. Her duet with Robin, 'I know a youth who loves a little maid', is a wholly charming piece in an Old English pastoral mode, reminiscent of 'Prithee, pretty maiden' in *Patience*. But her duet with Richard, 'The battle's roar is over', is most unconvincing and is usually cut in performance. Sullivan's attempt at an operatic love theme simply does not fit these people or this situation. In addition, Richard, who until now has been the epitome of the slangy, plain-spoken sailor-lad, suddenly sounds nothing like his old self. A line like 'embrace thy tender lover, O my love' is as alien to him as etiquette would be.

Among the act's set pieces, Sullivan's atmospheric introduction to Mad Margaret's 'Cheerily carols the lark' is distinctive, with its virtuouso writing for the flute and apt orchestral accompaniment to her disturbed ramblings. (Mad Margaret herself was based on that classic study of female insanity, Ophelia in *Hamlet*.) But her ballad 'To a garden full of posies' is somehow awkward, Sullivan's melody sitting uncomfortably beneath Gilbert's rather clogged lyrics. Later in the act Sullivan presents a much more elaborate madrigal than his little gem in *The Mikado*. ''When the buds are blossoming'' has impressive sections, particularly those for the chorus alone, but on the whole it too is not quite convincing, out of place in Act I's uneasy emotional climate.

But Act II is, literally, a different story. For one thing it emphasizes not the satiric machinations of the characters, jostling for marital positions, but the hereditary curse of Ruddigore. As burlesque it is funny, and Sullivan gives Robin and his faithful servant Adam appropriately creepy music to announce their instant corruption into bad young Bart and steward. But soon an extraordinary change occurs.

Though his work in the first act is certainly well done, we have the feeling that Sullivan has been chafing on the sidelines, waiting for a chance for the music 'to rise and speak for itself'. His opportunity comes with the ghosts' revivification. Such a change of mood need not have taken place. Clearly Gilbert would have preferred that his partner turn out something relating the satiric and burlesque halves of the piece, rather than emphasizing the differences between them. He thought the scene could 'have been treated more humorously'. After all, the ghosts themselves say they are 'a jollier crew than you, perhaps, suppose'. But it is hard to argue with Sullivan's interpretation of Gilbert's lyrics, not just because the results are magnificent but because the lyrics are what they are. From the opening line, 'When the night wind howls in the chimney cowls, and the bat in the moonlight flies', the aura of mystery is established. As the song unfolds, other details make the mood not only mysterious but awesome. Gilbert may have intended a mock-ghostly effect, but his reference to tombstones where 'are gathered the bones that once were women and men' is decidedly eerie and even moving. The same shiver attends the librettist's image of each spectral escort saluting his lady 'with a kiss, perhaps, on her lantern chaps. . .'. These are fairly hair-raising lyrics and might even have been in bad taste if Sullivan had not treated the scene with a solemnity at once robust and sensitive.

There is no question that the setting is one of his most remarkable achievements, with a tingling motif in the strings throughout, wonderful piping and shrieking in the woodwinds and really noble writing for the brass, especially at the close. The climax, with Sir Roderic and the chorus in full cry on 'high noon', is gloriously stirring. Despite Gilbert's doubts, this 'heavy music'—not really so heavy, but very impressive—introduces a much-needed new tone into the opera, besides being an unfailing show-stopper.

Sullivan takes a much more sombre line in the short anthem which opens and closes the scene:

> 'Painted emblems of a race,
> All accurst in days of yore,
> Each from his accustomed place
> Steps into the world once more.'

His setting is a lament of great dignity and yearning, and, simply reading Gilbert's words, we feel that this is the mood they require. The librettist seems almost to have put the idea of a comic opera before what he was actually inscribing. Sullivan has got inside the real atmosphere of the scene, in which these departed spirits suddenly return to the world, and all at once the 'comic opera' takes on another dimension.

Though a first-night critic declared that everything after the ghost scene was anti-climactic, the remainder of Act II contains at least two classics. Despard and Mad Margaret's born-again duet, 'I once was a very abandoned person', is sheer delight. Sullivan captures exactly their very strait-laced, very careful, rather precarious view of their reformed condition, as if the old mental goblins might still come back (for Margaret at least, they are very close at hand). The music is spare and subtly asymmetrical, with beautifully paced openings for woodwind commentary. The whole effect is of a sedate country dance gone ever so slightly awry.

One of *Ruddigore*'s clear triumphs is the well-known 'matter, matter, matter' patter trio for Robin, Despard and Margaret. It is a kind of offshoot of the 'short, sharp shock' number in *The Mikado* but is utterly unique. Each of the singers has his and her solo challenge—a roller-coaster verse to negotiate alone which the others launch with a sympathetic series of 'matters'. Then the three share a hearty climax to the classic statement 'This particularly rapid, unintelligible patter/ Isn't generally heard, and if it is it doesn't matter.' It is a truly perfect G & S collaboration, the idea clever and resourceful, the words funny and exact, the music witty and effective.

Finally, just before its conclusion, the opera gets its first taste of tenderness. Predictably, because this is *Ruddigore*, the circumstances are somewhat macabre—Dame Hannah sings to her old lover Sir

Roderic, who has just come back from the dead to renew his suit. But Sullivan takes the full measure of the moment, and 'There grew a little flower' becomes a deeply felt ballad of old devotion. It is most affecting in its refrain, with the reunited couple exchanging 'lackadays' in the best tradition of English folk-song.

Ruddigore has always had enthusiastic partisans, some for Gilbert's subversive libretto, some for Sullivan's dextrous settings and in particular the way he suddenly commandeers Act II. The two men themselves were proud of their respective contributions, though they were not sure about the other fellow's, and the discrepancy shows in the piece. Probably each man saw in the other's share the aspect of his colleague he most distrusted. With Gilbert it was Sullivan's hunger for grand emotions, with Sullivan, Gilbert's penchant for satire of a heartlessly mechanical type.

The disagreement was not long in surfacing once more. *Ruddigore*'s checkered fortunes meant the Savoy would require a new piece soon. As a first proposal Gilbert poured out the die-hard lozenge. Sullivan half-heartedly consented to let his partner work it up to a more finished form before passing judgement. But four months later his diary told the same old story: 'It is a puppet show, and not human. It is impossible to feel any sympathy with a single person. I don't see my way to setting it in its present form.' In at least part of *Ruddigore*, he had been there before.

10

The Yeomen Of The Guard;

or, The Merryman and his Maid

All the Savoy operas inspire affection, but reverence is reserved for *The Yeomen of the Guard.* Critics speak of it as 'the serious opera'. Reginald Allen, in his fascinating *The First Night Gilbert & Sullivan,* points out that, while all its predecessors' programmes contain some descriptive word before the title—*Ruddigore,* for instance, is 'An Entirely Original Supernatural Opera'—*Yeomen* is simply 'A New and Original Opera'. The difference is subtle but striking, as though the collaborators were coming out of the closet at last. When Gilbert abandoned his beloved lozenge and informed his partner of his plans for an historical subject, Sullivan saw at once that it was 'an entirely new departure'. A year later, a critic reviewing the work's opening night used exactly the same phrase. Here was a Savoy piece untainted by burlesque elements, essentially free from the topsy-turvy whimsy of the past. Of course there was wit, but there was also gravity, solemnity and pathos. It was, said another reviewer, 'a genuine English opera'. Convinced it was genuinely grand, both Gilbert and Sullivan believed it was their finest work together. Unfortunately it was not the most popular, despite early enthusiasm. Its record of 433 performances was better than *Ruddigore* though still 'not so good as *The Mikado*', which disappointed its creators, who hoped their ambition would be suitably rewarded. It has been, since then, by the devotion of many Savoyards. But *The Yeomen of the Guard* does seem to be a mixture of impulses, an attempt perhaps to do too many, and even contrary things. A later critic refers to 'that curious incompleteness which is both its strength and its weakness', but its strong moments are still some of the finest in the Gilbert and Sullivan *oeuvre.*

At first glance, it is curious that Gilbert, after his complaints about *Ruddigore*'s 'heavy music', should have been so willing to provide his partner with a chance for more of the same. But Sullivan's discontent was clearly not going to go away and required some kind of outlet if the partnership was going to survive. In addition, despite his keen sense of the theatrical marketplace, Gilbert cherished some heavy ideals of his own. They appear to some extent in the operas, in his satiric onslaughts against human folly, but even more openly in his later plays. Closest to his heart were *Broken Hearts* (1875) and *Gretchen* (1879). The first is a fantastic work about four ladies, three of them wounded by love, who have renounced man *Princess Ida*-style and sequestered themselves on a desert island. To make up for their loss, they transfer their affection to inanimate objects—a fountain, a sun-dial and a hand-mirror. Nothing about the play, including Gilbert's wooden blank verse, augured success, and it had a mercifully short run. The 1879 piece was a sentimental Gilbertian version of the Faust legend. It ran for fourteen nights. With so brief a life it was easy to miss, and an acquaintance, having only heard about the ambitious drama, asked its author what it was called. Gilbert did not spare himself. 'I called it *Gretchen*,' he said. 'The public called it rot.'

The satirist took these failures badly, because they were his bid for serious consideration as a playwright. They only confirmed his low opinion of public and critical taste, and he went back to wearing the cap and bells—and carrying a bare bodkin—at the Savoy. But he always hankered for another chance to display his depths rather than his shallows. He may have been encouraged as early as 1882, when, after *Patience*, an article in *The Athenaeum* exhorted him to 'pen a dramatic poem suitable for the exercise of the highest musicianly art . . . a lyric drama in which poetry and music shall be blended, neither being permitted an advantage at the expense of the other'. And, after *Ruddigore*, another writer urged him to stop churning out the same ten-year-old fare and attempt 'a real comic opera, dealing with neither topsy-turveydom nor fairies, but a genuine dramatic story, written with all Mr. W. S. Gilbert's masterly power, and set to such music as Sir Arthur Sullivan alone can compose. . .'.

It might have been a commission for *The Yeomen of the Guard*. At any rate Gilbert's muse was as eager for higher flight as Sullivan's. Specific inspiration arrived in a flash, as it supposedly had for *The Mikado*. Waiting on a railway platform, the librettist noticed a poster advertising the Tower Furnishing Company with a picture of the Tower of London. It was a short step from the old fortress to the image of a richly garbed beefeater, and, as he told a later interviewer, it occurred to him that 'a beefeater would make a good picturesque central figure for another Savoy opera.' His first inclination was 'to give it a modern setting, with the characteristics and development of burlesque—to make it another *Sorcerer*'. But almost at once deeper conceptions began stirring, and he 'decided to make it a romantic and dramatic piece, and to put it back into Elizabethan times'.

The subject was ideal, with opportunities for an imposing set of the grim old fortress, and all its associations of history, heroism and tragedy. In addition, Gilbert deeply admired sixteenth- and seventeeth-century writing, particularly the prose of the King James Bible (he had satirized Rose Maybud from the heart) and the lyric poets. His one gigantic blindspot was Shakespeare, of whom he registered his disapproval on several occasions. He told George Grossmith he did not find the bard 'rollicking', informed a correspondent that the great man's works 'should be kept off the boards' and in his last years called *King Lear* 'monstrous'. An Elizabethan motif would offer a chance of correcting Shakespeare, as well as paying homage to a period and style he loved.

Of course an Elizabethan play demanded a merryman, a figure automatically appealing to Gilbert. Shakespeare's clowns he found impenetrable and unfunny, and he had already created Jack Point's ancestor for an early issue of *Fun* magazine, in a character called Jumbles the Jester. His youthful career also came to his aid in the *Bab Ballad* 'Annie Protheroe', a touching story of a girl engaged to the Public Headsman, who jilts him for the man he is about to execute.

Doing his usual meticulous research, Gilbert read widely and pondered deeply. But the most valuable part of his preparations consisted of many trips to the Tower itself, during which he imbibed the atmosphere of the ancient edifice, making copious notes and sketches and feeling his own saga of the legendary place take shape.

As it turned out, Gilbert's period piece was not 'Elizabethan'. He gives its date as the sixteenth century, but Wilfred Shadbolt's reference in Act II to pleasing his king means the tale predates Good Queen Bess. Despite that quibble it is full of Tudor colour, intrigue and romance, as well as Gilbert's on-again, off-again attempts at imitating sixteenth-century speech.

The action opens in a plaintive key, presenting not a men's or women's chorus but Sergeant Meryll's daughter Phoebe alone at her spinning-wheel on Tower Green. Her sighing soliloquy is interrupted by the brutish Wilfred Shadbolt, head jailor and assistant tormentor of the Tower, who knows she is pining for a man she has only seen from a distance—the handsome Colonel Fairfax, a brave soldier and ingenious alchemist who later that day will be executed for 'dealings with the devil'. The jealous jailor also knows Phoebe regards him and his office with loathing, in spite of his love for her. Sure enough, she snubs him again, and he calls her a 'heartless jade'.

In come a crowd of townspeople and a band of the noble Yeomen of the Guard, old soldiers all. The Yeomen greet Dame Carruthers, the matronly but tough housekeeper to the Tower who describes the preparations for the beheading of 'poor Colonel Fairfax'. The beefeaters lament him, and Phoebe bursts into a tirade against the injustice of the sentence, and 'this wicked tower' as well. But Dame Carruthers staunchly defends the ancient bastion and its associations both grim and glorious.

Left alone, the agitated Phoebe is joined by her father, Sergeant Meryll, who tells her that a hoped-for reprieve has not yet arrived. However, her brother Leonard, recently appointed a Yeoman for gallantry in battle, may yet bring it when he comes from Windsor Castle. The Sergeant is determined to save Fairfax, who has twice saved him, and when his son appears without the pardon, he concocts a spur-of-the-moment scheme. Since Leonard has arrived unseen, Fairfax might be able to take his place among the Yeomen undetected. But first the colonel must be freed, and the Sergeant gives the coquettish Phoebe the task of spiriting the keys away from her loutish admirer Shadbolt.

Leonard departs, but Fairfax himself enters under guard before the Merylls can put their plan into action. His philosophic calm upsets Phoebe all the more, and her father leads her off weeping. But Fairfax has a scheme of his own to enact—not to escape the block but to keep the unscrupulous kinsman who trumped up the charge against him from inheriting his estate. It passes to him only if Fairfax dies unmarried; hence, the colonel wants a bride. Though she will be a widow within an hour, he will thwart his kinsman, and she will be 100 crowns richer. The Lieutenant of the Tower agrees to find the colonel a temporary wife.

The atmosphere of intrigue is shattered by the raucous entrance of Jack Point and Elsie Maynard, two 'strolling players', pursued by a crowd of rowdy townspeople. The mob is barely pacified by their singing and dancing, and only the appearance of the Lieutenant and his guard rescues them. When the officer learns that the jester and his pretty fiancée are trying to earn money to treat her sick mother, he proposes that Elsie wed Fairfax. The pair are taken aback but accept when assured that the colonel will die in half-an-hour. Elsie is led off blind-folded, while Point tries out his routines on the Lieutenant. When Elsie returns, she is married.

With Fairfax's plan accomplished, the Meryll's plot gets under way. Phoebe soon has Shadbolt eating out of one hand while, with the other, she passes his keys to her father. The besotted jailor notices neither their removal nor their return and stumbles after Phoebe, amazed at her unexpected wooing. Straightaway her father appears, followed by Fairfax, free, clean-shaven and in Yeoman's uniform. The deception seems successful as his fellow beefeaters parade in and hail him as the valiant Leonard Meryll. After a moment of mystification he 'recognizes' his sister Phoebe and meets the smitten Shadbolt, who doesn't mind a few innocent kisses between a girl and her brother. But the pleasant reunion is interrupted first by the gloomy entrance of the Headsman and his block, and then by shouts that his intended victim has escaped. The act ends in consternation as the Yeomen hunt the fugitive, and Jack Point and Elsie realize with horror that she is still a wife. Ironically, as the curtain falls, Elsie faints into the arms of 'Leonard Meryll', the very man she married.

Confusion still reigns in Act II. Dame Carruthers scolds the warders for their laxity. Jack Point mopes about and half-heartedly pokes fun at the disgraced Shadbolt. But the jailor's interest in the merryman's craft gives Point an idea for regaining his fiancée. In return for instruction in the secrets of jesting, Shadbolt agrees to claim he has shot Fairfax, while the fugitive was swimming the river.

Fairfax himself, still in disguise, bemoans his hasty marriage to an unknown woman. Then, coincidentally, Dame Carruthers reveals that, while she was nursing the delirious Elsie Maynard, the girl babbled phrases that make the Dame sure she must have married the escaped man. Sergeant Meryll is amazed and questions Fairfax, who denies everything. But the colonel resolves to test his newly found wife's principles. Alone with Elsie, 'Leonard Meryll' proclaims his love, denounces her missing husband and begs her to fly with him. Terrified, Elsie resists, when a shot is heard. Shadbolt has carried out Jack Point's ruse, and he and the jester describe Fairfax's demise.

The merryman observes hopefully that Elsie is now free to choose again. Fairfax offers to give him a lesson in wooing but actually pleads his own suit as Leonard, and Elsie accepts him. Point is undone again, and Phoebe, who wanted Fairfax for herself, is heartbroken. When Shadbolt asks the reason for her tears, she blurts out enough to make him realize that Leonard is Fairfax. Resourceful Phoebe saves the day first by reminding the jailor that he has sworn he killed Fairfax, and then by offering him if not her heart at least her hand, in exchange for his silence.

Suddenly her brother rushes in, with news that the colonel's reprieve, maliciously held up by the ubiquitous kinsman, has come through at last. Sergeant Meryll joins in the celebrations, learning at the same time of his daughter's forced pact with Shadbolt. The old soldier grimly declares that, though it is too bad, she must suffer for letting the secret out. But he suffers the same fate at the hands of Dame Carruthers, who has overheard him and will reveal all unless he marries *her*.

One more crisis remains. As everyone assembles for Elsie's second wedding, the Lieutenant announces that the bride's first husband still lives. The sorely tried maiden is stunned again, but her anguish is quickly relieved when it turns out that first husband and second husband-to-be are the same man. The final, general rejoicing is marred only by the tremulous figure of Jack Point, who makes a last appeal to his former fiancée before falling insensible at her feet.

As Sullivan's diary entry for Christmas 1887 showed, he was as attracted by the possibilities of the new project as his partner was: 'Gilbert read plot of new piece (Tower of London); immensely pleased with it. Pretty story, no topsy-turveydom, very human and funny also.' It seemed just what he had been asking for, the very departure Gilbert had promised. Yet some three months later, the composer was writing to the librettist that he had had another crisis of artistic conscience: he wanted to write more substantial works than the Savoy format permitted. Another comic opera, *Dorothy* was enjoying a *succès fou* in London; obviously pieces of the type so far associated with Gilbert and Sullivan were no longer their exclusive property. Sullivan wanted to move to grander opera, with a new theatre and a new company, and Carte, who still had his dream of reviving English opera, supported him.

But Gilbert would not be budged. In reply to his colleague, he cited their long string of successes, the ideal operation they had built up over many years, and their status: ' . . . we are world-known, and as much an institution as Westminster Abbey—and to scatter this splendid organization because *Dorothy* has run 500 nights is, to my way of thinking, to give up a gold mine.' Commerce and reason prevailed, the Savoy remained and the new opera proceeded. Relations between the three partners, however, could not be called tranquil. Gilbert and Carte had a considerable row, when, through a misunderstanding, the librettist arrived late for a rehearsal. Carte wired the vacationing Sullivan that he did not 'really see how things are to go on', though two days later he reported 'peace for the moment'.

The personal bond that Carte and Sullivan shared, and from which Gilbert was to an extent excluded, showed itself in April 1888, when Carte married his secretary, Helen Lenoir, with the composer as best man. A month later Sullivan's sense of artistic responsibility—from which Gilbert was also rather excluded—was fired by a passing comment from his Sovereign. He conducted *The Golden Legend* at the Albert Hall, in the presence of Queen Victoria, who told him afterwards, 'At last I have heard *The Golden Legend*, Sir Arthur! You ought to write a grand opera—you would do it so well.'

Personal and professional strains continued to surface during the new opera's creation. In mid-August Sullivan wanted part of Act II rewritten for the sake of musical effectiveness. By letter, Gilbert refused, protesting it was too late. Sullivan, as he told his diary, 'wrote him back a snorter', saying he 'wouldn't set the piece as it was'. Gilbert, though, turned 'mild and conciliatory', and a crisis was averted. But a month later the librettist's martinet side exploded, inciting a 'regular flare-up' at rehearsal. His long-suffering partner complained: 'He worried everyone and irritated me beyond bearing . . . I can't stand it any longer, and get as angry and irritable as he is.'

However, they patched this quarrel up too. Meanwhile Sullivan was having somewhat unaccustomed difficulty in composing. In one instance the cause was Gilbert's dissatisfaction. He balked at his collaborator's first two tries at the melody for Fairfax's song 'Is life a boon?', and Sullivan produced the present version only four days before opening night. He had much more trouble with the duet for Jack Point and Elsie Maynard, the famous 'I have a song to sing, O.' 'That blessed jingle', as he called it, stumped him for two weeks. For once his fluency failed, and as he picked away fruitlessly he told a friend, 'My dear fellow, I have a song to set-O, and I don't know how the dickens I'm going to do it.' Finally he turned to Gilbert for help, asking if a particular tune had suggested the lyrics to him. In fact, the librettist had got the germ of his idea from a sea shanty sung by the men on his yacht, and Sullivan insisted he hum it to him. As Gilbert said later, 'Only a rash man ever asks me to hum, but the situation was desperate.' Sullivan had his breakthrough almost immediately, exclaiming 'That will do—I've got it,' and hurried off to write his melody down. Gilbert thought perhaps his humming was simply more than his partner could bear, but Sullivan told him, 'It was the only time in your life when you were responsible for the music as well as the words.'

The Yeomen's opening night was set for 3 October 1888. Jitters were bound to increase as the date approached, and they were multiplied by the new work's novel character. Gilbert was even unsure what to call it. It had been *The Tower of London*, then *The Tower Warder*. In September he told Sullivan he was 'convinced . . . that *The Beefeaters* is the name for the new piece. It is a good, sturdy, solid name . . .'—very like beef, in fact. But Sullivan vetoed it as ugly, with perhaps a subconscious thought that a naked reference to meat was getting too close to *Ruddygore*.

In its review of the première, *Punch* observed that the ultimate title, *The Yeoman of the Guard; or, The Merryman and his Maid,* emphasized the curious, mixed nature of the work. 'Is it serious, or isn't it?' its critic wanted to know. The same question bedevilled Gilbert right up to the opening, and even beyond. On the morning of 3 October he gave Sullivan official notice that he thought the opening series of numbers was inappropriate. Even if a nostalgic song for Sergeant Meryll was deleted—as it was, after the first night—the sequence was still suspect: 'The act commences with Phoebe's song—*tearful in character*. This is followed by entrance of warders—*serious and martial in character*. This is followed by Dame Carruthers' "Tower" song—*grim in character*. This is followed by trio for Meryll, Phoebe and Leonard—*sentimental in character*. Thus it is that a professedly Comic Opera commences.'

Sullivan might have said the librettist had had plenty of time to consider how comic he wanted his opera to be. But it seems clear that Gilbert was simply suffering severe cold feet about having moved away from the old formulas. He and Sullivan did make some changes in the Act I finale only a few minutes before the overture. Then he carried his anxieties to Jessie Bond, the Savoy star whose responsibility it was to begin the whole opera, solo, as Phoebe. In her memoirs she recalled, 'He was almost beside himself with nervousness and excitement. . . . 'Gilbert kept fussing about, "Oh, Jessie, are you sure you're all right?"—Jessie this—Jessie that—until I was almost as demented as he was. At last I turned on him savagely. "For Heaven's sake, Mr. Gilbert, go away and leave me alone, or I shan't be able to sing a note!" He gave me a final frenzied hug, and vanished.'

The miserable librettist spent most of the evening staring at *The Armada*, a Tudor pageant by someone else at Drury Lane. But he returned to the Savoy in time for an ovation that was largely repeated in the next day's Press. Though a number of critics pointed out the resemblance between *The Yeomen*'s plot and that of *Maritana*, an opera by Vincent Wallace that also revolved around a mysterious prison wedding, almost all hailed the bold stroke the latest G & S opera represented: ' . . . the music follows the book to a higher plane,' one critic declared, and others welcomed it as 'more or less in the nature of an experiment'. Only *Punch* voiced the awkward question of its total effect, and the *Times* remarked on 'the weakness of the plot', going on to say that, though his lyrics were 'suave and good to sing', Gilbert had 'not written a good play' and that the piece's success would 'no doubt be largely due' to Sullivan's score.

Nonetheless, Gilbert told his partner he found 'the notices . . . very gratifying'. He would also have been gratified by the special reputation *The Yeomen* enjoyed in years to come, attracting praise of a kind very different from the other Savoy productions. Jessie Bond called it 'the most beautiful of all the Gilbert and Sullivan operas'. Chroniclers have referred to the 'high and natural tone of this magnificent masterpiece', to this 'perfect work of art'. One of the most famous of Jack Points, Henry Lytton, saw it as 'of all operas ever written, the one most essentially English', epitomizing the 'happy spirit of old Merrie England'.

That spirit certainly accounts for much of its appeal; Gilbert was as astute as ever in picking his subject and setting. The aura of England's Golden Age is hard to beat, and he piles on the associations: the implacable Tower with its picturesque citizens, the noble figure unfairly condemned, first one, then two maids yearning for him, and a series of intrigues and bizarre episodes that smack of Elizabethan tragedy. He also makes the most of the potent combination of tears and laughter, focussed on the one Savoy character who comes closest to representing Gilbert himself, poor Jack Point. Lovers of *The Yeoman* especially love the unfortunate jester and feel his pathos is responsible for the opera's uniqueness. Sullivan's music is, of course, indispensable and unique as well, worthy of the libretto's grand and diverse possibilities. (One distinguished critic has called it 'almost miniature *Mastersingers* at times'.)

All these elements are there, without a doubt. But finally, do they work? Does the piece hang together, giving a unified effect—like *The Mikado* or *Iolanthe*—or does Gilbert's uncertainty about that effect show? Is it a series of theatrical touches, veering from Wagner to, say, *The Student Prince*, *Gone with the Wind* and *The Beggar's Opera*, with the basic Savoy philosophy trying to hold the disparate arrangement together?

The Savoy aspect is prominent, evidently. *The Yeomen* may be neither burlesque nor topsy-turvy, but it does have affinities with its forebears. It is a natural extension of the Old English mood of *Ruddigore*, with Sir Rupert's writhing witches become the victims of the Tower. And it has obvious similarities of plot to *The Mikado*: the background of cruel justice and the prospect of beheading, the comic baritone unluckily giving up his fiancée (Ko-Ko for a month, Jack Point for half-an-hour), a faked death graphically described and forced marriages of inconvenience at the end. How do these resemblances square with the darker mood and more grandiose ambitions of 'the serious opera'?

At the beginning of *The Yeomen*, the Tower looms just like the Mikado's image in the earlier piece. It is not merely painted on the backcloth; its actual torments come forth in Phoebe's denunciation of the brutal Shadbolt. He is master of its 'racks, pincers, and thumbscrews' and such horrors as the 'Little Ease', a dungeon cell so small the prisoner could neither stand nor lie down. It is the Tower where the unjustly accused Fairfax will meet his doom, like so many others before him. Phoebe makes an even more direct and impassioned attack on 'this wicked Tower' to Dame Carruthers, comparing it to 'old Blunderbore', 'a cruel giant in a fairytale' who 'must be fed with blood'.

This is formidable stuff, creating a deep sense of the casual cruelty that was one of the traits popularly associated with the Middle Ages. The grim mood is made even grimmer by 'When our gallant Norman foes', the Dame's defence of the Tower, which for her symbolizes the often violent, but always glorious history of England. It 'tells of duty done and duty doing', she stoutly maintains, whatever the cause and whatever the cost. Alert Gilbert-watchers may well look for satire here, given his suspicions of blind 'duty' in other operas, but there does not seem to be any. The Tower is what it is; 'a sentinel unliving and undying', the embodiment of inevitable suffering and heroism. The awesome point is most strongly put in the refrain, in which the Tower itself speaks:

> 'The screw may twist and the rack may turn,
> And men may bleed and men may burn,
> O'er London town and its golden hoard
> I keep my silent watch and ward!'

The song is very fine, and Sullivan's setting—like all his music in the opera's first scenes—captures its subject's inexorable force.

The gravity of the atmosphere is deepened by the predicament of Colonel Fairfax, who is an ideal Tudor figure, soldier, philosopher and man of science at once. Gilbert may have modelled him loosely on one of the Tower's most famous prisoners, Sir Walter Raleigh. His first song, 'Is Life a boon?', is one of Gilbert's most highly regarded lyrics, a serenely stoic meditation on life's transience—the first lines of which, years later, the librettist would contribute as a memorial to his partner Sullivan.

But Fairfax is also handsome, and in a way that quality is more important to the plot than his gifts and virtues. It is not long before the weighty resonances of the Tower slip into the background—and rather far into the background—and we are more concerned with affairs of the heart than with the 'many gallant hearts' that have perished in its precincts. Gilbert uses the Tower solely as a means of evoking atmosphere (by contrast, the character of that other 'cruel giant', the Mikado, remains central to the action of his opera). After the first scene, the keep really ceases to play any part, except as a source of dramatic colour.

But because of its first importance, we may expect something more from the plot, in something like the same key. What we get instead is Meryll's plan to free Fairfax, which may seem slightly far-fetched, except that the switched prisoner-ploy was actually practised once or twice in the Tower, if not in precisely this form. Fairfax's request for an instant wife appears a little more credible, perhaps, though we might wonder why Elsie's blindfold is necessary, except to keep her from recognizing 'Leonard' later. Both plots, however, do change the mood considerably. When, in a cunning and typical Gilbertian stroke, they overlap, Colonel Fairfax becomes a very different character indeed. Impersonating Leonard, he seems to have abandoned all the high-mindedness that distinguished him in captivity. His Act II song, 'Free from his fetters grim', complaining of his bondage to an anonymous wife, appears an unworthy reaction from a man who only a little while before was under sentence of imminent death. Even more unworthy in his reaction when he discovers her identity. His cat-and-mouse game with the afflicted Elsie is distinctly unchivalric. It may make an entertaining theatrical episode, but it does not connect with what has gone before. Like the image of the Tower—or the stark appearance of the Headsman in the Finale of Act I—it is 'effective theatre' without necessarily contributing to an effective play.

In general, Act II becomes the marital scuffle that is the standard Savoy pattern. (In an odd way it resembles *Patience*, with Jack Point and Shadbolt in cahoots instead of Bunthorne and Lady Jane.) Dame Carruthers is after Sergeant Meryll, Shadbolt is after Phoebe, Phoebe Fairfax, while the colonel and Point pursue Elsie. We are a long way from 'the screw may twist and the rack may turn', and it is appropriate that the only violence threatened or performed in the act is a sham—Shadbolt's round from the arquebus, though again that is titillatingly atmospheric.

The pervading atmosphere is troubled romance, not tragedy. Fairfax's turnabout wooing of Elsie takes Phoebe and Jack Point completely by surprise, producing the perplexed little quartet 'When a wooer goes a-wooing', a deft exposition of conflicting reactions. We feel sympathy for Phoebe, who, throughout the opera, has been honest, resourceful, witty and pert. She is very likeable, though—or perhaps because—she inclines to the more worldly-wise female character represented by Yum-Yum, Phyllis and, notoriously, Rose Maybud. She is a bit of a flirt, who fears her brother's strictness; she declares she is not 'a poor nun who has renounced mankind'. Her father sums her up as 'a feather-brain, but . . . a good lass'. Her feather-brain and distress at losing Fairfax drop her at least nominally into Shadbolt's clutches, though she is quick to implicate him in his plot with Jack Point. We have a feeling it may be some while—'A year—or two—or three, at the most', she tells him—before she makes any binding commitment. (Her father, similarly trapped by Dame Carruthers, may be less agile.)

The noble Fairfax—or at least Act I's noble Fairfax—is probably better suited to Elsie Maynard, who represents the innocent wing of Gilbertian womanhood, most purely seen in the character of Patience. Elsie spends most of the opera in girlish turmoil, first as a result of her mother's illness and the dangerous life of a strolling player, then as veiled bride to an unknown and soon-to-be-executed man. His escape induces a nervous seizure, after which she is subjected to the mischievous wooing of her husband in disguise. Then her supposed husband is reported dead, and she accepts her importunate suitor. The final twist of the screw comes in the opera's finale, when Fairfax's unconventional sense of humour leads him to proclaim his resurrection as Fairfax before revealing his identity as Elsie's Meryll. The poor girl stands it all very well and in her way is as attractive as Phoebe. Both of them demonstrate some of Gilbert's best character-drawing.

Of course the most renowned figure in *The Yeomen of the Guard* is Gilbert's alter ego, Jack Point. He is a worthy addition to the long line of literary and dramatic jesters (an even more disastrously star-crossed funnyman appeared in *Pagliacci* four years after *Yeomen*), and he is one of his creator's finest achievements. From his first entrance, harried by a jeering crowd, the merryman epitomizes Gilbert's view of the travail of the humorist's life. Though the librettist settles a few scores, the final picture is bleak. (Despite its prevailing atmosphere of contention, Gilbert's life seems to have been quite happy. But his favourite work of literature was *The Book of Job*.)

One of the most striking things about the jester is that he does not derive much personal pleasure from his humour. An element of strain is always present; Gilbert might well say this is the reality of the funnyman's position. Many of his quips are rather feeble. Often he makes conventional jokes at the expense of his own real feelings. It is all too clear, for instance, that he does care for Elsie, but on their first appearance, when asked if they are man and wife, he dutifully sneers, 'No, sir; for though I'm a fool, there is a limit to my folly.' But his bargain with the Lieutenant for Elsie's hand—an offer very hard to refuse—will turn out to be even more foolish.

According to Point, the jester's life is constantly precarious, a search for patrons whom he must amuse without offending. In 'I've jibe and joke' he can boast,

> 'I ply my craft
> And know no fear
> But aim my shaft
> At prince or peer.'

But the comic 'should always gild the philosophic pill' if he knows what's good for him. His Act II song, 'Oh, a private buffoon is a light-hearted loon', clearly shows how completely he is at the public's mercy. Not only must he please all senses of humour, but suppress whatever personal anguish he may be suffering.

By the end of the opera, poor Jack's anguish is, of course, profound and darkens our response to the whole piece. We may not have returned to the world of the rack and screw, but his distress is no joke. Is it merely another effect? How seriously are we to take it? The role has been played in very different ways, based on different interpretations of what Gilbert meant by saying that Jack 'falls insensible' at the feet of the betrothed Elsie and Fairfax. Does he die or swoon? Those who want to milk as much tragic emotion from 'the serious opera' as they can, opt for fatality. (Comedians love the chance to play Hamlet.) Henry Lytton acted the scene in the grandest style, stumbling, falling, kissing the hem of Elsie's dress, and then every one of its ribbons, before making a sign of blessing and passing away. It was not how George Grossmith originally acted the part. Grossmith was praised for his restrained poignancy, but he does not seem to have given the impression that Point would never rise again. Gilbert, however, said that Lytton's interpretation was just what he wanted: 'Jack Point should die and the end of the opera should be a tragedy.'

But this does seem excessive, a sudden shift from mixed melancholy and merriment to disaster, while, since the opening, the whole opera has been heading in the opposite direction. It may be that, again, Gilbert was not sure what he wanted, or what the public would bear. When Lytton's conception was successful, he may have been happy to go along, pleased at having his serious side receive recognition.In 1897 he changed the opera's finale slightly but significantly, so that, when Elsie and Jack sing their farewells in 'I have a song to sing, O', she acknowledges his grief by describing herself as 'a merrymaid . . . who dropped a tear/At the moan of a merryman. . .'. But in the opera's first version the callous creature merely 'laughed aloud'—an ending much less conducive to sentimentality. Perhaps this is the final example of Gilbert's uncertainty about *The Yeomen*, a mystification at exactly what final effect it would, could or should have.

Not surprisingly, the libretto's patchwork quality is reflected in the score. When Sullivan has an opportunity for grandeur, he is very grand, and he takes full advantage of the Tower atmosphere at the beginning of the opera to produce some marvellously sonorous music. In fact, the overture gives him a chance for a solo meditation on the operatic mood before Gilbert gets in an imitation-Tudor word. Sullivan tended to be rather offhand about the Savoy overtures, sometimes even leaving their composition to others. At their best they are jolly medleys of very good tunes. But *The Yeomen* was a different kind of piece, and its overture had to be as well. Sullivan took pains with it and was justly proud of the result. It begins with the magnificently martial theme that will be associated with the Tower throughout *The Yeomen*, though it never appears as a melody. (The sole exception occurs at the very end, where the composer tries to pull the diverse threads of the work together by setting marital lyrics to the Tower's music, but the effect is unconvincing.) Sullivan's use of a recurrent orchestral motif obviously shows a debt to Richard Wagner, about whom he had mixed feelings, though he once declared that *Die Meistersinger* was the greatest comic opera ever written. After the Tower, the composer weaves the melodies of Phoebe's 'Were I thy bride' and Point's 'A private buffoon' into an artful and subtle symphonic movement, ending with the mighty Tower theme restated.

Though the opera begins with Phoebe's wistful spinning song 'When maiden loves', the ancient keep dominates the action at first, and Sullivan carries that mood from his overture into the splendid chorus of the warders, 'In the autumn of our life', and Dame Carruthers' stirring solo 'When our gallant Norman foes'. (The numbers are related in more than mood; Sullivan gives them the same basic dotted rhythm as the Tower theme.) But Phoebe's song has foreshadowed the opera's real direction—toward romance rather than tragedy—and the music adroitly and serviceably follows.

Thus, despite the Wagnerian beginning, Sullivan's later orientation turns more Italian and French than German. The difference shows at once in the Meryll's trio 'Alas, I waver to and fro' and that for Jack, Elsie and the Lieutenant, 'How say you, maiden, will you wed'. Closer to home, Act II's quartet, 'Strange Adventure', is very English, a pleasant Sullivan madrigal of the type that had become *de rigueur* in the operas. English of a later vintage are the two songs for Colonel Fairfax—both slightly perfunctory if graceful ballads of the Victorian drawing-room variety.

Phoebe, a much more substantial character than the colonel, also has much more of value to sing. In addition to her lovely opening solo, Sullivan gives her one of his finest songs, the sweetly come-hither 'Were I thy bride'. Both partners fit it perfectly to her character, at once romantic and coquettish. It seems a pity that she has to paint this idyllic picture for the loutish Shadbolt. But the solo is a little Sullivan masterpiece, marked by that exquisite sense of pace and timing that illuminates his later work in the Savoy series. The notes setting that key phrase, 'Were I thy bride', are crochets, twice as long as most of the others in the tune (quavers), which creates a subtle feeling of anticipation every time the title line appears. Sullivan increases that impression by holding back and varying the placement of the phrase. Delightful in itself, this delicate asymmetry also gives a subtle image of Phoebe tantalizing her eager suitor.

Phoebe's happier sister, Elsie Maynard, has a touching solo in ''Tis done, I am a bride', an Italianate reflection on the strange fate that has suddenly changed her from maiden to wife. But her moment in the Act I finale may even be finer, as she introduces and leads the 'Oh, mercy' chorus that follows the Headsman's entrance with his block. Some of the finale seems rather forced, with Sullivan trying to emulate Gilbert in what the librettist once called 'pumping up' various emotions. But the funeral march and the chorus that succeeds it can elicit real pity and produce real goose-bumps. The finale also contains a small connoisseur's delight of the kind Sullivan fans are always alert for, in the delectable writing that accompanies the reunion of Phoebe and her supposed brother, Fairfax/Leonard. Their attraction to each other is not familial, of course, and Sullivan's comments in the orchestra are quietly tongue-in-cheek, musically charming and—in their chromaticism—surprisingly 'modern'.

Sullivan plays a secondary role in characterizing Jack Point, at least as far as the jester's solos are concerned. His settings are light and lucid, giving Gilbert's witty words maximum exposure. But his part in introducing Jack and Elsie, pursued by the mob, is decisive. Indeed, according to Thomas Dunhill, Gilbert's contribution to 'Here's a man of jollity' should rank as one of 'the worst lyrics ever offered to a composer', but Sullivan saves it, making the most of sharply vigorous rhythms—even shifting at one point from common time into $5/4$—and creating a sense of rowdy excitement. (Sullivan's first concern in rendering Gilbert's lyrics was always getting the rhythm right, trying out various possibilities before selecting the most interesting.)

Composer and librettist share the honours in the Act II quartet, 'When a wooer goes a-wooing', with Point, Elsie, Fairfax and Phoebe. It is an ensemble not only of perplexity but of poignancy, the moment at which two of the group's expectations have been crushed, while the other two are blissful. The bitter-sweet tune turns the opera serious again. We feel Phoebe's resilience will stand up to the shock just as she subsequently stands up to Shadbolt; the merryman's lot is much more precarious.

His solitary desolation at the end gives *The Yeomen* its distinctiveness. The Tower's ominous presence may have receded, but Point's fate brings back some of its aura of cruelty and injustice. The moods may not be the same, and may be weakened by the intervening sequence of comedy and romance, but there is no denying the effect of the jester's last pathetic appeal, whether he dies at its conclusion or not. Nothing could be more telling than the reprise of Point's 'I have a song to sing, O' duet with Elsie as the form that appeal takes. The song establishes itself immediately in its first appearance in Act I. It is the strolling players' sure-fire hit. Known as 'The Merryman and his Maid', it is also a tale of a jester's poetic justice, one tender victory in an otherwise anxious life. It should be the story of this merryman and merrymaid too, but in the opera's story the lord succeeds in enticing the maid away, and the 'love-lorn loon' is left at the mercy of 'the mocking throng'.

Sullivan's initial difficulty in setting Gilbert's lyric was richly compensated. He matches the piquant, homely folk quality of the verse exactly, making subtle changes in the melodic line as each stanza is lengthened. Based on a folk-song, it seems a folk-song itself. It is unquestionably one of the gems of all Gilbert and Sullivan, just as Jack

Point is one of the enduring Savoy characters. Any opera that includes them among its strengths is bound to succeed, at least to a degree. But opinions as to how complete that success is will always diverge. The people who thrill to Sullivan's Tower music, enjoy the Tudor flavour of Gilbert's plot and characters and, having laughed, finally weep at Jack Point, go away from *The Yeomen* convinced they have had a great theatrical and musical experience. Those who find the piece forced and diffuse, a series of not quite coherent, though impressive effects, and tear-jerking withal will disagree. (In the '20s, when *The Yeomen*'s reputation was high and tragic, one iconoclastic Savoyard declared the piece was 'over-rated' and Jack Point 'a sentimental bore'.)

But despite this ambiguity, it is impossible to imagine it any other way, and there is nothing like it. Indeed, Gilbert, at least, recognized there could not be. Proud as he was of his 'new departure', its success did not warrant another attempt. Like Jack Point, he knew that he was 'paid to be funny', and whatever Sullivan's restlessness, their next opera had to follow proven paths.

Four of the principals from *The Yeomen*: Colonel Fairfax, Wifred Shadbolt, Sergeant Meryll and Jack Point — the latter played by George Grossmith, well-known 'society clown'. The head of his stick represents that no-nonsense jester, W. S. Gilbert

A caricaturist's tongue-in-cheek view of the two stalwart 'Yeomen of the Savoy'

The irrepressible Phoebe Meryll charms Wilfred Shadbolt out of his keys and most of his wits

Gilbert's illustration from his Bab Ballad 'Annie Protheroe', in which the headsman's axe is 'far less like a hatchet than a dissipated saw'

A contemporary survey of *The Gondoliers*. Marco and Giuseppe choose their brides in blindman's buff at the top, rule in tandem at bottom left and are instructed by the prosperous Duke of Plaza-Toro at bottom right. The saturnine Don Alhambra points in the direction of Casilda

Two Gilbertian sketches for songs from *The Gondoliers*, the first showing how Don Alhambra 'stole the Prince, and . . . brought him here', the second how the Duke of Plaza-Toro 'led his regiment from behind'

A regular royal occasion for *The Gondoliers*: the stage is set in Waterloo Chamber at Windsor Castle for a performance before Queen Victoria on 6 March 1891

11

The Gondoliers;

or, The King of Barataria

Though Gilbert and Sullivan produced two more operas after it, *The Gondoliers* broke once and for all the golden Savoy thread. The new opera was preceded by the sharpest dispute yet about art and authority and was followed by a catastrophic row over money and power. The last, so-called 'Carpet Quarrel' aroused such bitterness that the partnership could never be the same. But *The Gondoliers* itself reflects not a hint of acrimony. It is the brightest and most untroubled work of the Savoy series, a classic that epitomizes much of what was best and most sympathetic in Gilbert and Sullivan, just at the point when the differences between the two men—and their colleague Carte—were proving irreconcilable. Critics welcomed the piece as a return to the great days of *The Mikado*, audiences flocked to 554 performances, and Queen Victoria commanded the D'Oyly Carte company to act the work at Windsor. Yet within a year of its opening Gilbert was suing his collaborators, and an unprecedented Savoy drama was taking place in court.

Despite the concession to seriousness represented by *The Yeomen of the Guard*, Sullivan began 1889 with a fresh resolve to free himself from the restrictions of the Savoy formula, which he had lately referred to as 'this slavery'. He told Gilbert he wanted 'to do some dramatic work on a larger scale', with his old partner if possible, 'but that the music must occupy a more important position than in our other pieces'. He wanted subtler rhythms and rhymes to work with, 'words that would give a chance of developing musical effects', and 'a voice in the musical constructions of the libretto'.

No longer surprised by such sentiments, Gilbert wrote patiently to the composer that, while he understood and sympathized with his desire for 'Grand Opera', such a project would not suit either the Savoy company or Gilbert himself, since 'the librettist of a grand opera is always swamped in the composer'. Besides, experience had shown that their lighter, 'more reckless and irresponsible' pieces had best pleased the public. The moderate fortunes of *Yeomen*, 'a step in the direction of serious opera', had not proved that more earnestness was worth attempting. But couldn't Sullivan write two different kinds of work at once? He had done it before. Gilbert closed by recommending another librettist as a possible collaborator.

However, Sullivan's reply showed that his grievances ran deeper than had first appeared. He seized on Gilbert's notion that in serious opera the librettist must necessarily sacrifice himself to the composer. This, he claimed, was 'just what I have been doing in all our joint pieces, and, what is more, must continue to do in Comic Opera to make it successful'. He was tired of comic opera, tired of the standard Savoy types. He stressed again that he wanted 'to do a work where the music is to be the first consideration'. Could Gilbert suggest a way out of the impasse?

Gilbert could not. Sullivan's letter filled him 'with amazement and regret' and seemed to demand he occupy a position subsidiary to the composer's. This was impossible. 'If we meet,' he said, 'it must be as master and master—not as master and servant.'

A few days later Sullivan wrote two letters, expressing perhaps the same points, but with dangerously different emphasis. His message to Gilbert was mild and placating, insisting that their differences could be 'so easily arranged'. He merely asked that his views 'should have some weight with you in the laying out of the *musical situation*', that he should have some say in staging musical numbers and arranging rehearsal time to save the singers' voices. He also mentioned by the way that he had sent another letter to Carte, citing a few specific disagreements, which the manager would probably repeat to the librettist.

But Sullivan's letter to his friend Carte was just the sort of blast that might sink the partnership completely, and, out of thoughtlessness or perversity, Carte simply forwarded it straight to Gilbert. Employing nothing like the tone of sweet rationality he had used to Gilbert personally, Sullivan complained his co-worker reigned supreme while the operas were being staged. He called rehearsals when he liked, wasted people's time, tired out their voices. Except during specifically vocal or orchestral rehearsals, Sullivan had no part in the proceedings. He was no more than 'a cipher in the theatre'; the operas were Gilbert's pieces with music added.

Feeling rage now more than amazement and regret, Gilbert found Sullivan's peevish, hectoring tone insupportable. He charged him with 'unreasonable demands and utterly groundless accusations', reminded him of the many times the staging had been altered to suit Sullivan's wishes and closed with a magnificently rolling period: 'I say that when you deliberately assert that for 12 years you, incomparably the greatest musician of the age—a man whose genius is a proverb wherever the English tongue is spoken—a man who can deal *en prince* with operatic managers, singers, music publishers and musical societies—when you, who hold this unparalleled position, deliberately state that you have submitted silently and uncomplainingly for 12 years to be extinguished, ignored, set aside, rebuffed, and generally effaced by your librettist, you grievously reflect, not upon him, but upon yourself and the noble Art of which you are so eminent a professor.'

That broadside was followed by small-arms fire in both directions for the better part of a month. But by the end of April, a truce was in the making. Gilbert granted that Sullivan should have a hand in planning and staging the pieces and that the music and words should have equal importance, though he maintained that this was precisely the position he had adhered to in the past. Whether these terms were new or old, they were sufficient for Sullivan. He had decided he could indeed do serious and comic opera simultaneously and had arranged with Carte and another librettist that he would produce his *magnum opus*, *Ivanhoe*, at the new theatre Carte was building solely for English grand opera.

On 9 May, Sullivan noted in his diary that he and Gilbert 'had a long and frank discussion . . . shook hands and buried the hatchet'. For the moment. A few days later the composer wrote to encourage Gilbert to work up the subject Carte had told him the librettist was considering—a Venetian theme, which Sullivan found particularly appealing since he had visited the fabled city in the spring and had been intoxicated by its atmosphere, though not by its Opera. On 8 June he reported that Gilbert had read the sketch plot of *The Gondoliers*. It was all he could have hoped—'bright, interesting, funny and very pretty'. Having their next project so readily agreed put the seal on their peace treaty, and the two men got on with their separate work in perfect harmony.

One of the first night reviews of *The Gondoliers* surmised that the work was written '*con amore*'. So it seems to have been, the relief of the reunited partners shining through every musical and verbal line.

The opera's setting could not be more immediately cheerful. It takes place in the piazzetta in Venice, with the Ducal palace in view. The time is 1750. We think of sunny canals and carefree people in an age before the bustling pressure of modern life, and the first Venetians we meet are a band of pretty *contadine*, making bouquets of red and white roses. They are all in love with the two handsomest gondoliers in Venice, without being bothered that most of them must be disappointed. The other gondoliers, strolling in admiringly, are also quite content to choose their mates only after their charismatic colleagues.

Into this charming, good-humoured atmosphere come Marco and

Giuseppe, the *contadine*'s favourites. They and the girls exchange compliments, and the gondoliers get to the not-too-serious business of selecting their brides. Since all the girls are young, fair and amiable, the lads let fate decide, in a game of blindman's buff. In the ensuing merriment Marco and Giuseppe catch Gianetta and Tessa, and everyone dances off to the altar.

The next party to appear is a good deal more subdued. From a gondola disembark the Duke of Plaza-Toro, his Duchess, their pretty daughter Casilda and drummer Luiz. Their shabby finery shows they have fallen on hard times, and they complain of arriving from Spain without a stately welcome, not to mention having to make do with an entourage consisting of one drummer. However, things may well look up. The Duke reveals to his daughter that she was married in infancy to the baby son of the King of Barataria. When that monarch became a convert to 'Wesleyan Methodism of the most bigoted and persecuting type', the Grand Inquisitor stole the little Prince and brought him to Venice. The Methodist King himself has just perished in a revolution, leaving the throne open to his son and to Casilda, as soon as the Grand Inquisitor can produce her royal husband.

Meanwhile the Duke has plans to transform his own fortunes. He may have no money, but as 'a Castilian Hidalgo of ninety-five quarterings' he still has influence. He intends to set himself up as a commercial company—The Duke of Plaza-Toro Ltd—and market his connections. His daughter objects that the prospect is degrading. She seems to have a very keen sense of her rank, which she exercises most often in abusing Luiz, the family's lowly drummer boy. But when the two young people are alone, it turns out that her rough treatment is a ruse to conceal their passion. Unfortunately, the couple's love appears hopeless, since Casilda feels bound to accept her infant betrothal.

Casilda's father returns with the saturnine Don Alhambra, the Grand Inquisitor. The Don explains a slight complication in bringing the royal pair together. He had intrusted the Prince to a gondolier, who confused him with his own son. To ascertain which of the young men is the new king, he has sent for their old nurse—by odd chance the mother of Luiz.

Don Alhambra next approaches the lucky gondoliers, who turn out, of course, to be Marco and Giuseppe. They have just returned blissfully with their new wives. The Grand Inquisitor is taken aback at the alliances and also slightly bemused at the gondoliers' ringing praise of republicanism and denunciation of monarchy. But the newly-weds change their tune when Don Alhambra springs his surprise. Given the chance, and without swerving from their principles, they would be kings and queens quite happily. They are less happy when the Don (keeping to himself the awkward matter of Casilda) says that for the moment only Marco and Giuseppe will go to Barataria. For a few months they will reign side by side. By then their old nurse will identify the real king, and the couples can be reunited. Because it is only a few months, all accept, and the gondolier-kings and their friends get a rousing send-off.

Act II takes place in the Baratarian court. Marco and Giuseppe have been ruling contentedly for three months. As courtiers, the other gondoliers do what they please. Whatever their rank, all are equal, and the two Kings are careful to ask their permission for royal necessities as well as helping out with the chores.

The twin monarchs are reflecting that the only blot on their pleasant existence is the absence of their wives, when all at once the ladies appear with the other *contadine*. Everyone celebrates by dancing a cachucha, which is interrupted by Don Alhambra. He is amazed at the democratic disorder and advises Marco and Giuseppe that their noble scheme has been tried before, with dismal results: 'When everyone is somebody, then no one's anybody.'

The purpose of his visit is to announce the arrival of the Plaza-Toros and to reveal at last that Casilda is included in the Baratarian throne. Tessa and Gianetta overhear and immediately protest. But which of their husbands has two wives will be known soon enough: Luiz's mother, the former nurse, has arrived as well.

The Duke, Duchess and Casilda make a magnificent entrance; obviously the Duke's business venture has gone well. Despite the assurances of her parents that you can love anyone if you put your mind to it, Casilda declares that she can never give her heart to either Marco or Giuseppe. When the ex-gondoliers appear, the Duke gives them his own lesson in proper regal behaviour, before leaving them alone with his daughter. Casilda confesses that she is already 'over-head and ears' in love with someone else; Marco and Giuseppe declare that they are in the same boat. In come Tessa and Gianetta, and the quintet mull over the inconvenient state of affairs together. But its amazing resolution is only an instant away. The nurse Inez reveals that the Prince was never taken to Venice at all. When the kidnappers arrived to snatch him, she deftly switched him with her own son; the true King of Barataria is—Luiz! Stunningly garbed, the former drummer ascends the throne, he and Casilda embrace, and the gondoliers and their ladies return merrily to Venice, with only the faintest twinge of regret.

The Gondoliers took shape over the summer and autumn of 1889, with its creators happily back in harness. Gilbert was assiduous, Sullivan again more haphazard. Sometimes he would turn out a song, or even two, in a single session; sometimes he would do nothing for days except loll in his summer retreat. His mind was also on grander prospects: his *Ivanhoe* librettist, the very man Gilbert had proposed, delivered his part of the work by the end of July.

True to their 'cipher' agreement, Gilbert went out of his way to consult his partner in relating words and music. His willingness to accommodate the composer showed in the notes he sent along with his lyrics. One concluded, characteristically, 'If the verses won't do, send them back and I'll try again.'

By the autumn, Sullivan had shifted into a higher gear. The opera's opening was set for 7 December, and he spent November locked in the familiar back-breaking, all-night, every-night routine. The combined pressure of composing, scoring and rehearsing took an even heavier toll than usual. Alarmed at the state of Sullivan's health, Gilbert and Carte suggested the première be postponed, but the musician soldiered on, though he acknowledged that *The Gondoliers* had been the most gruelling of the operas for him.

Gilbert meanwhile had the rehearsals firmly in hand, while carefully making allowances for his colleague's wishes. But he did not make many allowances for the cast. The main reason for *The Gondoliers'* novel structure—double male and female leads, and a large number of rather small but distinctive parts—was the librettist's irritation with the stars of the company. George Grossmith had left to resume the solo career he had abandoned years before to become John Wellington Wells, and pretty, clever Jessie Bond wanted more money. She got it, too, supported by Carte and Sullivan against Gilbert's objections. The librettist forgave her, finally, because of his fondness for her and delight with her performance as Tessa, but at rehearsals he refused to speak to her, except to intone 'Make way for the high-salaried artiste' when she came on stage. He was happier dealing with Decima Moore, who played Casilda. She had no prior acting experience, therefore, as he said, 'nothing to unlearn', and also no exaggerated sense of status. He schooled her in proper Gilbertian delivery, demonstrating the rhythm he wanted in a speech by clapping his hands: 'I've no patience (clap) with the presumption (clap) of persons (clap) in his plebian (clap) position (clap).' The whole company was guided with equal exactness; Gilbert spent three days getting the blindman's buff sequence alone machine-perfect.

Despite Sullivan's distress and (or perhaps because of) this necessary grind, the run-up to opening night proceeded smoothly. The title was not fixed until 2 December, but Sullivan was pleased with it. He was also pleased at the 'beautiful effect' of the first full band rehearsal. At the same time, Gilbert removed any possibility of giving offence by deleting certain 'dangerous dialogues' from the finale. Five nights later, the première was an unqualified triumph. Sir Arthur recorded that 'everything went splendidly, with immense 'go' and spirit. . . . Gilbert and I got a tremendous reception—we have never had such a brilliant first night.' The critics whole-heartedly agreed. One said flatly that, '*The Gondoliers* is one of the best, if not the best of the Gilbert-Sullivan operas. Another declared it was 'not opera or play, it is simply an entertainment—the most exquisite, the daintiest entertainment we have ever seen'. The uncertainties of the preceding works had been resolved. As the *Illustrated London News* observed, 'Mr. W. S. Gilbert has returned to the Gilbert of the past, and everyone is delighted.' As for the almost infallible Sullivan, one writer stated that the new work 'surpasses all his previous efforts'.

The Gondoliers seemed to presage a whole new chapter in the Savoy story. A year after its opening Queen Victoria granted it royal recognition, commanding a D'Oyly Carte performance at Windsor on 6 March 1891, the first theatrical occasion since the death of her beloved Prince Albert thirty years before. She recorded her pleasure in her diary, and it was obvious enough to those present: the 'little, squat figure in black' was seen smiling and keeping time with her fan. (G & S mythology has it that the Windsor production slighted Gilbert, his name having supposedly been omitted from the printed programme. In fact it was there, as prominent as Sullivan's, and Her Majesty mentioned the librettist appreciatively in her diary.)

The Gondoliers' jubilant reception inspired a rush of warmth between its creators. After opening night Gilbert wrote to Sullivan: 'I must thank you again for the magnificent work you have put into the piece. It gives one the chance of shining right through the twentieth century with a reflected light.'

Sullivan wrote back at once: 'Don't talk of reflected light. In such a perfect book as *The Gondoliers* you shine with an individual brilliancy which no other writer can hope to attain. If any thanks are due anywhere, they should be from me to you for the patience, willingness, and unfailing good nature with which you have received my suggestions, and your readiness to help me by according to them.'

Sadly, that mood of shared euphoria and esteem was shortlived. But it still radiates from the work that engendered it. *The Gondoliers* is the brightest of the Savoy series, the most cheerful and pure of heart. 'Sunny' is the word most commentators attach to it, and it is an ideal description. In it Gilbert recovers his old sense of proportion. There is none of the cynicism of *Ruddigore* or the rather confused emotions of *Yeomen*. *The Gondoliers* celebrates youth, happiness and, above all, love and marriage—all of which Gilbert freely admits are fine things. There is a bit of satire, witty but basically innocuous, and enough topsy-turvydom to keep devotees of nonsense happy. The piece has the same kind of effortless consistency as *The Mikado*. It creates its own charming and timeless world, free from the shadows that make the Japanese opera more interesting but which would mar its own unique lustre.

Without question much of that lustre is due to Sullivan. Like *The Mikado, The Gondoliers* finds him sustaining an almost continuous level of high musical quality. The opera begins, in fact, with a segment unprecedented in the Savoy cycle: eighteen minutes of score unbroken by dialogue. This is Gilbert allowing the music to speak for itself with a vengeance. But it also thoroughly establishes the special mood of the piece. This varied and utterly delightful sequence of song and dance epitomizes the spirit of *The Gondoliers* as surely as the image of the Tower in *Yeomen* or the title character in *The Mikado.*

The opening situation recalls *Patience*—a chorus of love-sick maidens pining, probably hopelessly, for their ideal man—or men, in this case. But the resemblance is only superficial and immediately dispelled. The *Patience* girls are morbid, self-dramatizing and silly; they make love itself seem a forced and unnatural emotion. But the *contadine* are as healthy as sunshine, as untroubled as the blue sky. Marco and Giuseppe will choose two of them, the others will pair up elsewhere, and everything will be fine. The chorus of gondoliers feels exactly the same way. Their disappointment at playing second gondola to the girls' favourites passes in an instant: there is plenty of love and happiness for everybody.

The feeling that love is a kind of sweet natural resource that does not even require discrimination appears when Marco and Giuseppe let Fate do the choosing. If love is blind, he might as well be blindfolded too. Their gentlemanly conviction that 'a bias to disclose would be indelicate' is a wonderful extension of republican principles into romance. The whole scene exudes delight and contentment, and the unbroken singing and dancing make it seem like a staged ritual of courtship, a little masque on its own. The Venetian setting heightens the effect. Most of its flavour is Sullivan's doing, as he throws in one Italian dance form after another, each sounding perfectly authentic. But Gilbert does his imaginative bit (in addition of course to devising the whole scene) when he has his lovers exchange simple compliments in Italian. It is a pleasant and effective ploy, increasing the native aura, as his potted Japanese did in *The Mikado.*

All the opening music is infectious, from 'List and learn', the pulsating waltz sung by the *contadine* (worlds away from the lugubrious opening strains of *Patience*) to 'For the merriest fellows are we', the men's romping tarantella, filled with joyous tra-la-las, and Marco and Giuseppe's well-known duet 'We're called gondolieri'. The latter number, as T. F. Dunhill points out, is in a Neapolitan style but more importantly 'shows so close a resemblance to the real Italian folk-song type that it is difficult to believe it is by an English composer'. The dazzling sequence ends with a Sullivan *tour de force*, an advanced variation on his old trick of pitting one chorus with one melody against a second with its own. In 'Thank you, gallant *gondolieri*', introduced by Tessa and Gianetta, the ladies deliver a rising line with two beats to the bar, which the men accompany with three-beat tra-la-las. The exhilarating cross-rhythms sweep both choruses away to be married *en masse*. Throughout the opera, as in this first scene, marriage is the natural and blissful result of love, a sentiment Gilbert does not try to undermine in any way. Here, as Gianetta sings in the Finale to Act I, 'Woman's heart is one with woman's hand'—a view precisely opposite to Phoebe's in *The Yeoman of the Guard*. In fact the newly-weds regard their wedding day as their true birthday.

The Gondoliers cost Gilbert a good deal of effort, but it shows in the plot's cunning construction and lightness of touch rather than any laboriousness. After the opera's basic mood of idyllic love has been created, he brings on its second, satiric motif and also introduces the topsy-turvy notion of switched babies and double monarchs. The Duke of Plaza-Toro in a way embodies aristocratic posturing, but Gilbert presents him quite mildly and affectionately. A nobleman putting on airs may be exasperating; a penniless nobleman trying it is simply funny. Besides, the Duke does have a sense of *noblesse oblige*, which shows in his treatment of Luiz, whom he defends against Casilda's feigned high-handedness. Both his daughter and his redoubtable wife seem more arrogant than he, though he would have liked to make his Venetian entrance on horseback—not having been told about the canals. Despite his rank, he reminds us more of Ko-Ko than of the truly pompous Sir Joseph Porter, especially when he recalls his military exploits in 'In enterprise of martial kind': retreating and hiding were his strong points.

A more tantalizing satiric thrust works in two directions—first toward the idea of the nobility's influence rather than its actual rank, and second toward the marketing of that vague but powerful commodity. Gilbert does not take the concept very far, but the implications are potent and amusing, an oddly modern venture into the world of public relations, commercials and endorsements. It is just the kind of attitude he would mistrust: a product that is not a product, but pure pretence and sham. It is the new snobbery, given mass appeal. Of course it is also a spin-off from the old snobbery, as the Duke and Duchess recount in their witty second-act duet, 'Small titles and orders', which lists the typical services that (like Pooh-Bah) they sell to the lower ranks—everything from obtaining honours to appearing at card parties to lending a touch of class to interments ('We enjoy an interment', His Grace remarks). Sullivan's genteelly bouncing accompaniment makes it all the funnier and gives added tang to Gilbert's verses:

'In short, if you'd kindle
The spark of a swindle,
Lure simpletons into your clutches—
Yes; into your clutches,
Or hoodwink a debtor,
You cannot do better
Than trot out a Duke or a Duchess.'

Pure pomposity is represented by Don Alhambra, the Grand Inquisitor, who does the same kind of double-act with the Duke as Pooh-Bah did with Ko-Ko. But the Don also has a slightly forbidding side that relates him to that other very heavy man, the Mikado. There is not enough of it to cast even a momentary pall over the untroubled surface of the opera, but he does evoke the uneasy mood of the Inquisition with its torture chambers, like the one where Inez waits to be interviewed (Don Alhambra assures a worried Giuseppe that 'she has all the illustrated papers'). The other, darker association in the work is the insurrection in which the old King of Barataria perished. But the effect of this is less striking than the image of a Spanish king suddenly becoming a Methodist, a wild Gilbertian stroke that almost smacks of the Marx Brothers.

The Grand Inquisitor's basic function in the plot is acting as emissary between the new Queen and her family and the unknown gondolier-King. Of course he is more at home with the Plaza-Toros, giving them a lively account of the prince napping and its confusing aftermath. His jolly narrative—as jolly as his augustness permits—'I stole the prince and I brought him here', contains one of Gilbert's familiar catch lines: the Don concludes each verse of tale by asserting:

'Of that there is no manner of doubt—
No probable, possible shadow of doubt—
No possible doubt whatever.'

His meeting with Marco, Giuseppe and their brand-new brides is a classic encounter, one of those sly Savoy confrontations between rank and cheekiness. Perhaps it most resembles Pooh-Bah's pained exchanges with the little maids in *The Mikado*. Here the grave Spanish grandee engages the blithe Venetian republicans. First they think this *éminence noire* is an undertaker; then they address him as 'my man'; then Giuseppe subjects him to a purple peroration on republican virtue and monarchical vice while the others cheer. But the Don laughs last by exposing the shallowness of these noble sentiments when tested by the offer of an actual throne.

Thus, rather late—there is nothing in the long opening sequence about politics at all—occurs the other half of Gilbert's satire, which is also very mild. The gondoliers are not hypocrites, just innocents. Their excited speculations about the pleasures and powers of royalty are endearingly child-like. Of course they will be model monarchs, and of course they will give their friends places at court—to which the experienced Don replies drily, 'Undoubtedly. That's always done.'

Their delight at this astounding turn of fate produces some very good songs—Tessa and Gianetta's girlish fancies about their future, 'Then one of us will be a Queen', and Marco and Giuseppe's two-man royal proclamations, 'Replying we sing as one individual' and 'For every one who feels inclined'. The first is a wide-eyed view of the delights of being 'a regular Royal Queen'. Gilbert knows his girls very well and likes them: scratch a republican teenager and you find Marie Antoinette. His details are bright and convincing, Sullivan's setting perfectly bubbly. (This number was one of the great hits of the show's opening night. The crowd demanded that 'All of it!', not just the last verse be encored; then the gallery whistled the melody between the acts.) 'Replying we sing' begins with a hilariously rustic oom-pah-pah introduction, after which the two could-be Kings cleverly divide a single oration between them, sometimes even splitting single words. They follow this with a statement of their commitment to a reign both royal and republican: in their court 'all shall equal be'.

Gilbert's shift from idyllic romance to wry satire is by no means total. Love is still at the heart of the piece, tenderly evoked in Tessa's 'When a merry maiden marries', which she sings when the newly-weds first appear. Sullivan's setting for Gilbert's pretty lyrics is delicate and subtly varied. (But he was accused of plagiarizing his melody, or part of it. He protested he had never heard the other tune, and at any rate he and its composer had only the same seven notes to choose from.)

The Finale to Act I is distinguished by two further tributes to married love. The girls are heart-broken that the first effect of their rise in the world is separation from their husbands. Gianetta's touching 'Kind sir, you cannot have the heart' expresses the absolute bond between man and wife, and also a woman's acceptance that marriage is not a republic. 'Marco', as Gianetta says, 'is my king.' Finally, somewhat comforted that they will 'not be parted long', the girls, in the duet 'Now, Marco dear, my wishes hear', make some sweet wifely requests, which are all summed up in the last line of the refrain: 'Do not forget you've married me.'

Gilbert focusses on the republican satire only at the beginning of Act

II, again in the mildest terms. When he first broached his idea to Sullivan, he said he wanted to show the 'absurdity' of a court in which everyone is equal, and he does. When the curtain goes up on the royal pavilion at Barataria (a mythical kingdom Gilbert borrowed from Don Quixote), we see the two Kings busy polishing up their sceptres, while their courtiers lie about higgledy-piggledy doing whatever they like. It does not look at all the way a kingly court should be run, and the spectacle is funny. But the satire really goes no further than the humour of the spectacle. Obviously, all courtly positions should not be equal; the King(s) should not have to insist loudly on their right to tea for two. If Gilbert had really wanted to test republican principles, he could have proposed the equality of the monarch and the man in the street, not just the members of his court (though it is briefly mentioned that Marco and Giuseppe's subjects do nod to them as they walk about). But his satire is not meant to challenge anything, really; it is aimed much more at manners than at politics. *H.M.S. Pinafore* is a good deal more radical because Sir Joseph actively preaches the equality of captain and crew. So is *Iolanthe*, with its spoofing of the privileged House of Peers.

It is very easy for Don Alhambra to point out the drawbacks of the Baratarian arrangement. His mock-Handelian solo, 'There lived a King, as I've been told', describes the failure of just such a philosophy. Its moral is succinct: 'When everyone is somebodee, then no one's anybody', a home truth to which any Victorian would agree. Marco and Giuseppe agree as well and also see the wisdom of the little lesson in courtly manners they receive from the Duke of Plaza-Toro. Their amusing gavotte, 'I am a courtier brave and serious', counsels a middle course, neither too unbending nor condescending, which absolutely characterizes the politics of *The Gondoliers*. It is the pleasant ideal of the status quo, very well suited to English good sense, chuckling at both red-hot republicans and pompous grandees. The monarchy's value is unquestioned—after all, the original Baratarian insurrection ended as soon as Marco and Giuseppe took the throne. No wonder Queen Victoria enjoyed *The Gondoliers*.

But it is of course love that reigns supreme. Even at the height of their kingly but co-operative power, Marco and Giuseppe pine for their little wives. No sooner has Marco sung the lilting 'Take a pair of sparkling eyes'—which was an immense Victorian hit, despite Gilbert's describing a maiden's hand as 'fringed with dainty fingerettes'—than the little wives descend. Another free-wheeling dance ensues, this time a quasi-Spanish cachucha (*The Gondoliers* has not only two sets of stars but two exotic locales as well—and two shades of political satire). All is bliss once more, though consternation briefly obtrudes in the shapely form of Casilda. But compared to the complications that threaten the lovers in other operas, this is a mere technicality. It does provide an opportunity for two good ensembles, Sullivan's showpiece 'In a contemplative fashion', where the two couples express their perplexity in highly wrought counter-point, and their superbly gay quintet with Casilda, 'Here is a case unprecedented', which sounds more like Rossini than Rossini.

But at last everything is resolved as ideally as it should be. Inez unveils her fabulous secret, and Luiz and Casilda gain Barataria and each other (we are left to wonder which of the gondoliers is Inez's real son). Obviously, the dénouement is only a slender variation on the topsy-turvy climax of *Pinafore*. Gilbert told Sullivan he wanted to alter it, though it is hard to see what else he could have done. It is more consistent than the nautical play, and both the lovers turn out to be of noble blood instead of just one. We have seen very little of Luiz and not much of Casilda—though their first-act duet, 'There was a time', has a seriousness and beauty unique in the opera—but it really seems not to matter who a king and queen are, as long as they are the king and queen. In *The Gondoliers*, everyone has his or her place and is perfectly contented in it. Everyone shares youth, love and happiness, or at least happiness. The opera does create a 'Golden Land' where life is reduced to its simplest terms. Gilbert's attitude in the piece—and, audibly, Sullivan's too—is summed up in the Act I madrigal sung by the Plaza-Toro party and Don Alhambra, which is a mutual G & S masterpiece:

> 'Life's a pudding full of plums,
> Care's a canker that benumbs.
> Wherefore waste our elocution
> On impossible solution?
> Life's a pleasant institution,
> Let us take it as it comes!'

Unfortunately for the partnership, Gilbert was not the man to take stage advice, even his own, as words to live by. The notorious 'Carpet Quarrel', which began to unroll within a few months of *The Goldoliers*' glorious opening and comradely salutes, epitomized 'impossible solution', but that did not stop Gilbert from pursuing it with fervent zeal. It produced care on all sides, and the chief victim was that 'pleasant institution' the Savoy operas.

A carpet, of course, was only the most superficial *casus belli*. The real conflict was personal, principally involving Gilbert and Carte. They had had disagreements before, always relating to money and the question of who had the right to oversee expenses. The first joint contract for the Savoy stipulated that all three partners would share the costs and divide the profits, but that Carte alone would bear any losses. As owner of the Savoy, he would rent it to the trio for £4,000 a year, an expense they would also share, though the money in fact would go to Carte. The agreement seems fair enough, but Gilbert could not let it pass without remarking, in Hesketh Pearson's words, 'that as Carte the partner was paying one-third of the rent to Carte the proprietor, it was a sound investment for Carte the capitalist'. But Carte told Sullivan that the acid *bon mot* hurt him more than he could say.

Periodic strife continued. During the run of *Patience*, Gilbert expressed outrage at the nightly expenses and demanded they be trimmed. During *The Mikado* he took Carte on even more directly, insisting that he and Sullivan be given more of a say in the administration of the theatre. Carte pointed out that three-way consultation on every business decision was impossible; such decisions were his contribution to the operas. He told Gilbert he did not see himself as anything more than 'the tradesman who sells your creations of art'.

But soft answers had little effect where money was concerned. It was not that Gilbert was penny-pinching, but he wanted as much control over where his pennies were going as he had over the production of the operas. Part of this was his meticulous and military nature. But part of it also stemmed from his professional view of himself. He wrote for money, pure and simple. He had tried writing from conviction without success. Therefore, whether he liked it or not, his bank balance was his justification as an author. He was not ashamed of it. It was a fact of life he acknowledged every time he put a new work in the post, saying, 'Here goes five pence or five figures.'

He earned the money by hard and careful labour. This was particularly true at the Savoy, where he was responsible for writing, directing and, at least sometimes, design. He also coped with Sullivan's discontent and did what he could to accommodate it. Under no illusions as to what the devotees of 'high art' thought of the operas—he himself dismissed *The Gondoliers* as 'ridiculous rubbish' a week after it opened—he still knew they were well done and unprecedentedly successful, in no small part through his efforts, and he expected his full reward.

If Gilbert was suspicious of Carte's manipulating, behind-the-scenes hand on the purse-strings, he was also suspicious of the manager's special understanding with Sullivan, and their attachment to projects like Sullivan's new grand opera, which would inaugurate Carte's new grand opera house. That world had nothing to do with him, and it may be that he did carry a slight chip on his shoulder at its putative superiority. The fact was that Carte and Sullivan's dream of art would be funded to a large extent by Gilbert's Savoy librettos and stage labour. The comic-opera author did not begrudge that, but he did want his financial reward by way of recognition.

The Carpet Quarrel ignited all these simmering sources of bad feeling. It began with Gilbert's astonishment at the statement of preliminary expenses for *The Gondoliers*—£4,500, with £500 of that to cover new carpets for the auditorium. He thought the figure ridiculous and objected violently to the carpet purchase since technically he and Sullivan were liable only for repairs, not replacement. He and Carte went at it hammer and tongs in a stormy interview; Gilbert said he had made Carte what he was and demanded a new agreement, Carte threatened to raise the rent, and one or the other declared Gilbert would write no more for the Savoy.

Gilbert went off to enlist Sullivan's support when the composer returned from holiday, but found to his great chagrin that his creative partner sided—though rather uncomfortably—with the manager. Feeling betrayed, Gilbert announced the collaboration was finished and that he was withdrawing permission for any performance of the Savoy operas for anyone, let alone Carte, after *The Gondoliers*. A three-way interview followed which only hardened the divisions and concluded with Gilbert shouting that his colleagues were not gentlemen and charging from the room using, Carte said, 'shocking language'.

Carte had already defended himself by asserting that the large expenses were due to Gilbert's own lavish outlay on *The Gondoliers*, that the cost of the carpet was £140, not £500, that he leased the Savoy to his partners at below the market rate, that all lessees were liable for wear and tear and that Gilbert did very well by their arrangement. But by now Gilbert had put matters in his solicitors' hands. He demanded his regular payment from the Savoy, which Carte's solicitors had held up pending resolution of the expenses question, then argued successfully that the sum presented was £1,000 too low. Carte had to pay up, and the librettist applied for a receiver to check into the financial workings of the Savoy. Of course, all the aggravation was now going on in public, much to the bemusement and amusement of the newspapers. As one commentator said, 'When Mr. Gilbert does quarrel with anybody they know it. . . . Sir Arthur did not want to quarrel with Mr. Carte or anyone else. He declined to quarrel with Mr. Carte. Consequently he got into a quarrel with Mr. Gilbert. . . .'

Poor Sullivan was trying to work on *Ivanhoe* throughout the dispute. He ran further afoul of his partner by swearing an affidavit, in all good faith, that turned out to be false, and Gilbert badgered him for months to confess it. There were attempts at reconciliation, at one point even Gilbert admitting he might have been overhasty. The composer declared himself 'physically and mentally ill over this wretched business' and later made a cordial offer of tickets to *Ivanhoe*, which Gilbert, still brooding over the affidavit, curtly declined.

In all, the dispute dragged on for a year and a half, with residual flare-ups even after that. But in October 1891 the two men shook hands. They had each tried other collaborators with no great satisfaction. They shared professional respect, but also a suppressed sense of having been ill-used by the other. They would return together to their very profitable work, as agreeably as possible, but the days of the Savoy partnership were effectively over. The lovely light of *The Gondoliers* came from a setting, not a rising, sun.

12

Utopia, Limited;
or, The Flowers of Progress
The Grand Duke;
or, The Statutory Duel

Though it may not have seemed precisely so when they were produced, *Utopia, Limited* and *The Grand Duke* were mere postscripts to the Savoy saga. *Utopia* opened on 7 October 1893, more than two years after *The Gondoliers* had closed, by far the longest break in the celebrated sequence that had begun with *The Sorcerer* in 1877. Two years after Utopia's early demise, *The Grand Duke* lagged along, to fade even more quickly. That was quite clearly the end. From then on, 'Gilbert & Sullivan' would mean only revivals and new versions of the classics. Fortunately or unfortunately, those revivals hardly ever included the duo's last two operas. *Utopia, Limited* and *The Grand Duke* have turned out be failures once and for all, vanishing almost without trace after their shaky première runs. The swan-songs of the most renowned operatic partnership are almost as unknown as *Thespis*, the forgotten work that had launched them twenty-five years before.

The aftermath of the Carpet Quarrel did remind its protagonists of their value to each other. Sullivan's dream of proving himself a serious operatic composer collapsed when *Ivanhoe* closed after 160 performances. It was doomed by lavish expense, its own weaknesses and the folly of assuming that a grand opera could attract crowds night after night, like a Savoy production. As it was, a run of 160 nights was remarkable, but far short of what Sullivan and Carte had hoped for. Carte shared Sullivan's disappointment at the failure as well as its consequences. Not long after *Ivanhoe*'s departure, he abandoned his dream of presiding at the renaissance of English grand opera and sold his plush opera house to a music hall consortium. Renamed the Palace, it has flourished ever since, with shows like *Jesus Christ Superstar*.

Gilbert had predicted that the scheme would fail and chided Sullivan as 'the sort of man who will sit on a fire and then complain that his bottom is burning'. The composer himself admitted that 'a cobbler should stick to his last' and returned to the Savoy, but not at first with Gilbert. After weathering a near-fatal attack of illness, he completed *Haddon Hall*, with libretto by Sidney Grundy, which opened a very moderate run in September 1892. Gilbert meanwhile had had only slightly better luck with *The Mountebanks*, which employed his cherished lozenge plot, to music by Alfred Cellier.

It was clear the old magic could only be awakened by the old team, and a reconciliation was arranged. Some lingering dust from the Carpet had to be dispelled, and there were fresh disagreements about a new contract (and even briefly about whose idea it had been to get back together in the first place), but basically all three partners were eager to promote harmony. Sullivan wintered on the Riviera and sent Gilbert a box of Christmas sweets with an admonition (thinking of his partner's chronic gout) not to make himself sick. Gilbert sent Sullivan a book on billiards, declaring that careful attention to its principles had made him what he was in the game.

The rather determined good feeling carried over into the new project. Gilbert read his story to Sullivan and his friend Sir George Grove, who agreed it was the best plot he had done. Later on, the author returned the compliment, saying the setting for the Act I Finale was Sullivan's best. But there were problems as well. Sullivan may have recorded his pleasure at working with his old partner again—'after all, there's no one like him'—but he found Gilbert's verses for the Act II Finale utterly unfathomable. The librettist finally gave up trying to redo them and told the composer to write the music first; for the only time in their collaboration the words would follow.

The composer was also bothered by the overwhelmingly satiric nature of the new piece. Accordingly Gilbert changed and softened lyrics and added songs that would give his colleague a chance for greater expression. He also yielded on a classic Gilbertian point. Sullivan objected to his dramatic treatment of Lady Sophy, yet one more addition to the Savoy line of middle-aged dragons. The librettist objected in turn that to make her 'a grave and dignified lady' in Act II would distort the character he had been shaping in Act I. Nevertheless, he did grant Lady Sophy 'pathetic interest' in accord with his partner's wishes. Perhaps influenced by his experience with *Ivanhoe*, Sullivan's final complaint concerned the cost of the production, but here the author-manager held firm. He sympathized with the musician's alarm and promised that he would practise whatever economies he could 'without cramping the piece'. But the piece was the thing, and the cast 'must be dressed *somehow*'. The Savoy opera had a reputation for spectacle; the first new work in four years had to maintain it.

In addition to Sullivan's occasional fits of discontent, Gilbert had his gout to contend with. He had to direct the cast on crutches or from a wheelchair, saying at one point that he had been unable 'to do anything but swear for the last eighteen days'. But for all that, rehearsals went smoothly, and the final dress rehearsal marked a great departure for the Savoy. Instead of imposing the web of secrecy that had surrounded earlier productions, Gilbert opened the theatre to the Press. They were struck by the glamour and stage-readiness of the new opera; also, no doubt, by the 'many references to the state of England and . . . hits at existing abuses' which Gilbert mentioned to one reporter. He said the piece was only vaguely political and had 'nothing of a party character. It doesn't do to divide the house.' But there was no question that his topical slings and arrows were much more direct than they had been for some time.

However, *Utopia, Limited*'s setting could not be more un-English. In a palm grove on a tropical isle, languorous maidens lounge in perfect contentment. The Vice-Chamberlain tells them even better days are coming. Princess Zara, eldest daughter of King Paramount, has spent five years at Girton College, Cambridge, and is returning to instruct her simple homeland in all the arts that have made England 'the greatest, the most powerful, the wisest country in the world'. One of the maidens objects that they are better off un-anglicized, living carefree lives under a benevolent despot, but the others praise the superiority of 'English institutions, English tastes, and oh, English fashions!'.

Suddenly in rushes Tarara, the Public Exploder. Under the eccentric Utopian constitution, the King's conduct is subject to the scrutiny of two Wise Men, who are bound to report any 'lapse from political and social propriety' to this officer. He then blows the King up with dynamite and rules in his place. Tarara is constantly practising for his big moment by setting off holiday crackers. Just now he is in a rage because he has seen a copy of the *Palace Peeper*, which accuses the King of the sort of shady activities that should get him exploded; but the Wise Men have not reported them.

Tarara runs off, swearing in Utopian, which the King has officially banned in favour of English. With great pomp, Scaphio and Phantis, the Wise Men themselves, enter and reflect proudly on the effectiveness of the native scheme for controlling despotism. But Phantis confesses his self-control is helpless where Princess Zara is concerned. Scaphio assures him that he shall have his heart's desire, though

Phantis is fifty-five and Zara is returning 'from a land where every youth is as a young Greek god'. The King, after all, is in their power.

A fanfare introduces the Utopian monarch, who in turn presents his younger daughters, Nekaya and Kalyba. They have been 'finished' by their English governess, Lady Sophy, and will now 'daily be exhibited in public', to provide models of 'maidenly perfection'. On the best English plan, the girls have been trained to be 'demurely coy—divinely cold'.

Meanwhile the King has requested an interview with Scaphio and Phantis. He says he does not mind being forced to invent all the scurrilous articles that appear in the *Palace Peeper*, but does object to the Comic Opera he has just had to produce, containing a burlesque portrait of himself. The King habitually looks on the humorous side of things, but he is worried about what Zara or Lady Sophy might think if they saw the opera or the *Peeper*—although he always buys up every copy of the scandal-sheet himself. And in short order this is exactly what happens. Brandishing a *Peeper*, Lady Sophy demands to know why, if its accounts of His Majesty's conduct are false, the offending scribe is not punished. Paramount hems and haws and pleads for her understanding.

After another fanfare, the whole court heralds the arrival of Princess Zara and her special escort, Captain Fitzbattleax and four Life Guards. The local maidens ogle the Guardsmen, while the Princess and the Captain exchange endearments. Unfortunately, now Princess Zara has smitten *both* Wise Men. Phantis accuses Scaphio of betrayal, but Fitzbattleax straightens out the squabble. Under the 'Rival Admirers Clauses Consolidation Act', he will hold Zara in trust until one of her elderly admirers kills the other in a duel—which he is sure will never take place.

In private, King Paramount confesses to his daughter how Scaphio and Phantis humiliate him. Zara has the remedy; she has brought with her the 'Flowers of Progress', 'Six Representatives of the principal causes that have tended to make England . . . powerful, happy and blameless' in the eyes of all Europe. They will reorganize Utopia and rescue the King from his persecutors. The Flowers include Captain Fitzbattleax, a clever representative of the logical and mathematical arts, a Lord High Chamberlain and a County Councillor who will take charge of censorship, a Company Promoter who will modernize commerce, and Captain Edward Corcoran of the Royal Navy, formerly of *H.M.S. Pinafore*. The Company Promoter, Mr Goldbury, suggests that the whole realm be set up as a limited company to ensure progress without liability. King and Country will become a corporation, free from the whims of the Wise Men and Public Exploder. These three mutter dark threats, but everyone else is delighted.

In Act II reform has triumphed. The Utopian army and navy are pre-eminent, poverty and hunger, crime and divorce are abolished, commerce and English fashions abound. While Scaphio, Phantis and Tarara fume and plot, Mr Goldbury convinces the young Princesses that the well-starched manners they have been taught really do not resemble those of 'a bright and beautiful English girl', and the King reveals the truth about the *Palace Peeper* to a relieved Lady Sophy, who can now love him.

All at once, Scaphio, Phantis and Tarara arrive with an angry mob. They declare that reform has been a disaster for Utopia. There are no more wars, and doctors and lawyers are starving. The country is 'swamped by dull Prosperity'; they demand a return to the old ways. But Zara recalls that she has omitted one vital factor of anglicization: Government by Party. Parliament and political factions will promote the necessary amount of confusion and unhappiness to ensure real contentment. The Wise Men are foiled and everyone hails the replacement of Utopia (Limited) by a Limited Monarchy on the true English plan.

Utopia, Limited's première was a sentimental triumph from the moment Sir Arthur Sullivan appeared and received a sixty-five-second ovation, to the fairy-tale tableau at the end, when he and Gilbert, after several solo bows, came together in centre stage, shaking hands to tumultuous cheers and applause. The reaction was a combination of delight, nostalgia and relief at what one paper called 'the prosperous restoration of the historic triumvirate of Gilbert, Sullivan and Carte'. It indicated approval of the opera only in part. Critics recorded the audience's pleasure at the magnificent sets—Act I's 'tropical landscape of bewildering splendour', Act II's veritable fairy palace, illuminated by some hundreds of incandescent lamps. Widely praised as well were two speciality pieces in Act II, the meeting of the Utopian Cabinet Council, which was presented like a minstrel show, the court officials accompanying themselves with banjos, tambourines and bones, and a sumptuous re-creation of a royal reception at Buckingham Palace. No satire was intended here, simply spectacle for its own sake, an eye-filling pageant of gowns and uniforms inserted in the middle of the opera.

But individual numbers seemed not quite convincing. There were encores, but by far the most raptuous response went to the re-emergent Captain Corcoran, whose song contained a quote from *H.M.S. Pinafore*. Not just a quote, in fact, but *the* quote. The Captain—now *Sir* Edward KCB, equal in honours to his old nemesis Sir Joseph Porter—claims, 'We never run a ship ashore', to which the assembly obviously has only one reply. A hearty 'What, never?' leads to the jolly

Pinafore chorus. According to T. F. Dunhill, who was present, 'the first-night audience . . . rose to it as to nothing else', with 'an outburst of enthusiasm which drowned the singers and orchestra'. Again, part of the appeal was nostalgic, but the happy snatch of the first great G & S success was also about the freshest bit of music heard that night.

Most critics, like the crowd, wished *Utopia* well, trying to find as much as they could to praise. Several protested mildly that the First Act, of Wagnerian proportions at one hour forty-five minutes, wanted pruning. But a few refused to bargain with sentimentality at all. One said bluntly that Gilbert's piece was 'a mirthless travesty of the work with which his name is most generally associated. . . . The quips, whims, jests, the theory of topsy-turvey, the principle of paradox, the law of the unlikely, seem to have grown old in a single night. . . .' The shadow of the same crushing opinion appeared in another critic's view of Sullivan's score: 'It would be altogether unreasonable to expect the musician of more than a dozen comic operas to go on producing strains new in character and expression.' In other words, he hadn't. Less tolerantly, a third cited 'a dearth of fetching tunes' and 'instrumentation . . . of the sketchiest and most perfunctory description'.

These are the very basic reasons why *Utopia, Limited* ran for a scant 245 performances and why it has so rarely been revived since. It is much more a revue than a comic opera, with (to quote one last notice) 'no coherence, no ordered sequence'. It is Gilbert at his most Gilbertian, the barbs flying in all directions, but lacking focus and finally force. Sullivan's music is no more than serviceable and occasionally less than that. Partly this is due to the overridingly waspish nature of the libretto; but partly to weariness of invention as well.

What is Gilbert satirizing? Everything English, it seems, with a vengeance. But much of his attack is simply name-calling. He appears most suspicious of his country's rank and power in the world: in 1893 Britain and her empire did occupy a 'pre-eminent position among civilized nations', and the Utopians are just the kind of native population that were being drawn into the imperial fold at every turn. By having the awe-struck islanders apply superlatives like 'greatest', 'most powerful' and 'wisest' to the nation, Gilbert hoped to encourage a more sensible perspective in people who revered Britain uncritically. The Finale to Act II (rewritten yet again after opening night) sums up the librettist's basic concern:

> 'Let us hope, for her sake,
> That she makes no mistake—
> That she's all she professes to be!'

The Utopians' anglomania produces some easy satiric hits; they firmly believe that every Englishman thinks for himself, that English conversation 'of the very meanest is a coruscation of impromptu epigram', that strong language is never heard. In the Gilbertian vein of *Princess Ida,* the islanders aver that a Girton College education puts all the keys to culture at a girl's fingertips.

The natives themselves give Gilbert a chance for some darker nonsense. Their quaint system of 'Despotism tempered by dynamite' must have had a slightly uneasy effect in a Europe already familiar with bomb-throwing anarchists. Such humour is of the 'shocking' variety most associated with *The Mikado.* Like Ko-Ko, the Public Exploder is working up to his ultimate professional detonation by stages—in his case by the holiday crackers he sets off and presents to others. In another Gilbertian in-joke, King Paramount actually mentions the Mikado, telling Lady Sophy he has asked the Emperor to advise him as to a punishment that will fit the crime of libelling the royal name in the *Palace Peeper.* (The whole idea of royal behaviour attracting the breath of scandal would have reminded the Savoy audience of the light-hearted doings of their own Prince of Wales.)

The Utopian monarch seems both a kind of Mikado-figure himself, with his 'humorous' outlook, and one of Gilbert's spokesmen. Paramount is forced to be funny in print too, after all, and has just written a comic opera. When he declares, 'Properly considered, what a farce life is, to be sure,' he echoes his creator's own notions, at least some of the time. 'First you're born', the King's bleakly pithy description of an average human existence, moving helplessly from one absurdity to another, is vintage bitter-Gilbert, right down to the hollow 'Ho-ho-hos' that punctuage each chorus.

Almost equally bitter, though in another key, is his scornful depiction of the courtship practices of proper English girls, at least those brought up by governesses like the prudish Lady Sophy. The Princesses have learned to snub any suitor who is too 'active', and they have always known both how to behave and how to seem to behave:

'English girls of well-bred notions
Shun all unrehearsed emotions.
English girls of highest class
Practise them before the glass.'

On the other hand, one of the paradoxes in the play is Mr Goldbury's hymn to the 'bright and beautiful English girl' in Act II. It opens as if he intended to mock the aggressively hearty style of English maidenhood as well as its demure opposite:

'A wonderful joy our eyes to bless,
In her magnificent comeliness,
Is an English girl of eleven stone two,
And five foot ten in her dancing shoe!'

No suitor would be too active, or maybe active enough, for this Amazon. Gilbert portrays her bounding over hedge and brook after the hounds, playing cricket, golfing, rowing, singing and dancing with healthy high spirits:

'Down comes her hair, but what does she care?
It's all her own and it's worth the showing.'

Suddenly you realize that Gilbert is serious. This modern maiden, free from prudery and false modesty, is his ideal.

'Her eyes they thrill with right goodwill—
Her heart is light as a floating feather—
As pure and bright as the mountain rill
That leaps and laughs in the Highland heather!'

And now the song's refrain, which seemed sarcastic at first, sounds almost fulsome:

'Go search the world and search the sea,
Then come you home and sing with me
There's no such gold and no such pearl
As a bright and beautiful English girl!'

Evidently any country with women like this is all right. Mr Goldbury's—and Gilbert's—advice to the Princesses is to drop all rigid codes of conduct and 'be nobody else but *you*', because 'Art is wrong and Nature right'. (The same truth was to have been demonstrated by Lady Sophy, in a wild and precipitate expression of love for King Paramount, before Sullivan insisted she be left with a shred of dignity.) This may be good counsel, but it is not clear what it has to do with the English institutions Gilbert is attacking. It also makes his view of his country somewhat contradictory—'a mixture of satire and fervour', as one critic has said.

The same contradictions appear in the two special scenes from Act II. The minstrel show-cabinet meeting is obviously wicked in intent; the implication that ministers are blackfaced clowns presided over by the King as interlocutor is quite delectable. The scene also shows the

'Flowers of Progress' lightly mocking Paramount's native gullibility. The monarch asks if arranging the chairs minstrel-style across the stage is in accordance with the practice at the Court of St James's, and is told it is the practice at the Court of St James's *Hall*—the theatre where the famous Christy's Minstrels regularly performed.

The Drawing-Room Scene, however, oozes respectful opulence. The ceremony may be English, but it is very impressive, though, as one critic observed, its function in the opera 'is not quite apparent'. In fact its only function is dazzlement, anticipating similar scenes in later extravaganzas like the Ziegfeld Follies and MGM musicals. Curiously, in one small detail Buckingham Palace was supposed to have copied its stage imitation. In 'a cheap and effective inspiration', the Utopian court offered its guests 'the cup of tea and the plate of mixed biscuits' to help them through the ritual. After the opera opened, just such modest refreshments appeared at Queen Victoria's receptions for the first time. (Rumours to the contrary, the royal family's only objection to *Utopia* was the Prince of Wales' mild complaint that in the second act King Paramount wore both a Field-Marshal's uniform and the Order of the Garter, which only the Prince was permitted.)

Some of Gilbert's most obvious satire arrives with the Flowers of Progress, those models of culture who bring with them the secrets of England's greatness. Her army and navy were considered the best in the world, and Gilbert was always ready to attack militarism. Indeed some critics took Captain Corcoran's reference to running ships ashore as a callous allusion to a recent disaster during manoeuvres.

Gilbert's feelings about censors, represented by the Lord High Chamberlain and the County Councillor, should be clear enough, considering the trouble they had given his plays. (In his old age, however, the librettist became a pillar of the community on the subject, testifying in favour of censorship as a bulwark against agnosticism and free love.) Of course, a man like Gilbert, who wanted yea to be yea and nay nay, would look suspiciously at the master of rhetoric, logic and arithmetic who can confound the simple meanings of things—usually in court, and for a price.

But Gilbert's real *bête noire* in the opera is peculiarly specific—the Joint Stock Company Act of 1862, which permitted corporations to escape liability for financial losses above a certain declared limit. (It was this same act that the Duke of Plaza-Toro used to such good advantage.) The idea of being able to evade responsibility for financial failure seemed to Gilbert monstrously immoral. Therefore, when Mr Goldbury suggests applying the principle to the entire kingdom of Utopia, the satire shifts from England as a whole to a particular English commercial practice, and one already over thirty years old. It seems curious, and rather confusing, especially when Mr Goldbury announces in Act II that every citizen of Utopia has become a limited company in his and her own right.

But at least the procedure frees King Paramount from the crabbed grip of Scaphio and Phantis. It also creates a Utopian boom. The success of the Flowers of Progress permits further broad jibes at the state of things in the mother country. Since Utopia has been completely Anglicized, there are no divorces, no preferential treatment for rank, no low women in high places, no slums, no unemployment, no poverty or hunger—'just as in England'. In addition, artistic merit is always rewarded, and entrance to the peerage is based on intellect, not heredity.

Perfection, of course, is dull, and dangerous for the professions, and only the introduction of Parliamentary government will redress the balance. Princess Zara's speech on the subject was termed 'about the bitterest thing Mr Gilbert has ever penned'. In its original form it ran: 'Government by Party! Introduce that great and glorious element—at once the bulwark and foundation of England's greatness—and all will be well! No political measures will endure, because one Party will assuredly undo all that the other Party has done; inexperienced civilians will govern your Army and your Navy; no social reforms will be attempted, because out of vice, squalor, and drunkenness no political capital is to be made; and while grouse is to be shot, and foxes worried to death, the legislative action of the country will be at a standstill. Then there will be sickness in plenty, endless lawsuits, crowded jails, interminable confusion in the Army and Navy and, in short, general and unexampled prosperity!'

This is savage stuff, and Gilbert cut the references to inexperienced civilians and political capital. In any case, the blast is so comprehensive it is hard to relate to Gilbert's other criticisms. He might even be proposing an absolute monarchy that would not be troubled by Parliament and parties. (George Bernard Shaw, however, no lover of G & S till then, thought Gilbert was supporting socialism and gave *Utopia* a warm welcome.) Finally, like much of Gilbert's satire, it only seems a fit of rage against general human folly. There is no plan or programme behind it, and, as its original critics saw, little pattern to the opera as a whole.

For his part, Sullivan seems lost in the proceedings. He has his moments—the minstrel setting is merrily ironic, with a lot of tambourine shaking and slapping. The trio which Scaphio, Phantis and Tarara sing as they moot subversion in Act II is brisk and lively, though it recalls the dragoons' 'aesthetic' trio in *Patience*. Indeed, there are many passages in *Utopia* that produce an unintentional feeling of *déjà entendu*. Almost nowhere is there a sense of discovery in the music, none of the little felicities that brighten the other operas. Even that favourite set-piece, the sonorous, Old English-sounding chorus, here called 'Eagle high in cloudland soaring', fails to get off the ground. The love-songs for Zara and Captain Fitzbattleax are feeble and artificial, inserted for romantic interest, like the characters themselves. (Zara's part was expanded to feature Nancy McIntosh, an American discovery of Gilbert.) However, Act II opens with an eccentric and witty solo by the Captain, the ultimate Gilbertian pot-shot at tenors, which requires him to muff his high notes: he can't do himself justice, he says, because he is in love.

Unhappily, Sullivan does not do himself justice either. The opera does seem, as the composer had complained before *Gondoliers,* a piece by Gilbert with music added by Sullivan. But neither the music nor the piece is distinguished, in spite of Gilbert's feverish attempts to lampoon everything in sight. *Utopia, Limited* is hectic and diffuse, as if the librettist in particular were trying too hard with too little. Too much of the time it is, as a first-night critic said, 'a weary business', a sad sign that the Savoy partnership, like one of the limited companies Gilbert loathed, was 'winding up'.

The Grand Duke took up where *Utopia, Limited* left off. It is unquestionably the last and least of the Savoy operas. None of the series has had such a unanimously negative press since its first production. Critics otherwise very partial to the G & S achievement have dismissed their final effort as 'a vastly dull affair of which the less said the better', or found in it 'no appeal whatever', or hoped that 'in justice to Sullivan's memory, as well as Gilbert's it . . . will never be heard again'. That plea for merciful oblivion has effectively been granted, for the piece has had almost no performances since its original short, stumbling run of 123 nights. Only the libretto and a recorded version by D'Oyly Carte give an impression of what must at any rate be a Savoy curiosity.

The response to *The Grand Duke*'s opening night on 7 March 1896 was more hopeful, with the usual excited audience and some critical praise, particularly for Sullivan. But even then a number of commentators concurred in feeling that 'the rich vein which the collaborators . . . have worked for so many years is at last dangerously near exhaustion.' So it was. Neither of them had really been eager for the new production. After *Utopia*—which Gilbert defiantly ranked as one of his favourite librettos—there had been further dissension, mainly to do with what role Nancy McIntosh, Gilbert's protégée, would play in any future works. Once again, both men took other partners and turned out separate comic operas. Neither was successful, though Gilbert wrote to Helen Carte that his effort, *His Excellency*, 'would have been a second *Mikado* if it had had the advantage of your expensive friend Sullivan's music'.

An agreement was patched up and a libretto rather half-heartedly presented in 1895. Sullivan set it early the following year, and it sailed determinedly through rehearsals and into the customary glossy première. Sullivan's diary recorded he thought 'parts of it dragged a little' and found the 'dialogue too redundant'. But his main reaction was 'Thank God [the] opera is finished and out.' He might have said the same for the Savoy partnership. He had had enough. Vacationing in Monte Carlo five days after the first night, he wrote to a friend, 'Another week's rehearsal with W. S. G. and I should have gone raving mad. I had already ordered some straw for my hair.' As for Gilbert, even before the opera was produced, he had announced that this libretto would be his last.

That *The Grand Duke* was not written *con amore* is clear enough from a simple recital of the plot. Gilbert's main inspiration seems to have been a dogged professionalism, and the result is a mixture of old gimmicks taken to absurd lengths, painful nonsense and strained effects.

The opera opens in the marketplace of Speisesaal, capital of the Grand Duchy of Pfennig-Halbpfennig, in 1750. Ernest Dummkopf's theatrical company is sharing a wedding breakfast for Ludwig and Lisa, two of their colleagues. Unfortunately the wedding hasn't happened yet. The despotic Grand Duke has summoned all the local clergy to discuss his own marriage tomorrow, so the young couple cannot be joined until just before curtain-time that night.

The Grand Duke, however, is in for more than marriage. The Dummkopf company are all members of a conspiracy against him, and if it succeeds, the manager will become Grand Duke and all places at court will be filled by his actors—according to their rank in the troupe, of course. For instance, Dummkopf's leading lady, the English comédienne Julia Jellicoe, has scoffed at his romantic attentions to her. But she grudgingly admits that, if he becomes Grand Duke, her standing in the company requires that she play the Grand Duchess, so she must become his wife.

But all at once it seems as if the whole conspiracy is undone. One of its bizarre peculiarities is its secret sign—every member is required to identify himself by eating a sausage roll before discussing their plans. Ludwig rushes in to confess that he has just spilled the plot to a stranger, because he ate *three* sausage rolls—but turned out to be the Grand Duke's own detective.

Things look desperate, but the local notary, the conspiracy's solicitor, springs a remarkable proposal. The laws of the duchy provide for Statutory Duels, in which, instead of fighting, the combatants simply pick cards. The loser becomes officially dead, and the winner assumes all his legal obligations. The curious statute has fallen into disuse and indeed has only another day to run before it expires, having been on the books for the regulation one-hundred-year term. If Ludwig and Ernest fight such a duel, the loser can disappear into legal death, while the survivor can denounce him to the Grand Duke as the brains behind the conspiracy and receive a full pardon for his evidence. When the Act expires tomorrow, the dead man can come back to life, beyond the threat of capital punishment because he has already officially died once. Ludwig and Ernest agree and draw cards, with Ludwig's ace beating Ernest's king.

After the relieved company dance off, the target of their plot dodders in. Grand Duke Rudolph is anything but a commanding figure—weak, ill and poorly dressed, though his shabby garments are festooned with decorations. His condition is his own fault: he is abysmally stingy, though fond of ceremony too. His bride-to-be, the Baroness von Krakenfeldt, is as much a miser as he is, as well as possessing a large fortune. When she arrives, she brings with her a copy of the local paper, which reveals Rudoph's infant betrothal to the Princess of Monte Carlo. But the contract is void unless she weds before she comes of age, which will occur at two o'clock tomorrow, and for years her father has been too debt-ridden to leave his house for fear of arrest.

The Baroness also brings a letter from Rudolph's detective, which contains a more serious threat—his report on the conspiracy. Roaring with laughter at Ludwig's naïve confidences, the policeman forgot to do his duty, and the plotters are still at large. Rudolph is paralysed with terror. As he weeps in distress, Ludwig trots in to make his confession. When Rudolph wails that he would gladly kill himself if he could find a cheap way of doing it, the foxy actor immediately suggests a Statutory Duel. If Rudolph dies today, his opponent will have to bear the effects of the conspiracy. Then, when the act expires, he can resume his office in safety. Ludwig volunteers to be the Duke's victorious opponent and guarantees the duel's outcome by putting an ace up his sleeve. Rudolph agrees, the two stage a quarrel, the duel transpires and the 'deceased' Grand Duke slinks away, mocked by his former subjects.

However, as soon as he has departed, Ludwig renews the law on Statutory Duels to run for another hundred years—making himself Grand Duke for life. But his sudden elevation has an unhappy result. Since the Dummkopf company rules Pfennig-Halbpfennig, even without Ernest, they must play their proper parts. Julia must still be Grand Duchess, which means that poor Lisa must give up her Ludwig, since she is only a supporting player. Despite Lisa's tears, Ludwig declares his court will be a jolly one and calls for new court attire—the 'Athenian' costumes the troupe were going to use for their production of *Troilus and Cressida*. The act ends with the company extolling the new Duke.

Act II begins with a grand procession in Grecian garb in the hall of the Ducal Palace, following the marriage of Ludwig and Julia. Ludwig proclaims his neo-Athenian reign, Lisa commits him to Julia's care, and Julia ponders how to interpret her new role. But confusion ensues with the arrival of the Baroness von Krakenfeldt. Since Ludwig has taken on all Rudolph's responsibilities, he has taken her on too. Ludwig admits her claim, apologizes to Julia and goes off to be married again.

Meanwhile Ernest, the first statutory victim, has been wondering what is going on. He meets Lisa and then Julia, who both flee in horror since he is technically dead. But finally Julia reveals Ludwig's bloodless coup, which the irate Ernest calls 'the meanest dodge I ever heard of'.

In comes the joyous procession from the marriage of Ludwig and the Baroness. No sooner has the champagne popped than a stately herald announces the approach of the Prince of Monte Carlo, his daughter and their hired entourage. Ludwig and company hide and jump out at the royal band, by way of 'official ceremonial'. Then, as the Prince explains that roulette has enabled him to pay his debts and that his daughter wishes to make good her infant betrothal, it looks as if another wedding is imminent.

But the act's third enraptured nuptial chorus is cut off by the sudden entrance of Rudolph, Ernest and the notary, who announce that Ludwig's rule is over. In statutory duels, an ace is the lowest, not the highest card. Thus Rudolph is reinstated, never having died, and the confusions of Ludwig's reign are resolved. Everyone pairs up properly, and 'all dance off to get married as the curtain falls'.

Many of *The Grand Duke*'s critics have observed that it seems mock-Gilbert and Sullivan, a monster self-parody of the Savoy formula. Certainly Gilbert had recycled motifs from previous operas before; he was famous for 'economy'. But never had he thrown together such a fantastic and ill-assorted bag of old tricks. The basic premise of the tale—a company of actors taking over a government as if they were playing dramatic parts—comes from the very first G & S production, *Thespis*. The idea of making death a legal fiction is based loosely on the Mikado's power to make reality whatever he wants. As Ko-Ko says, when the Emperor sentences a man to death, he 'is as good as dead . . . and if he is dead, why not say so?' Topsy-turvy government and impoverished noblemen also come from *The Gondoliers*, as does the infant betrothal ploy, used before in *Princess Ida*. *Ruddigore* presents the same cynical view of marriage and romance. But in *The Grand Duke* none of these elements fits naturally. The parts are mechanically imposed on one another and welded together by coincidence, producing only incredulity. This is not the humour of the absurd; it is just an absurdly laboured attempt at humour.

In addition to being ungainly in construction, much of *The Grand Duke* is simply silly. Even in his early burlesques, for instance, Gilbert cannot have offered a more desperate gambit than his sausage roll or more dubious taste than the conspirators' struggles to get the offensive pastry down. Equally strained is the Statutory Duel device, played out not once but twice, then seized on to contrive an ending so artificial it makes *Pinafore*'s baby-switch seem a model of dramatic logic.

Satire in the piece is catch-as-catch-can. Gilbert mocks actors' airs and aristocratic penny-pinching, but the glut of marriages in Act II strikes us as more a parody of Gilbert's own happy endings than an effective sneer at people's compulsive view of the institution.

Of course it is wrong to demand a kind of classical 'consistency' from Gilbert. His art of the topsy-turvy explicitly denies that kind of preconception. At his best he establishes his own credibility, creating a fanciful or eccentric situation that is consistent with itself. But it is just that Gilbertian consistency that *The Grand Duke* lacks. The librettist is determined to be funny at any cost. A prime candidate for most embarrassing moment in the Savoy operas is the surprise welcome Ludwig's court inflicts on the Prince of Monte Carlo and his suite. It is something out of a high school show, this hiding behind curtains, bursting out madly, swinging into a wild dance that leaves everyone breathless—all apropos of nothing.

The songs betray the same flaws as the scenario. Like the whole opera, most of them are much too long, as Gilbert obviously tries to inflate quantity into distinction. Sometimes, as in the sausage roll sequence, they are in dubious taste. Another nadir is Rudolph's recital of his precarious physical condition from excessive 'low living', which sounds altogether too much like an old person's graphic recital of the little humiliations of decrepitude. (Rudolph's age is another case of illogicality. He seems utterly ancient, but, since he was betrothed in infancy to a girl not yet of age, he must be barely twenty-one.)

One of the lyrics' most obvious difficulties is the failure of Gilbert's muse to come up with plausible rhymes. An occasional strained coupling is permissible and can even be passed off as a source of humour in itself. But when it happens again and again, the audience takes back the benefit of the doubt. One critic of the première made Gilbert's distortion of ghost into 'ghoest' for the sake of a rhyme the premise of his whole review, observing rightly that *The Grand Duke* was a "ghoest" of a Gilbert and Sullivan opera'. 'Ghoest' may be the most flagrant example, and Gilbert's attempts to flaunt it into acceptability do not work. Neither does his distortion of 'sich' for 'such', 'diskiver' for 'discover', 'shoeses' for 'shoes' or 'yallow' for 'yellow'. Neither do the stilted speeches he puts into almost everyone's mouth, frantic coinages like 'matrimonially matrimonified' or such hopelessly limp verses as these from the first Statutory Duel:

> 'He's drawn a King!
> How strange a thing!
> An excellent card—his chance it aids—
> Sing Hearts and Diamonds, Spades and Clubs—
> Sing Diamonds, Hearts and Clubs and Spades!'

The opera includes a number of lengthy, brittle patter songs, all too often examples of 'rhyme without reason', as an early critic complained. There is one good comic idea: Gilbert's use of an actress with a German accent—in the original production the Hungarian Mme Ilka von Palmay—to play Julia Jellicoe, the supposedly 'English' member of the Dummkopf 'German' troupe. But even this is overdone. For the rest, there is only spectacle, the last infirmity of noble stage-managing. With his Greek wedding processions Gilbert hoped to salvage some audience approval, but his stratagem had too much to contend with.

Sullivan fared better from the critics initially. One has even said that *The Grand Duke* contains 'music as good as any he ever wrote', but that is surely wishful thinking. The score has the kind of general competence to be expected from a master musician, but very little stands out. Sullivan too seems tired and strained, so that one welcomes 'a tiny fragment of graceful melody', as T. F. Dunhill described Lisa's Act II song 'Take care of him'. But Sullivan has his lapses too. His vocal writing is sometimes literally strained, with tenors and sopranos sounding particularly stretched in the top range. He is even unsure of his favourite technical devices. For instance, the opera's opening chorus, 'Won't it be a pretty wedding', is given a contrapuntal treatment almost from the beginning, so that the words are obscured, a *gaffe* the younger Sullivan would never have committed. His humorous touches betray a surprising coarseness, as one critic noted, such as a too literal fidelity to Gilbert's description of the stomach distress that comes from too many sausage rolls, or Rudolph's bodily complaints. At other times, as in the closing chorus of Act I, he too seems to be parodying the old Savoy practice, pumping up enthusiasm with forced harmonic sequences.

To give both collaborators their due, *The Grand Duke* does contain one number that, if not exactly a gem, transmits a certain sparkle. It is the 'Roulette Song' delivered by the Prince of Monte Carlo in Act II. In a way the piece has very little to do with the opera—being another attempt at spectacle for its own sake—and is quite different stylistically from almost anything else Gilbert and Sullivan wrote—a romping imitation of a French café song, complete with built-in leer. Each

A Savoy ritual coming to a close: Gilbert reads his libretto for *Utopia Limited* to the company in the presence of Sullivan and Carte

Rosina Brandram, Emmie Owen and Florence Perry as Lady Sophy and the Princesses Nekaya and Kalyba, shunning 'all unrehearsed emotions' in *Utopia Limited*

The fetching Ilka von Palmay, Gilbert's Hungarian 'English comedian' in *The Grand Duke*

Gilbert's designs for *The Grand Duke*'s Prince of Monte Carlo and his motley, hired entourage of 'nobles'

The composer as social animal: Sullivan at a house party at Blenheim Palace in the '90s. Standing below him, holding cup and saucer, is his lifelong friend Mrs Ronalds

Sullivan: only in his fifties, but exhausted and prematurely aged

Gilbert in Edwardian contentment — at home at Grim's Dyke holding one of his pet lemurs, with the lawn laid out for croquet

Gilbert in Edwardian dignity, even pomp, as Deputy-Lieutenant of Middlesex

refrain is entirely in French, a Gilbertian pastiche of a Monte Carlo croupier's patter as the wheel goes round. With Sullivan's love for the place and the game, it is no surprise he catches exactly the Gallic flavour of the occasion—so exactly in fact that some first-night critics were slightly taken aback. Such thorough Frenchness seems an admission of how weary both partners had become of grinding out the old English-eclectic formula. But despite the song's jolly *élan*, when Gilbert bowed to the critics who said the first thing wrong with *The Grand Duke* was its length, this was one of the numbers he cut.

That kind of uncertain judgement is as symptomatic of Gilbert's state of mind as the general indifference and artificiality that doom *The Grand Duke*. Indeed, the librettist knew he had failed, writing to a friend after the opera's opening: ' . . . now that the baby is born I shall soon recover. . . . I'm not at all a proud Mother, and I never want to see the ugly misshapen little brat again!'

It was clear now that there would be no more G & S operas. Musical comedies with simple plots, romantic lovers and fall-about comedians were beginning to prevail over comic opera, though Savoy revivals of G & S were still a great draw. But even if the audience had remained unchanged, Gilbert and Sullivan were content to become, as a team at least, classics of the past, to leave the partnership as a historical institution. As for the men themselves, after the failure of *The Grand Duke*, they never spoke to one another again.

In the years that remained to them, the world-renowned collaborators led completely separate lives. They did meet once, in 1898, taking a silent bow at *The Sorcerer*'s gala revival on the twenty-first anniversary of its original production. The rest of the time their personal courses were as different as they had always been. Sullivan did debonair service to both music and high society. He composed and played for Queen Victoria's Jubilee in 1897, for which Her Majesty rewarded him with a twenty-minute private conversation. His musical output included a ballet, songs and two comic operas, *The Beauty Stone*, which failed in 1898, and *The Rose of Persia*, which succeeded moderately in 1899.

He found composition increasingly difficult, and the time he devoted to it was reduced by his glittering social life and by bouts of his old illness. Mrs Ronalds was, as ever, his constant companion. He went to the races and the theatres and presided at musical evenings graced by royalty. There were trips to the Continent and long nights at the roulette table. But there was no question that his health was declining. Pain and fatigue, fits of restlessness and idleness, and the sense of failing powers all conspired to make him depressed, anxious and irritable. In the late summer and autumn of 1900 he was at work on another comic opera, *The Emerald Isle*, but soon found the going almost impossible. He spent October in Tunbridge Wells, ill at ease and in pain, unable to produce a note. In his diary he recorded he had 'done nothing *for a month* . . . first from illness and physical incapability, secondly from *brooding* and nervous terror about myself'.

The graceful *joie de vivre*, the old facility in life and art, had deserted him. He returned to London on 15 October, making his last diary entry: 'I am sorry to leave such a lovely day.' Though he was too ill to attend the revival of *Patience* on 7 November, which would have reunited him and Gilbert, he did receive an affectionate note from his old partner, saying that, but for his own 'enfeebled condition', he would have liked to call on Sullivan before going abroad. Two weeks later, after growing steadily weaker, Sullivan died suddenly, on 22 November 1900. The host of international tributes, including a telegram from the Queen, testified to his public stature, and, despite his own wish for family interment, he was buried with great ceremony in the crypt of St Paul's Cathedral. His funeral procession wound past the house of D'Oyly Carte, where the third Savoyard lay bed-ridden from the disease that would kill him in a few months' time.

Of the old triumvirate, the irascible Gilbert had the longest and happiest old age. It would not have been Gilbertian if it had been tranquil, but it was vigorous. After *The Grand Duke*, he presented a drama, *The Fortune Hunter*, which was roughly handled by the critics. The author retaliated by giving an interview in which, as the paper recalled later, he 'did some noble slashing all round', delivering thumping judgements on actors, writers and the general state of the British stage. A theatrical magazine accused him of 'abnormal self-esteem' and Gilbert sued. The subsequent trial provided merry copy as the librettist had a field-day in the witness box, but the case ended, to Gilbert's chagrin, in a hung jury.

Gilbert's activities also included time on the other side of the bench. For the last eighteen years of his life he served as a Justice of the Peace, known for firm but fair treatment of offenders. Later on he was appointed Deputy-Lieutenant for Middlesex, a title that brought with it a handsome uniform. But probably his favourite role was that of country squire, overseeing his 110-acre estate, Grim's Dyke, guarding his privacy but entertaining freely, particularly enjoying the company of the children, who enjoyed in turn his collection of fascinating animals.

In what was really a period of retirement, he and his wife (and the American soprano Nancy McIntosh, whom they had adopted) travelled a good deal, though his need to seek healthier climes departed with his gout in 1902. His theatrical projects were limited. He wrote another play, *The Fairy's Dilemma* (1904), which only proved that the vogue for fairy fantasies was long dead. In 1909 a comic opera on the same kind of theme, *Fallen Fairies*, was no more successful. But Gilbert knew what his librettos really required. In 1903 he had written to a friend that, 'A Gilbert is of no use without a Sullivan—and I can't find one!' His final production could not have been further removed from comic opera—a grim one-acter about a condemned prisoner, called *The Hooligan*.

Perhaps the project dearest to his heart—and therefore liable to engender the greatest discord—was the revival of the G & S operas that Helen Carte undertook from 1906 to 1909. Gilbert rehearsed the pieces but was not consulted on casting and gradually felt that his authority was being treated with less respect than it deserved. But the operas were a great hit and a triumph for their only surviving begetter, who received rapturous personal ovations. He may have continued to feel that his comic works were 'twaddle' and that his holdings at Grim's Dyke represented 'the folly of the British public', but now it was harder to claim (as he had once) that 'posterity will know as little of me as I shall know of posterity.'

The Savoy renaissance was probably responsible for his receiving a belated knighthood in 1907—twenty-four years after Sullivan. Typically, Gilbert sniffed at the honour as 'a tin-pot, twopenny-halfpenny sort of distinction,' and accepted partly as a credit to his profession: no playwright, he said, had ever been granted a knighthood before 'for dramatic authorship alone'.

Thus, in spite of himself, Gilbert grew into a Grand Old Man. He pursued a hearty, happy life right up to the end, which occured on 29 May 1911. That beautiful spring day he lunched in London and, in a burst of good will, patched up a long-standing quarrel, then visited an actress who had been injured in a fall. She was recuperating in a darkened room, and her mother aplogized for the difficulty in forming any impression of her appearance. The lion of the Savoy delivered a last graceful quip: 'Her appearance matters nothing; it is her disappearance we could not stand.' In the afternoon he bathed with two young ladies in his pond at Grim's Dyke. One of them, frightened at being out of her depth, called for help. Gilbert immediately came to her assistance, but the strain was too much for his heart, and he died instantly. Like Sullivan's, his passing elicited an impressive array of eulogies and remembrances from distinguished admirers, but, in contrast to his partner's stately rites, Gilbert's funeral was a simple affair in the local churchyard.

Since the death of its founders, the Gilbert & Sullivan partnership has showed no signs of waning, in either Britain or America. Indeed, the hit version of *The Pirates of Penzance* showed that Yankee G & S may be the wave of the future. Some British devotees would gnash their teeth at that prospect, having found the production (with some justice) too brash, too Broadway, too electric, too ready to chop and embellish both score and libretto. But whatever its excesses, its basic fidelity to the text proved that a fresh approach can bring out the real theatrical virtues of Gilbert and Sullivan. The operas still work, which may come as a revelation to many who have ignored them as mere tradition, institutional entertainment and no more than that.

For three generations, the D'Oyly Carte family has served Gilbert and Sullivan nobly, but it is true that its determination to preserve Gilbertian conceptions of staging has made for a certain staleness. Lately, when there might have been the will to update the productions, there has not been the money: the company never benefited from government funding, struggling along on pure fortitude and a staff willing to work for very little. In addition, there has always been a breed of G & S fan chronically opposed to change. The D'Oyly Carte productions of the operas are a stay against the bewilderments and flux of contemporary life. After one mildly modernized version, a traditional supporter protested, 'Why can't they leave the bloody things alone?'

It is a fair question, but the answer is that the operas are extremely entertaining theatrical works, and they come alive only when presented with the energy and imagination—and taste—that good theatre demands. Regarding the Savoy series as an institution denies it its rightful existence. The kind of stylization that became associated with D'Oyly Carte severely limited the operas' effect—as the New York *Pirates* demonstrated. With D'Oyly Carte, the audience response was in danger of becoming as stylized as the performance. At the New York *Pirates*, the laughter and enthusiasm were spontaneous and genuine, like the production itself—as the first production of *The Pirates* must have been.

Certainly Gilbert knew what he wanted when he wrote the operas. One of the great innovators of stage direction, he planned his pieces with a total effect in mind and discouraged improvised contributions by his actors. But even he changed his conceptions. Rehearsing one of the Helen Carte revivals, he questioned a bit of stage business but was assured it had always been done that way, as laid down by W. S. G. himself. Rutland Barrington chimed in, affirming the sequence was classic. Gilbert raised an eyebrow. 'Oh, it's classic, is it?' he said. 'Well, we must not interfere with the classics.'

The old master might well have agreed with the young Beatle-haired musical director of an *H.M.S. Pinafore* presented in London in 1981, influenced by the Broadway *Pirates* but done with more refinement if no less verve and wit. 'What I want,' he said, 'is for people to come out of the theatre not saying "that was good G & S," but "that was good entertainment.''' This is obviously the philosophy which brought G & S into being—a new conception of what 'good entertainment' was. It is the only philosophy that will rediscover the virtues G & S so abundantly and uniquely contain.

The two Savoy masters are still great showmen. Between them they provide all the material necessary for inimitable theatre—high-spirited, eccentric, touching, jolly, sentimental, slightly barbed. But it demands something like the attention they devoted to their productions themselves, in bright, innovative staging, attractive costumes and sets, first-rate performers and, above all, a lively and tasteful theatrical instinct.

The future looks promising. New productions of the operas are coming forward, not all by any means on the New York model, but with a similar spirit of freshness. A hit *Mikado* joined *The Pirates* in London's West End even as this book was being written. The recently formed New Sadlers Wells Opera will regularly feature stylish, properly financed versions of the Savoy classics as part of their comic opera repertoire. It may be that some audiences, hitherto turned off by stodgy productions, will be amazed to find they like Gilbert and Sullivan, that the partners deserve their classic status not for reasons of reverence but for real delight. It was all they would have wanted. Given half a chance, the immortal Victorians will run and run.

SELECT BIBLIOGRAPHY

Allen, Reginald. *Sir Arthur Sullivan, Composer & Personage*, New York, 1975

Allen, Reginald. *The First Night Gilbert and Sullivan*, New York, 1958

Ayre, Leslie. *The Gilbert and Sullivan Companion*, London, 1972

Baily, Leslie. *The Gilbert and Sullivan Book*, London, 1952

Baily, Leslie. *Gilbert and Sullivan: Their Lives and Times*. New York, 1979

Benford, Harry. *The Gilbert and Sullivan Lexicon*. New York, 1978

Blom, Eric. *Music in England*, London, 1942

Brahms, Caryl. *Gilbert and Sullivan: Lost Chords and Discords*, London, 1975

Cellier, François and Bridgeman, Cunningham. *Gilbert, Sullivan and D'Oyly Carte*, London, 1914.

Cox-Ife, William. *W. S. Gilbert: Stage Director*, London 1977

Dark, Sidney and Grey, Rowland. *W. S. Gilbert, His Life and Letters*, London, 1923

Darlington, W. A. *The World of Gilbert and Sullivan*, New York, 1950

Dunhill, Thomas F. *Sullivan's Comic Operas, A Critical Appreciation*, London, 1928

Dunn, George E. *A Gilbert & Sullivan Dictionary*, New York, 1936

Fitzgerald, Percy. *The Savoy Opera*, London, 1894

Fitz-Gerald, S. J. A. *The Story of the Savoy Opera*, London, 1924

Gilbert, W. S. *The Bab Ballads*, London, 1882

Gilbert, W. S. *Original Plays*, London, 1902

Gilbert, W. S. *The Savoy Operas*, London, 1926

Godwin, A. H. *Gilbert & Sullivan: A Critical Appreciation of the Savoy Operas*

Goldberg, Isaac. *The Story of Gilbert and Sullivan*, New York, 1928

Grossmith, George. *A Society Clown*, Bristol, 1888

Hughes, Gervase. *The Music of Arthur Sullivan*, London, 1960

Hyman, Alan. *Sullivan and his Satellites*, London, 1978

Jacobs, Arthur. *Gilbert and Sullivan*, London, 1951

Jones, John Bush (ed.) *W. S. Gilbert: A Century of Scholarship and Commentary*, New York, 1970

Lawrence, Arthur. *Sir Arthur Sullivan: Life Story, Letters and Reminiscences*, New York, 1899

Lytton, Henry A. *The Secrets of a Savoyard*, London, 1922
Mander, Raymond and Mitchenson, Joe. *A Picture History of Gilbert and Sullivan*, London, 1962
Pearson, Hesketh. *Gilbert and Sullivan*, London, 1935
Pearson, Hesketh. *Gilbert, His Life and Strife*, London, 1957
Rees, Terence. *Thespis: a Gilbert & Sullivan Enigma*, London, 1964
Stedman, Jane W. (ed.) *Gilbert before Sullivan*, Chicago, 1967
Sullivan, Herbert and Flower, Newman. *Sir Arthur Sullivan, His Life, Letters & Diaries*, London, 1927
Sutton, Max Keith. *W. S. Gilbert*, Boston, 1975
Walbrook. H. M. *Gilbert & Sullivan Opera, A History and a Comment*, London, 1922
Williamson, Audrey. *Gilbert & Sullivan Opera, A New Assessment*, London, 1953
Wolfson, John. *The Last Gilbert and Sullivan Operas*, London, 1976
Young, Percy M. *Sir Arthur Sullivan*, London, 1976

INDEX

Italicized page numbers denote illustrations